Missouri Folklore Society Journal

Special Issue: Songs and Ballads

Volumes 27 - 28

2005 - 2006

Cover illustration:

Anonymous 19th-century woodcut used by designer Mia Tea for the cover of a CD titled *Folk Songs & Ballads* by Mark T. Permission for MFS to use a modified version of the image for the cover of this journal was granted by Circle of Sound Folk and Community Music Projects. The Mia Tea version of the woodcut is available at http://www.circleofsound.co.uk; acc. 6/6/15.

Missouri Folklore Society Journal

Volumes 27 - 28
2005 - 2006

Special Issue Editor
Lyn Wolz
University of Kansas

Assistant Editor
Elizabeth Freise
University of Kansas

General Editors
Dr. Jim Vandergriff (Ret.)
Dr. Donna Jurich
University of Arizona

Review Editor
Dr. Jim Vandergriff

Missouri Folklore Society
P. O. Box 1757
Columbia, MO 65205

This issue of the *Missouri Folklore Society Journal* was published by Naciketas Press, 715 E. McPherson, Kirksville, Missouri, 63501

ISSN: 0731-2946; ISBN: 978-1-936135-17-2 (1-936135-17-5)

The *Missouri Folklore Society Journal* will soon be available full text in:

The Hathi Trust Digital Library   Vols. 1-26; 1979-2004
(https://www.hathitrust.org/home)
This online repository will have the full text of Vols. 1-26 of this journal available at their website for free access and use. The current issue (Vols. 27-28, 2005-2006) and the following issue (Vols. 29-31, 2007-2009), which has already been published, will eventually be added, as will succeeding issues. The same volumes will also be available through https://openfolklore.org/journals.

The *Missouri Folklore Society Journal* is indexed in:

The MLA International Bibliography   Vols. 1-26, 1979-2004
Searchable by keyword, author, and journal title. The result is a list of article citations; it does not include abstracts or full-text.

RILM Abstracts of Music Literature   Vols. 13-14, 20; 1991-92, 1998
Searchable by keyword, author, and journal title. Indexes selected articles about music that appear in these volumes only. Most of the entries have an abstract. There is no full-text.

A list of major articles from every issue of this journal also appears on the Society's web site (http://missourifolkloresociety.truman.edu/MFSJcnts.html).

Notice to library subscribers and catalogers:
Though the cover date on this volume is 2005-2006, the issue is actually being published at the end of 2015.

The Society's board is working to produce enough issues to catch up with the journal's publishing schedule as quickly as possible.

© 2015
The Missouri Folklore Society claims the copyright to all materials published in the *Missouri Folklore Society Journal*, unless the author retains his or her rights by specifying this prominently in the manuscript or in written (printed or digital) correspondence with the editor(s).

Missouri Folklore Society Journal
Special Issue: Songs and Ballads
Volume 27-28, 2005-2006

Preface – "It's been a long time comin'…"   v

Music in Our Lives

A National Folk Festival Reminiscence   1
    Alex Usher

The McDowell Gold Jubilee: History of a Hootenanny   7
    Betty Craker Henderson

Freaks and Fiddle Tunes: The Early-1970s Folk Revival in St. Louis   18
    Paul J. Stamler

Songs We Know and Love

"Nancy Dill": Searching for a Song My Mother Sang   31
    Jim Vandergriff

The Dawg Song War   70
    Sue Attalla

John Henry and the Reverend Bayes   97
    John Garst

"Pretty Polly": A History of a Folk Song   124
    Beth Brooks

A Note on the Song "The Babes in the Wood"   146
    Steve Roud

Music and Customs in Our Region

Ozark Ballads as Story and Song   157
    Julie Henigan

A Shivaree in Thornfield, Missouri   187
    Pauline Greenhill

The Lasting Legacy of Jim Hickam – A Remembrance   208
    Lyn Wolz

In Memoriam

Adolf Schroeder: Co-Founder of the Reorganized MFS   214

Susan Pentlin   219

John Schleppenbach   220

Mildred Letton Wittick   221

Reviews   229

Adam Brooke Davis

Literary Legacies, Folklore Foundations: Selfhood and Cultural Tradition in Nineteenth and Twentieth Century American Literature. Karen Beardslee. University of Tennessee Press, 2001.

Legend and Belief. Linda Dégh. Indiana University Press, 2001.

Medieval Folklore: A Guide to Myths, Legends Tales, Beliefs and Customs. Carl Lindahl, John McNamara, and John Lindow, eds. Oxford University Press, 2002.

The Meaning of Folklore: The Analytical Essays of Alan Dundes. Simon Bronner, ed. Utah State University Press, 2007.

Jim Vandergriff

Family Fun and Games: A Hundred-Year Tradition. Carolyn Gray Thornton and Ellen Gray Massey. Skyward Publishing, 2002.

Living Sideways: Tricksters in American Indian Oral Traditions. Franchot Ballinger. University of Oklahoma Press, 2006.

Older Than America. An independent film directed by Georgina Lightning and produced by Adam Beach. IFC Films, 2008.

About the Authors / Editors   240

A Note from the Editors about the Term "Folk Song" >>>
Since we have not been able to find a definitive statement on which form of the term "folk song" is the "standard" form, we've chosen to use "folk song," rather than "folk-song" or "folksong," unless the term appears in a quotation or a title, where we have retained the original form.

PREFACE: "It's been a long time comin'…"

Welcome to this special "Songs and Ballads" issue of the *Missouri Folklore Society Journal*. We are excited about the lineup of articles we were able to solicit on this topic, ranging from fascinating personal experience narratives to in-depth scholarly investigations. This combination of academic articles and personal stories has always been a hallmark of the Missouri Folklore Society's publications and events, something we believe to be a strength of the Society that contributes substantially to its accomplishments and successes by building a community of those who cherish Missouri's traditional culture, no matter what their individual circumstances.

The topics of the ten articles we received seemed to fall naturally into three categories: "Music in Our Lives," "Songs We Know and Love," and "Music and Customs in Our Region."

"Music in Our Lives" contains three personal experience stories: from autoharpist Alex Usher, who performed at the National Folk Festival in the 1940s and '50s; from Ozark author Betty Henderson, who gives us a history of a "hootenanny" that has been bringing people together in southern Missouri for more than fifty years; and from folk music radio show host Paul Stamler, who gives us his take on how the folk music scene developed in St. Louis during the early 1970s. These authors allow us to explore with them the ways in which traditional music has influenced their lives.

The scholarly articles we received fell into two categories – those that explore the history of individual songs and those that delve into various aspects of songs in our region. We put the studies of individual songs into the section titled "Songs We Know and Love." The first entry in that category is from retired educator Jim Vandergriff, whose article recounts the journey of discovery he took while researching a song he heard his mother sing to his daughter. Next, we catch up with Sue Attalla's work on the history of "The Dawg Song," specifically her description of the "war" that arose in the early 1900s over conflicting claims about who actually wrote the song. After that, retired chemistry professor John Garst demonstrates his experimental use of logical proofs to determine the actual location and historical reality of events in the well-known American folk song "John Henry." College music professor Beth Brooks then traces the possible historic path of one traditional song found in America ("Pretty Polly") and the many changes it experienced over the centuries. Finally, finishing up this section is a brief article by Steve Roud, librarian, author, and folk song expert from London, concerning the history of the song "The Babes in the Wood," in which he speculates about how the song changed during its journey from England to Missouri.

The second category of scholarly pieces, titled "Music and Customs in Our Region," includes three articles about different aspects of regional culture. First, musician, poet, and scholar Julie Henigan gives us an overview of the types of ballads found in the Ozarks and the southern Appalachians. This is followed by Canadian professor Pauline Greenhill's account of a noisy shivaree (involving so-called "rough music") gone awry in a small southern Missouri town in the early 1960s. Finally, we close this section with a remembrance of MFS member Jim Hickam, who co-hosted a folk music radio show that influenced the traditional music scene around Cape Girardeau, Missouri, for many years.

Following these articles are our final two sections—*In Memoriam*, where we say good-bye to long-time MFS members and friends, and the *Reviews* section where Adam Davis and Jim Vandergriff offer their cogent comments on six books and one film in their areas of expertise.

You will have noticed that the cover date on this issue is 2005-2006, though it is actually being published in 2015. (The previous volume, which had a cover date of 2004, was actually published in 2008.) Obviously, the Society has been having trouble producing volumes of this journal on a regular schedule, but the MFS board is trying its best to catch up, already overseeing at least two more issues of this journal that are currently in process. Though many factors in this delay were beyond our control, we extend our apologies to everyone involved, including the authors, the members of our Society, and our institutional subscribers. Most of all, we apologize to the Schroeders, the founders of the modern incarnation of our Society, who faithfully shepherded this journal through the publication process for so many years.

As we "put this issue to bed" (as they say in the newspaper biz), it's good to know that the Society's loyal subscribers will soon see the results of our labors. We hope you enjoy it!

Lyn Wolz   *Elizabeth Freise*
Editor   *Assistant Editor*   Dec. 1st, 2015

Acknowledgements

I would like to express my appreciation to:

My colleague Elizabeth Freise for her excellent research and editing skills and wise perspectives on "life, the universe, and everything;"

MFS board members Jim Vandergriff and Adam Davis for answering my frequent questions about editing, technical glitches, and other topics;

Neal Delmonico of Naciketas Press, who got us through the home stretch;

And last, but certainly not least, Susan Bryson for her help and moral support on this project, as well as the Chez Coffeehouse Reunion and other folklore activities I've been involved with over the past 15 years.

Thanks, guys. I literally couldn't have done it without you! – *Lyn*

Introduction – "A National Folk Festival Reminiscence"

Alex Usher and her family band in the 1960s; Alex is playing a harp-guitar
(Used by permission of Mel Bay Publications, Alex Usher, and Gregg Miner;
http://harpguitars.net/blog/2011/01/more-harp-guitar-harmony-2; acc. 6/6/15)

A proud St. Louisan tells us about her appearances at "The National"

Our first article is a personal reminiscence by St. Louis musician Alex Usher about her performances at the National Folk Festival. Founded by recreation leader, community theater promoter, and social reformer Sarah Gertrude Knott in St. Louis in 1934, the National Folk Festival still exists as one of the most prestigious and longest-running celebrations of traditional music and dance in the United States. After that first year in St. Louis, founder Knott took her festival to Chattanooga, Dallas, Chicago, Washington, D.C., Philadelphia, and Cleveland before returning the National to its home at the Kiel Opera House in St. Louis in 1947, where it remained through 1955. One of the performers in 1949 was the Missouri Folklore Society's own Alex Usher, now familiar to people all over the world as an extraordinary autoharp player, though during the middle decades of the twentieth century, she was primarily known as a folk singer.

Alex has been collecting and performing folk songs for over fifty years, mainly in her hometown of St. Louis, but increasingly (especially after she and her husband Rich retired) collecting songs while they travel all over the country in their RV. In the early days of TV, Alex was a regular performer in several children's series on local educational station Channel 9. She also performed as part of a family band with her husband and their four children during the 1960s and '70s—Alex played guitar, concertina, and tin whistle, among other instruments, while her husband Rich played banjo, harmonica, and guitar, and their children played fiddle, banjo, and guitar. In the 1970s, Alex began entertaining staff and patients in hospitals, becoming known as "The Music Lady" for her twice-weekly stints at St. Louis Children's Hospital. She also played frequently at veterans' hospitals.

Though she bought an autoharp in the 1970s and occasionally played chords on it to accompany her singing, Alex began to approach it in earnest in 1987, teaching herself to play in a more complex melodic style. She captured the Southern Regional Autoharp Championship (Mountain View, Arkansas) in 1991, the National Autoharp Championship (Avoca, Iowa) in 1993, and placed in the International Autoharp Championship Competition at the Walnut Valley Festival (Winfield, Kansas) seven times, taking third place five times between 1993 and 2003, second place in 2001, and first place in 2004.

In addition to teaching private autoharp lessons at Music Folk, a store in the St. Louis suburb of Webster Groves where she lives, Alex has taught many workshops at Winfield's Walnut Valley Festival, as well as at the Mountain Laurel Autoharp Gathering, the Cranberry Dulcimer Gathering, the Wisconsin Stringalong, and the Memphis Dulcimer Festival, among others. She has also performed and taught countless times for Elderhostel (now Road Scholar), hospitals, church groups, libraries, schools, and other civic and cultural organizations. In recent years, she has also presented a program of folk songs called "Hand-Me-Down Music" for the Missouri Humanities Council, as well as sharing her love of music with her four grandsons. Here are her entertaining stories about her experiences playing music and singing on a national stage.

A note from Lyn: One of the delights of belonging to the Missouri Folklore Society is the chance to get to know some really fine musicians and singers from Missouri and elsewhere. I have been privileged to be at many meetings where Alex performed and talked about her experiences in folk music. When I announced that music would be the focus of this issue of the journal, I was very happy to hear that she wanted to write about the early days of the folk revival, specifically about her appearances at "The National."

For more info about Alex and her instruments, see *Autoharp Clearinghouse*, Aug.-Sept. 1997 (http://www.cyberpluckers.org/Autoharp_Clearinghouse/usher.php; acc. 6/6/15).

Alex Usher with one of her favorite autoharps
(http://missourifolkloresociety.truman.edu/emails.html; scroll down to "U"; acc. 6/6/15)

A NATIONAL FOLK FESTIVAL REMINISCENCE
Alex Usher

In 1949, I was invited by Sarah Gertrude Knott to participate in the National Folk Festival in St. Louis. How she got my name I have no idea, for I was merely a twenty-year-old beginning folk singer who had received a guitar and Carl Sandburg's *American Songbag* for Christmas the year before. Sarah Gertrude's whole life was devoted to encouraging the continuance of folk traditions in the United States and I suppose she saw me as a link in the chain.

It seemed to me that the other performers involved in the festival were people who had grown up in their traditions—ethnic dancers or singers from the backwaters of the country comfortably singing the songs that had been passed down for generations. These folks all paid their own way to the festival and performed *gratis* just to display their heritage with pride.

The festival, which was sponsored by the *Globe-Democrat* newspaper, went on for several days with performances at the Keil Opera House in downtown St. Louis. What went on behind the scenes was as important as what happened on the stage. There were workshops where everyone participated—not the modern-day "workshops" which simply showcase an individual performer, but opportunities for people to share their repertoires. The first folk song workshop I attended was a gathering of perhaps fifteen people who sat in a circle and shared their songs. Most of the singing was *a cappella* and it included a lot of the old ballads. I remember one rendering of "The Brown Girl" which elicited variations from many of the other singers. One of the participants was Booth Campbell, a lawyer from a small Ozark town, who wore a pair of miniature false teeth as a tie clasp and knew a plethora of the old songs. May McCord from Springfield, Missouri, sang some of her vast repertoire of the old songs and sometimes, with a twinkle in her eye, would suggest that people might want to get a handkerchief out for a particularly heart-wrenching verse.

As you might imagine, the shows were not too popular with the general public, who were looking for something more polished, but there were some unexpectedly entertaining happenings. There was a group from Louisiana one year that re-enacted a Cajun Mardi Gras celebration on stage that was perhaps a bit too authentic. The re-enactors had imbibed liberally before they got on stage and were happily prepared to celebrate at length in their new venue. There was a live chicken involved in this chaos and it was running frantically around the stage. Poor Sarah Gertrude as the emcee was doing her best to end the debacle and I think some stage hands had to help escort the revelers off.

This was the same festival that was attended by a very pretty blond folk singer for the first time. One of the Cajun men walked up to her and started a conversation. The only problem was that he was speaking a Cajun patois and she couldn't understand a word of it. In an effort to be polite, she smiled and nodded pleasantly. The next day he returned, walked up to her, pulled out a large wad of money, and started counting it out. Suddenly feeling somewhat panicky, she found an interpreter. It seems that the day before, she had agreed to become the wife of a young man back down in the Louisiana bayous for whom there was no local prospect available and this was the agreed-upon dowry she had nodded "yes" to!

Most of the National Folk Festival programs were lackluster. The presenters were not polished performers, but simply everyday folk who had kept the old traditions going in their communities. The object of the festival was to keep those traditions healthy in their home settings by giving them some national airing and prominence, and this aim was accomplished. The festival also presented these arts to a wider audience that they might be appreciated and spread. The scope of the programs was broad and included ethnic and regional folk dances as well as every other folk art. The festival succeeded in its purpose of encouraging the participants, but the shows were not too exciting to the audiences who were used to the expertise of professional performers. The programs tended to run overtime as well.

The audiences during the daytime shows were primarily schoolchildren, and I assume that many of the teachers had classroom applications that paralleled the programs. As I said, the *Globe-Democrat* sponsored the festival for some years, but Sarah Gertrude was difficult to deal with and eventually the management tired of her outbursts and demands and the festival had to find other sponsors and venues.

Though it was inaugurated in St. Louis, the National Folk Festival moved periodically to new cities, sometimes being held in a city for only one year, sometimes for several, before being relocated to a new venue. One year, I attended the festival in Covington, Kentucky, where my husband Rich met Paul Cadwell, a Princeton-graduate lawyer who played classical banjo. Paul's sidekick was a wizened little bow-legged cowboy who played guitar and delighted in packing a pistol, which he loaded with blanks and fired off at times. This caused considerable alarm among the local police.

The year that the festival was in Florida, Rich and I were awakened at three o'clock in the morning by Sarah Gertrude who assigned us the task of having breakfast with the Russian embassy delegates. How they were involved with the festival, I have no idea. I just remember the Russians arrived at our hotel at the appointed hour in a chauffeur-driven limousine, and we sped through downtown St. Petersburg at seemingly the speed of sound, running red lights and riding on diplomatic immunity.

Another year the festival was in Nashville, Tennessee. The performances were not well attended, probably because everyone thought the music was just a poor relative of country-western. Again, Sarah Gertrude issued an all-points bulletin to various of her trusted circle that the Native American performers were missing. When last seen they were somewhere downtown window shopping and unaware that they were due shortly on stage for the afternoon show. We criss-crossed the downtown area and were relieved to finally get the word that they had landed safely and were on time for their performance.

It was in Nashville that I heard shape-note singing for the first time. The group consisted of about thirty to forty members, many of them white-haired, who sang the hymns in the old manner the first time around—using the names of the notes (sol, fa, etc.)—and then roared the verses out in harsh backwoods voices. Many of the group beat time with a hand. Perhaps the beginnings of the shape-note revival that has spread across this country can be attributed to Sarah Gertrude Knott.

In the 1960s, suddenly there was a "folk revival" and pseudo-folk songs erupted out of Tin Pan Alley. Professional performers took over the field and the National Folk Festival that had heretofore been ignored by the commercial music world became an object of great interest. The National Park Service took over the festival and it became primarily a showcase for well-polished performers.

The last time I saw Sarah Gertrude Knott was at the National Folk Festival in Wolf Trap Park Farm in Washington, D.C. in 1970. It was now in the hands of a board that reflected a more commercial policy in programming. Gone were all the everyday homespun folks that had traveled from far and wide in the old days, and in their places were the professional big name performers of folk music. Eighty-something Sarah Gertrude was wandering around the grounds on a miserably hot humid summer day dressed like a proper Southern lady in a pink linen dress, corseted and wearing stockings, while the rest of the world spun by in tie-dye t-shirts, jeans, and a variety of other hippie garb. She looked so lost and out of place. She died in her hometown of Princeton, Kentucky, in 1984, but will forever be remembered as the founder of the National Folk Festival, the event that still brings traditional music and dance to new audiences every year.

Sarah Gertrude Knott, founder of the National Folk Festival
(National Council for the Traditional Arts Collection;
http://www.loc.gov/folklife/news/pdf/afcnews-winter-2002.pdf [p. 4]; acc. 6/6/15)

To learn more about the National Folk Festival...

Participants at the 15th Annual National Folk Festival in St. Louis, 1949
(http://www.loc.gov/folklife/news/pdf/afcnews-winter-2002.pdf [p.5]; acc. 6/6/15)

Grosby, Jane. "The First National Folk Festival," *Missouri Folklore Society Journal*, 8-9 (1986): 115-122; also in *M.F.F.A.*, 4 #1 (Summer 1976): 1-3.

Knott, Sarah Gertrude. "The National Folk Festival—Its Problems and Reasons," *Southern Folklore Quarterly*, 3 (1939): 117-124.

Knott, Sarah Gertrude. "The National Folk Festival after Twelve Years," *California Folklore Quarterly*, 5 (1946): 83-93.

Wallace, Andrew. "The National Folk Festival: The Sarah Gertrude Knott Years," *Folklife Center News*, 24 #1 (Winter 2002): 3-6.

Williams, Michael Ann. *Staging Tradition: John Lair and Sarah Gertrude Knott* (Urbana: University of Illinois Press, 2006).

Books and Recordings by Alex Usher

Basic Melodic Autoharp Solos (Pacific, MO: Mel Bay Publications, 1997).

Children's Song Favorites (Pacific, MO: Mel Bay Publications, 2003).

'Harps of Gold: An Instrumental Autoharp Christmas (CD; RT Audio, 1997).

Scottish Airs and Ballads for Autoharp (book/CD set; Mel Bay, 2003).

Side Splitters (Pacific, MO: Mel Bay Publications, 2008).

Introduction – "The McDowell Gold Jubilee"

An Ozark author traces the history of a long-running rural music party

Author, musician, and long-time Missouri Folklore Society member Betty Craker Henderson gives us her description of a local "hootenanny" that she has helped run in the tiny community of McDowell, Missouri, for more than thirty-five years. McDowell is a township in Barry County about 45 miles southwest of Springfield and about 15 miles southeast of Monett, where Betty lives. According to the 2010 census, this unincorporated area has a population of 288, though the Jubilee often draws musicians and spectators from quite a distance—even occasionally from other countries.

Barry County, Missouri – the location of the McDowell Gold Jubilee
(http://en.wikipedia.org/wiki/Barry_County, Missouri; acc. 6/6/15)

The McDowell Gold Jubilee, like other music gatherings in the Ozarks, is steeped in tradition. Whether they're called hootenannies, music parties, or jam sessions, these events trace their roots to old-time house parties where family and friends would gather to play music and visit. In this article, Betty documents the importance of these music-centered get-togethers to small rural communities.

A former children's librarian and newspaper editor, Betty is passionate about the Ozarks and its cultural heritage and enjoys writing about the history of the area for both adults and children. She is a member of the Missouri Writers' Guild, the Springfield Writers' Guild, and is a charter member of the Ozark Writers League. Drawing on a lifetime of living in the Ozarks, Betty writes short stories, novels, and non-fiction. (See a list of her publications after this article.) For several years, she also acted as a hostess for Elderhostel and presented programs in character as Granny Dingle, a country woman who sings her way through a day in the past. Betty also plays upright bass and sings in her husband's band, Country Color, as well as using her musical skills to conduct workshops for local children, teaching Ozark songs and stories.

People are drawn to Betty's quick wit and storytelling abilities, her great sense of humor, and her charming descriptions of life with her husband Ben, three kids, two sons-in-law, five grandchildren, and her "poet mother, as well as countless supportive friends, forty acres of junk cars, and a cat who believes he's God." Those who know her can easily picture her life as the still center of a large extended family—as she tells us, "My husband says I'm the busiest person he knows who doesn't have a real job."

Betty sent us this note with her manuscript and we thought it would give readers some insight into her life-long loyalty to the culture and people of her native Ozark region:

> Those who know me understand that I have no training as a folklorist. I'm only an Ozark woman with a lifelong interest in the traditions, songs, and stories of my forebears and the history of those who came before me and how it shapes the lives of those who travel the world today. Therefore, my knowledge is scattered and I have looked to my sources for information both personal and recorded. I've perused the works of Vance Randolph, Otto Rayburn, Milton Rafferty, Bill McNeil, Robert Gilmore, etc.; listened to miles of tape from the collections of Hunter, Lomax, and others; and embraced the rewritten 'folk' music of the later years and I know what I like. I also know that I'm not alone, even though I'm in a minority. But that minority may once again rise and it is the duty of those of us still around to preserve what we can for those to come. The history we have with us today is what will be looked to in the future. So I have given you this tidbit to do with as you will, done in my 'folksy' free-lance style…but not scholarly! Good reading, y'all!

A note from Lyn: Since becoming acquainted with Betty at the Missouri Folklore Society's annual meetings, I have come to cherish her friendship. Her smile lights up the annual MFS get-togethers and helps to make them the special events they are for all of us. Though we see each other only once a year, we are like long-lost family—reuniting, catching up, and enjoying each other's company. I bet it's like going to one of the McDowell Gold Jubilee shows…..may they keep going strong for another fifty years and more!

> > > Definitions of the Word "Hootenanny"

Webster's Third New International Dictionary of the English Language
(Springfield, MA: Merriam-Webster, 1986; p. 1089)

> **Hoot·e·nan·ny** [origin unknown]
> Gathering at which folk singers entertain, often with audience participation

OED: Oxford English Dictionary
(2nd ed., 1989; online – http://www.oed.com/view/Entry/88354; acc. 6/6/15)

> **Hoot-en-an-ny** *from U.S. dialect* [origin unknown]
> An informal session or concert of folk music and singing
> "A hootenanny is to the folk singer what a jam session is to the jazzman."

THE MCDOWELL GOLD JUBILEE: HISTORY OF A HOOTENANNY

Betty Craker Henderson

Musicians perform in an old schoolhouse, the home of the McDowell Gold Jubilee
(Photo taken in the summer of 2000; used courtesy of Drew Beisswenger and Betty Henderson; http://library.missouristate.edu/projects/jamsessions/mcdowell.htm; acc. 6/6/15)

In the hills and valleys of the Missouri and Arkansas Ozarks, the old ways have been disappearing at a rate that is alarming to old-timers and folklorists alike. No more is heard the quaint Elizabethan pronunciations, the children no longer roll hoops nor play at marbles, old men do not "spit and whittle" in front of country stores. Instead, TV antennas and satellite dishes sprout like weeds from homes and the elderly as well as the young carry cell phones as easily as the shotguns of earlier days. One ancient custom, however, still persists in a modernized form and appeals to some younger persons, as well as to the older ones who frequent these events. Music parties, popularly known as hootenannies, are no less than the remnants of a custom that goes far back in Ozarks history.

The casual observer may notice, here and there throughout the Ozark hills, a number of cars and trucks parked willy-nilly around a small building in a hollow a bit off a little-traveled road. No doubt there is a well house nearby and a small propane tank, as well as a couple of utilitarian outbuildings. Coming closer, the driver opens the window and hears…yes, music.

In the homes of the early settlers there was little to look forward to but hard work. Each day brought its own set of problems and the only relief came from the religious gatherings and the social get-togethers taking place in the humble homes of neighbors. Here the folks would gather, bringing food and drink and any musical instruments they might be lucky enough to possess (often no instruments at all) and spend hours visiting, catching up with the news, singing, dancing, or playing games together, to lighten their daily lives. Although times have not been as hard in recent years, the traditions are still observed at homes in countless communities across the Ozarks.

Just where Little and Big Flat Creeks converge in the tiny Barry County community of McDowell, Missouri, Norma Clevenger recently spoke about the origins of one of these long-lasting events—the McDowell Gold Jubilee. During the 1950s, all the friends and neighbors in the area made it a practice to gather often in each other's homes to play music, sing, visit, and just have a good time. Norma said that in 1961 her husband Raymond was visiting with a friend, Gerald Rickman, who lived about a mile southeast of the Clevenger family. "Raymond wanted to have a whole lot of folks come for a New Year's music party," she explained, "and there wasn't enough room at our house, so Gerald suggested talking with the school board at Purdy. The old McDowell schoolhouse was just up the road about a quarter of a mile and it was only used for elections and 4-H meetings after the rural schools were consolidated. Raymond told me it was a big mess and would have to have a really good cleaning, but it would be a good place to have a whole lot of people. The school board said if we paid the electricity and insurance and didn't allow any drinking or dancing it would be okay as long as we wanted to use the building. So, that's the way it all started – New Year's Eve, 1961."

Raymond Clevenger and Norma Hemphill Clevenger were each life-long residents of the McDowell area (Raymond suffered a stroke and heart attack in 1981 and died in 1985) and the couple raised three children—Shirley, Willis, and Wayne—who still live in the community. These three children have in turn raised a total of ten of their own children, several of whom have stayed there also, so the practice of staying where you are put is pretty well carried out in this family, with only a few going further afield.

Norma's family, she explained, was not musical. "Well, one of my brothers played a little guitar, but all eight kids in Raymond's family played something. Even Delmar played the Jew's harp."

Norma and Raymond's son Wayne plays guitar and a mean mandolin and sings—some hymns, but also some of the old-time tunes of long ago. One of the Jubilee's favorites is "Groundhog" and it's often requested.

"Willis and Shirley went to the music some, but Wayne always liked it," she said. "He started playing the guitar when he was about twelve and his bedroom was right next to ours and he'd be a-playin' and I was wishing he'd never found a guitar." She laughed. "There was so much drummin' on that guitar…every time he'd come in the house, he'd pick up that guitar."

The New Year's Eve music party was received by the neighbors with enthusiasm. "We had so many people show up that first night," Norma said. "They all wanted to come back the next week and keep on coming, but it was too much for us. We said we'd do it every two weeks, but that turned out to be too much also. Finally, we went to once a month."

"After we started, Willis and Wayne and Carl Moore, they painted the inside. It's been changed since then. There was a partition there in the middle. They used to have a high school in the west side. Raymond and Joe Roller and Sonny Stewart and the boys, they built the stage and that's when we moved it to the west end."

Norma's son Wayne remembered, "Rickmans would come, Heath and Brandon, and Cliftons, Doug, you know, and those Whisman kids....you talk about harmony. Red Perriman used to come down and play at McDowell a lot, him and Will Hudson. Tom and Joanne Patterson were here, too."

Once a birthday party got a bit out of hand and almost put an end to the whole thing. Folks were dancing and it nearly 'blew it up,' but times change and the music continued. In later years, a quite elderly woman, Mrs. Dodson of rural Cassville, the mother of twelve children, would come with some of her daughters and jig dance in the aisles. She had a wonderful time. Her son Robert played guitar for many years until his own death, and her daughter Eula May, herself elderly now, still sings old songs with her husband Gene. Another older couple, Gene and Suzie Carter of Fairview, Missouri, would often waltz in the aisle and individuals will still spontaneously jump up and break into jigging during a lively fiddle tune.

By this time, the Clevenger family had moved from the farm into the little town where they bought the local store and post office and began to operate them. Norma told me, "We were cooking for everybody down at the school...hamburgers and hot dogs. Sometimes people brought things, but mostly we cooked. It wasn't too bad when Bill [Ozbun] helped out. One night we ran clear out of food and Betty Holloway went out to her car and got out the hamburger meat she was taking home to eat and we cooked it all up, too."

From the beginning, there were large crowds and, according to Norma, lots of work, so after a while the Clevengers turned the responsibilities over to another local couple. That didn't last too long, though, and after a number of years, Raymond and Norma were forced to end the event and the schoolhouse once again stood empty.

Raymond joined a band called Country Gold to play for festivals and events in the area. One of the members, Ben Henderson of nearby Monett, became a good friend. When the group disbanded, the members began gathering at a second location—Pleasant Ridge about six miles north of McDowell—to play music with other friends.

Bob Nichols remembered, "We'd go to Pleasant Ridge and Raymond Thomas and Si Carpenter and I would sit on the back seat and Raymond wouldn't play, he'd just hold his fiddle on his lap. After a while, Ben comes in and then Harley Johnson comes in and I said, 'Now, we'll have some music.' Betty would sit there on the bench and read her book and wouldn't say a word back then."

When the little schoolhouse sold, Clevenger and Ben made a decision to re-open the McDowell hootenanny and the original schedule of every two weeks was started again in 1977. People were ecstatic that the fun was beginning again.

Arrangements were made for Paula and Alan Hightower of McDowell to manage the concession stand and the crowds began to gather. They turned out in droves and continue to do so to this day. "I can hear them all the way down here where I live," Norma said. "It would be clearer if it weren't for that little hill there, but it sounds really good." She hesitated. "I'd still go, but I've got too lazy. I'm 78 years old....I can, but I'm just too lazy."

"They were trying to decide on a name for it," she continued, "and the boys wanted to keep the 'Gold' from the band's name. They were playing for an event in Springfield and talking about it. The lady said, 'Why not the Golden Jubilee?' and that was how it came about. We were doing upholstery work and we made the sign for the front with the material that's still there...McDowell Gold Jubilee."

One family that "darkened the doors" for many years were the Carpenters—Si, Paul, Ava, Thelma, Chloe, Dorothy, Mary, Lillie, and nephew Gary and nieces Marie and Shirl. Of these, only Gary and Shirl are still alive to attend. Their signature white heads were recognized by all as they lined up in their special seats. Lillie said to me, "I lived in Neosho and come up here at the beginning. I never missed. Si and Gloria came right after that. I remember when the kitchen was on the west and there wasn't anything except benches to sit on. Alan Hightower was doing the concessions."

C. J. and Mary Borushasky of Wheaton, Missouri, began attending 26 years ago. He says, "I don't know where we'd get any better entertainment than this. I remember when Gary Cook was just a little fat boy and he and Coones' little girl always sang together. And out of all the years of coming, Marcele Craig is the closest to the ladies I grew up listening to."

Later, when Wayne's second son Wyatt was small, he would perch on the bench at the Jubilee and watch the movements of all the musicians, especially his grandfather, Raymond Clevenger. It was obvious he was going to become a musician and he was master of the mandolin before he was a teenager, going on to perform across the state and beyond with a well-known award-winning group, Downhome Bluegrass, before it disbanded. Wyatt is one of the many young people who have moved on to bigger and better things following their musical beginnings at the McDowell Gold Jubilee.

About 1975 or 76, Ben sponsored the addition of a hall and jam room on the southeast end of the building. A tiny bathroom with a pipeline that ran to the well was temporarily added but the traffic proved to be too heavy, so it was later removed. To this day, outhouses are updated regularly. Later, a well was drilled, but the old pump remains standing to the east of the building.

In 1985, when Raymond died, Ben took over the duties of Master of Ceremonies. A board was formed consisting of Bill Ozbun, Ben, and Bob

Nichols (at the present time a fourth member, Jim Daniels, is also serving) and their application for non-profit status was approved. Betty Henderson was put in charge of public relations work and keeping track of the acts. The rules were approved that each musician would be allowed three numbers or a group would be allowed twenty minutes on stage at a time. These rules apply to this day. Around that time, Raymond Thomas of Cross Hollow began traditionally opening each session with his fiddle music and continues to do so.

Sylvia and Bill Ozbun took over the concessions in about 1989 after assisting the Hightowers for a couple of years. At that time, the decision was made to do some additional remodeling. The kitchen was moved to the east side of the side wall and a warm-up room was added. The old wood heating stove was removed and Monett Sheet Metal donated a new furnace. Davis Plumbing of Monett gave the group a propane tank and installed it. Junior McKinley, who was mayor of Aurora, donated the big sign at the entrance to the lane. A roof was added. In 1993, old theater seats were purchased from Royce Campbell in Strang, Oklahoma, for $1.00 each and Ben, Bill, Bob, and Ken Langford borrowed a truck from Friend Tire of Monett and drove over to haul them back. Several years later, the roof had to be replaced a second time and, in addition to the generous donations of audience members, a good portion was given by the Pearl Foundation of Monett. Regular maintenance is kept up by donations and concessions.

There is seating in the main area for approximately 180 people with additional standing room and it is usually filled to capacity. The halls are full of happy, laughing people and the two added rooms are stuffed with musicians and listeners. Seats run around the perimeters of each room and they are always filled, as are the extra foldout chairs. Many times, it is difficult to hear the music for the laughter and talking.

The people who come range from the very young to the very old and they usually all enjoy it. Visitors have come from most of the states and many have returned again and again. There have been a number from other countries and they are entranced with the uniqueness of the program. A foreign exchange student from France came fairly regularly a number of years ago and more recently another from Belgium came to enjoy the music and the hands held out in friendship. Visitors from England, Mexico, and Canada have come to hear the music and most recently, two visiting music professors from Japan, teaching at Missouri State University (formerly Southwest Missouri State University) in Springfield, brought their interpreters and enjoyed an evening of listening to the offerings of the hill country folk here in the Ozarks, where there still remains a remnant of the way things used to be.

Some well-known names have entertained throughout the past years*, but of more consequence than these are the musicians who have learned to play and sing at the feet of their elders. Norma said, "Raymond told me he wanted a place for the young folks to go and have a good time and they wouldn't have to get out and run around and look for things to do and get in trouble." One of the things that is most important to a folklorist is the passing on of family traditions and over the more than fifty years that the McDowell Gold Jubilee has been doing the programs, the practice has been repeated frequently.[†]

So, Raymond Clevenger's wish, made in 1961, has come true and is still doing so. The music is alive and well and still going strong. Wayne summed it all up, "In a way, Dad sort of hated to start it up again…you know, the regular music. He and his friends, well, they'd go down to the James River and go fishin'…but, well, this was everybody's absolutely favorite thing to do. Over the years, the communication between the neighbors has died down. The school went away. The store went away. The church nearly has. There isn't any town here at all anymore. So everyone looks forward to the Jubilee, you know. It's the way things used to be. And that's good."

[*] Entertainers who have performed at the Jubilee over the years include:

Earnie Bishop
The Hammer Sisters
Curly and Speedy Haworth
The Johnson Family
Bill and Mona Jones
Gordon McCann
Harold Morrison
Leonard and Francis Smith
Bob Walsh
Slim Wilson
Sonny Woodring
Vern Young

[†] A partial list of families from the region who have played at the Jubilee:

Black (Fred, Jackie and Jimmie – "The Black Mountain Boys")
Butterfield (Gary, Angela, Holly)
Clevenger (Raymond, Wayne, Wyatt – "Downhome Bluegrass")
Coones (Lyn, Tonya, Eric – "Brightwater Junction")
Craft (Roy, Betty Jo, Mark, Kendra – "The Roy Craft Band")
Dunn (Lonnie, Donna; Gary Cook – "Downhome Bluegrass")
Johnson (Harley, Mike)
Keil (Fred; Will Hillburn)
Nichols (Bob, Bob Jr.)
Raley (Ken, Deanna, Tracy, Brandon, Grant – "Family Tradition")
Rickman (Gerald, Gary, Larry, Heath, Brandon)
Savage (James, Lori; Cody Cantwell – "Wilderness Road")
Stoneking (Fred, Alita, Lucas)
Thomas (Paul, Pauletta, Jimmy)
Whisman (Mike, Lyn, Stephanie, Shawn, Josh)

Every other Saturday from October to May, between 20 and 25 acts take the stage at the Jubilee. As performers arrive, Betty adds their names to her list.
(Photo taken in the summer of 2000; used courtesy of Drew Beisswenger and Betty Henderson; http://library.missouristate.edu/projects/jamsessions/mcdowell.htm; acc. 6/6/15)

To learn more about...

The McDowell Gold Jubilee and Other Music Parties

Galbraith, Art. "Music Parties in the Ozarks," *Ozarks Mountaineer*, 28 #6-7 (August 1980): 35+.

Henigan, Julie. "The McClurg Music Parties: A Living Tradition," *Old-Time Herald*, 4 #5 (Fall 1994): 20-22.

McEowen, Bob. "Hootenanny in the Holler: Three Decades of Music and Fellowship at the McDowell Gold Jubilee," *Rural Missouri*, 61#2 (Feb. 2009): 8-9; (also www.ruralmissouri.org/09pages/09FebMcDowell.html; acc. 6/6/15).

"Jam Sessions and Jig Dancing," *OzarksWatch Video Magazine* (Ozarks Public Television; KOZK, Springfield, MO; aired 1/22/2010); features Gordon McCann; (http://video.optv.org/video/1393139156; acc. 6/6/15).

Jam Sessions and Jig Dancing (VHS tape; Southwest MO State Univ., 1999); Gordon McCann, Art Galbraith; [different from item above with same name].

"Jam Sessions in Southwest Missouri: The McDowell Gold Jubilee" (http://library.missouristate.edu/projects/jamsessions/mcdowell.htm; acc. 6/6/15).

"A Music Tradition: The McDowell Gold Jubilee," *OzarksWatch Video Magazine* (Ozarks Public Television; KOZK, Springfield, MO, aired 1/13/13); features the Hendersons (http://video.optv.org/video/2332654351; acc. 6/6/15).

Patrick, Michael. "Ozark Music Parties," *Ozarks Mountaineer*, 26 #3 (April 1978): 26-27.

Author Betty Henderson plays bass with her husband and friends at the McDowell Gold Jubilee hootenanny
(Photo taken in the summer of 2000; used courtesy of Drew Beisswenger and Betty Henderson; http://library.missouristate.edu/projects/jamsessions/mcdowell.htm; acc. 6/6/15)

The Word "Hootenanny"

Seeger, Pete. "How Hootenanny Came to Be," *Sing Out!* #5 (1955): 32-33.

Tamony, Peter. "Hootenanny: The Word, Its Content and Continuum," *Western Folklore*, 22 (July 1963): 165-170.

Writings by Betty Craker Henderson

"A writer first of all, an entertainer at heart"
(http://owinc.webs.com/apps/profile/67420823; acc. 6/6/15; courtesy of the author)

"[Betty's website]" (http://bettycrakerhenderson.webs.com; acc. 6/6/15).

Child Support (Hard Shell Word Factory, 2001).
   Betty's first novel, it won an award from the Missouri Writers' Guild.

From Trash to Treasure: The Evolution of an Ozark Junkyard (St. Charles, MO: High Hill Press, 2010).
   A humorous memoir about how Betty lived her husband's junkyard dream.

Junkyard Bones (High Hill Press, 2011).
   A children's mystery novel.

Echoes of the Ozarks (Ozark Writers League, AWOC.COM Publ.); Vol. I (2005); Vol. II (2006); Vol. III (2007), Vol. IV (2010), Vol. V (2009).

Mysteries of the Ozarks (St. Charles, MO: High Hill Press, 2003-2011).
   Betty's stories appear in these two series of short story collections.

Introduction – *"Freaks and Fiddle Tunes"*

"Those were the days!" – the early 1970s folk revival scene in St. Louis

Paul Stamler, the author of this article, is one of St. Louis' multi-talented Renaissance men—a performer, an audio recording engineer, an adjunct professor, an independent scholar, and a freelance writer, among other pursuits. His expertise in audio engineering is recognized within his profession as witnessed by his being hired to teach recording classes in Webster University's highly regarded media program, where for many years he has been helping budding audio engineers hone their craft. He also shares his knowledge by writing articles for *Recording* magazine and *audioXpress*, among other professional publications. He has designed and built audio equipment, remastered hundreds of LPs and 78s onto CD to improve their sound quality, and engineered a variety of folk recordings, including *Jump Fingers, Face the Creek*, the Buckhannon Brothers' *Little River Stomp*, and Julie Henigan's *American Stranger*. He has also written occasional reviews and obituaries for periodicals such as *Sing Out!*, St. Louis' *FolkFire* magazine, and England's *Folk Music Journal*, in addition to articles on topics such as civil rights and peace. (See a selected list of Paul's writings on page 30.)

Paul's main avocation, however, is his radio show called *No Time to Tarry Here*, which has been broadcast weekly since 1987 on KDHX, an independent community-based radio station in St. Louis. Pablo Meshugi is his "nom d'air," as he calls it. The name came about because, when he began this show, Paul was also working for the local public television station and wanted to separate his radio and television personas. He took the first name from the Spanish name for Paul and the surname from the Yiddish word for nutty. The combination of ballads, dance tunes, gospel songs, politics, and nuttiness on his show gives us a sense of Paul's approach to life and music. The music he plays on *No Time to Tarry Here* demonstrates the breadth and depth of his interest in all aspects of folk music, though he is most concerned that his audience not forget the historical roots of American music. His show, currently broadcast on Sundays from 2:00 to 4:00 pm, is also available online at: http://kdhx.org/play/radio-shows/no-time-to-tarry-here. (An interesting side note – the show's title comes from a hymn collected by Missouri's Loman Cansler and recorded by MFS members Cathy Barton and Dave Para.)

A talented musician, Paul regularly plays guitar in The Original Speckled Band, a group that provides music for the St. Louis English Country Dancers, though he's also been known to jam with the crowd of regulars at the Missouri Folklore Society's annual meetings.

Paul also serves on the editorial board of the *Traditional Ballad Index* (http://www.fresnostate.edu/folklore/BalladSearch.html), in addition to being a frequent contributor to the Digital Tradition database and the Mudcat Café Forum, both of which appear on the high-traffic Mudcat Café website at http://mudcat.org, where you can find extensive information about folk songs, ballads, folksingers, and related topics.

Introduction   19

A note from Lyn:
I subscribe to an excellent listserv called "Ballad-L" where I had always enjoyed the comments of one Paul J. Stamler, a guy who was obviously knowledgeable about anything to do with American and British folk music. I got the chance to meet him in 2002 when I organized a panel of folk song database compilers and producers for the American Folklore Society's annual meeting, where Paul very ably represented the *Traditional Ballad Index*. When I decided to give a paper on Columbia's Chez Coffeehouse at the Missouri Folklore Society's 100th anniversary meeting in 2006, I wanted to add a comparative dimension and, knowing that Paul had been involved with the Focal Point Coffeehouse in St. Louis (a venue similar to the Chez), asked him to join us. He agreed and his paper so impressed me that I immediately asked him if he would be willing to write an article for this issue of the journal, which—luckily—he was and this article is the result. Enjoy!

Paul Stamler's band plays for English country dances in St. Louis
(Google image search, "Paul Stamler;" acc. 7/11/12; permission of the author)

>>> Definition of the Word "Freaks"

The Hippie Dictionary (John and Joan McCleary; Ten Speed Press, rev/exp 2004.)

freak a self-denigrating term used by hippies to describe themselves. Early on, the hippie counterculture was characterized as "a freak of society" by the straight culture, so, in defiance, hippies adopted the word 'freak' and used it themselves. (related def: **hippie** what straight people called the people who called themselves freaks!)

A hootenanny held in Gaslight Square in 1963
(Thelma Blumberg Collection, Photo Database [Photo #402.178];
The State Historical Society of Missouri Research Center-St. Louis
[http://tjrhino1.umsl.edu/whmc/view.php]; acc. 6/6/15)

Gaslight Square

Paul's article (which starts on the next page) mentions Gaslight Square, the name given to an entertainment district that built up in the area around Olive and Boyle Streets in the Central West End of St. Louis in the 1960s. The Square was known for its gas street lamps and Victorian architecture. It was a thriving entertainment district, home to many restaurants and venues where patrons could enjoy poetry, dancing, and theater, in addition to many types of music, including jazz, ragtime, blues, and folk. It attracted writers such as Jack Kerouac and Allen Ginsberg and entertainers such as the Smothers Brothers, Lenny Bruce, Tina Turner, Barbra Streisand, Mike Nichols and Elaine May, and George Carlin, as well as folk artists such as Ian and Sylvia. Sadly, flight to the suburbs and fear of crime killed the district by the mid-1970s.

To learn more about Gaslight Square...

Crone, Thomas. *Gaslight Square: An Oral History* (Wm. & Joseph, 2004).

Fuegner, Rich and David Roth. *Gaslight Square Illuminated* (Virginia, 2010).

"Gaslight Square" (https://en.wikipedia.org/wiki, search name; acc. 6/6/15).

"Gaslight Square" (https://youtube.com/watch?v=MAUA7st75ds; acc. 6/6/15).

Marren, Bruce. *Gaslight Square: The Forgotten Landmark* (film, 2002).

Marren, Bruce. *Gaslight Square: The Legend Lives On* (film, 2005). [View at: https://www.youtube.com/watch?v=F8I79nWo6h4; acc. 6/6/15]

FREAKS AND FIDDLE TUNES:
THE EARLY-1970s FOLK REVIVAL IN ST. LOUIS

Paul J. Stamler

When I arrived in St. Louis in 1967, the folk music scene could best be described as moribund. The "folk scare" of 1958-64 had been overshadowed by the explosion of contemporary rock and psychedelia and Gaslight Square had been exploited by the greedy and seedy and was on its last legs. On-campus coffeehouses sputtered into existence, and out again, while a political science professor would occasionally bring friends into the Washington University quadrangle to play bluegrass on warm days.

A small group of families, centered around Bill and Janet Boyer in suburban Kirkwood, kept the flame alive through an informal organization called the Folk Song Society. This group's membership and approach came from an earlier generation of the revival, one which predated the "folk scare." They were part of a movement within the revival that was anchored at the Fox Hollow Folk Festival in New York, an event founded by Bob and Evelyn Beers – Bob Beers was Janet Boyer's brother. The Folk Song Society put on occasional house concerts and jam sessions, held an annual campout in the Ozarks, and (I hope I'm not breaking confidentiality on this) on the day after Christmas would turn up at an unsuspecting friend's house at dawn, put on a mummers' play, and demand breakfast.

Aside from this group, however, the folk scene was quiescent. How came it, then, that half a dozen years later a popular folk music scene would flourish in this city? For, if you went into a St. Louis club in the early 1970s, you would be as likely to hear old-time string-band music, country blues, or bluegrass as rock or jazz, and concerts featuring blues or Celtic music performers unknown outside of specialist circles would draw packed houses on local campuses with minimal publicity.

In every community, the folk revival built on different institutional centers. In Chicago, it was the Old Town School of Folk Music, the Fret Shop, and the University of Chicago Folk Festival. In New York, it was the Greenwich Village club scene and concerts at Town Hall. In Columbia, Missouri, it was the Chez Coffeehouse and the University of Missouri. To all intents and purposes, in St. Louis the revival came about because of the convergence of five factors: a conscientious objector with time on his hands, a performer seeking a career change, a community radio station, a concert at Washington University's Graham Chapel, and a reel of recording tape.

The Conscientious Objector

Barry Bergey was a "PK" – a preacher's kid – from New Haven, MO. He had applied for and received conscientious objector status during the Vietnam War and was assigned to alternative service at a mental hospital in St. Louis; when his service was over, he stayed on and began looking for a job.

Barry was and is a quiet person with an uncanny knack for meeting and getting along with people and he had always been interested in traditional music. Around 1971, he got a phone call from one of the people he'd met – Johnny Shines. Shines, a transitional figure who'd traveled with Robert Johnson in the 1930s and went on to become a member of the first generation of Chicago blues players, had been stranded in St. Louis by a broken-down car and needed money to make it home to Arkansas, where he now lived. Barry began calling friends at Washington University, where he booked an on-campus lounge used for poetry readings and discussions with visiting scholars.

Washington University in those years was a pretty dead place on weekends. If a student wasn't a member of a fraternity (and most students in those iconoclastic years were not), there was nothing to do on Friday or Saturday nights; the huge variety of cultural events common on today's campuses simply did not exist. As a result, if you organized an event, people would attend.

The concert was a success, Johnny Shines made enough money to fix his car and get home, and Barry Bergey had learned some things. He'd discovered that concerts weren't all that hard to put on, he'd found that they could be successful, and he'd found that they could be fun to do. He wanted to do more, so he got together with a group of friends including blues singer Leroy Pierson, banjo player Jim Olin, and lawyer Francis Oates, and they created a not-for-profit organization called Missouri Friends of the Folk Arts or MFFA. (Barry's small-town roots were reflected in the "FFA" part of the abbreviation, while the more urban members of the group took due note of the fact that the initials could be pronounced "muh-fuh.")

MFFA put on more concerts—they helped bring the "Traveling Folk Festival" to campus, featuring Mississippi Fred McDowell and the Georgia Sea Island Singers; it was hosted by Mike Seeger. They did a multi-media weekend called "Ozark High," featuring music and culture from the Ozark mountain region, and every year they put on a cider-pressing party and jam session—somewhere Barry had managed to find an old-fashioned cider press. Then, in late 1971, he got a call from another person he'd met, Norman Blake.

The Musician

Norman Blake was born in Rising Fawn, Georgia, and (aside from a short time in the army) had spent his entire life as a musician. For many years, he'd worked as a session player in Nashville, playing guitar on Bob Dylan's influential *Nashville Skyline* album and working with Johnny Cash on his recordings and TV show. More recently, he'd toured extensively backing John Hartford. In the early 1970s, though, he was ready to step out on his own as a performer. For his first concert as a headliner, he lined up banjo player and orthodontist Ed Cullis as a sideman, recorded tracks for an album on the brand new Rounder Records label, and called Barry Bergey for a booking.

Barry obliged; he booked Graham Chapel on the Washington University campus, and MFFA sent out a newsletter and printed up a few fliers, which he posted on campus. I saw one of those fliers and decided to go to the concert; Blake's playing on Dylan's album was impressive, but what really decided me was that he had an album coming out on Rounder. I'd just discovered the label, having bought album #0002, and thought they showed real promise. Perhaps more significant than the newsletter and fliers, though, was that on the afternoon before the concert, one of his hosts took Blake down to the studios of radio station KDNA.

Staff of KDNA radio during the "Freaks and Fiddle Tunes" era
(KDNAstaff.jpg; gailpellettproductions.com; acc. 7/13/12)

The Radio Station

Community radio began in 1940s California as an effort by left-wing activists to get alternative political and cultural ideas onto a mass medium. The first generation of stations, run by what became the Pacifica Foundation, was strongly political: socialists, communists, Trotskyites and anarchists all stirred their ideas into a bubbling pot, along with alternative-culture advocates in what would become known as the "Beat Generation." (The Pacifica stations are still around; nationally, their best-known program is probably Amy Goodman's *Democracy Now!*)

In the 1960s, a second and very different generation of community radio stations arose; the inspirational figure in this era was a visionary named Lorenzo Milam. He founded a station in the Pacific Northwest and wrote what would become the bible of the new community radio movement, *Sex and*

Broadcasting. The book was noteworthy for many things, including the fact that it contained nothing whatsoever about sex; in the introduction, Milam explained that he'd put that in the title to attract attention and sell more books. What the book did contain, however, was a strong case for why a new kind of community radio was important and necessary, and clear detailed information about how to start a station.

Across the country, people did. In St. Louis, the person who took inspiration from Milam was Jeremy Lansman. Lansman and friends, working on a shoestring (and a loan from Milam), started an FM station operating out of an old house in what remained of Gaslight Square. (FM in those years was still the stepchild of the broadcast world; frequencies were reasonably inexpensive and easy to obtain. That would change within a few years as AM withered.) The station was called KDNA; the initials did not come from genetics, as most people thought, but from the fact that, when filling out an FCC license application, one was instructed to enter "DNA" in certain blanks as an abbreviation for "Does Not Apply."

KDNA was different from any radio station ever heard in St. Louis before or since. Where a modern community or public radio station might have programs devoted to jazz, bluegrass, classical music, political discussion, and poetry scattered across the dial, a KDNA listener could often hear all of those and more within the space of a single hour, perhaps tied together by a tape of ocean waves played in between cuts. One of the most eclectic program hosts was John Ross, a member of the Folk Song Society; on his program, you could hear, in succession, Bach (played on a synthesizer), Mississippi John Hurt, the Beach Boys, field recordings from Mozambique, and a group of rank-and-file dissidents mounting a challenge to the leadership of their Teamsters Union local.

In the living room of the house from which KDNA broadcast, there was an old, slightly rickety couch with a couple of microphones in front of it. On a Saturday afternoon, it wasn't unusual for a musician to wander down to the station, ring the doorbell, sit on the couch, and be put on the air. That's what Norman Blake did—for about an hour, he picked guitar, sang songs, and told stories on the radio while his hosts reminded listeners about his concert that night.

The Concert in Graham Chapel

The concert drew about 200 patrons, decent attendance for a virtually unknown musician. After a warm-up by a local trio, Blake and Cullis came onstage. Blake was wearing a long jacket, slightly at odds with his sport shirt and jeans; he began the concert by saying, "I hope y'all won't think I'm too formal tonight, coming out in my jacket, but I've got a rip in the seat of my britches...They say a performer should show something of himself to the audience, and I'd be getting off to a real good start."

As the crowd finished laughing, Blake tore into his song "Randall Collins" and for the next ninety or so minutes proceeded to show his audience more than they'd ever bargained for. His playing was phenomenal, without doubt, but what astonished and delighted the audience just as much was the world of new musical styles to which he opened the door. Names like Charlie Poole and the Delmore Brothers rolled off his tongue when introducing songs and tunes, names utterly new to most of his listeners. He played bluegrass, early country music, and the various styles lumped together as "old-time"; along with the old music, he mixed in his own compositions, brilliant songs that sounded a century old themselves.

By the end of the evening, the audience knew they'd seen something remarkable, and they reacted accordingly. It's said of the rock band The Velvet Underground that the reason they were so influential was that, although only 100 people bought their first album, every one of those people went out and started a band. It would only be a slight exaggeration to say the same about the 200 listeners at Norman Blake's concert that evening; they went home and called their friends, picked up instruments and tried out the new sounds they'd heard, and if not every one of them started a band, many of the people they phoned did.

The word of mouth from that evening was unlike any in my experience, but it wasn't the only factor in spreading the news about Blake and this new music so quickly. It had help.

The Reel of Tape

The sound person for Norman Blake's Graham Chapel concert was an electrical engineer employed at Washington University. He was also an audio hobbyist and had recently acquired his first professional tape recorder. He brought the recorder along, taped the concert, and got a release from Blake to play the recording over KDNA.

The recording aired twice, and I can assure you that on both occasions home tape recorders were running all over St. Louis. Those tapes, and copies of them, and copies of the copies, began circulating in the informal underground of tape collectors and musicians; the latter used them to learn tunes and songs, but also to glean from Blake's introductions the names of the old-time musicians from whose records he'd learned. Within a month, bands were forming and musicians were working out songs by Blake, Charlie Poole, and the Delmores. In six months, the bands were playing the local clubs and the music scene was off and rolling.

In fact, the boom was on. When MFFA brought Blake back to Graham Chapel, with minimal publicity, the building which would legally hold 1200 people saw at least 1400 come through the door before Barry decided to post the "sold out" sign. Every aisle was packed with seated fans; even the staircase to the balcony, where it was impossible to see the stage, was filled with desperate patrons. The atmosphere when Blake walked out was electric with anticipation to a degree I have never witnessed at any other concert in any genre, and Blake did not disappoint. This night was, if anything, more revelatory than the first; this tape, too, was made available to KDNA and promptly entered into the informal circulation network. (I suspect that there were more underground tapes of Norman Blake circulating in St. Louis in those years than there were of Bob Dylan, which is no small comparison.)

The Aftermath

For several years, the folk scene that was born from the Blake concerts flourished. MFFA put on a reunion concert featuring blues veterans Roosevelt Sykes and Henry Townsend, packing the chapel again with college students who had never heard of either, but who would come to anything the organization produced. MFFA brought a then-unknown Celtic group, the Boys of the Lough, and packed the house again. MFFA's activities created spin offs, including a still-active contra dance organization and the all-source-performer Frontier Folklife Festival, held for several years under the Gateway Arch.

Actually, this story is only half-finished; the peregrinations of the St. Louis folk scene would take more space than I have here. I've had to omit important threads, including the further contributions of Folk Song Society members, who founded two enduring institutions of St. Louis' folk revival: the Music Folk store and the Focal Point Arts Center. I would, though, like to quickly re-examine the importance of several aspects of this "creation story."

The events that created the folk revival of the early 1970s seem evanescent and random: a conscientious objector, a musician, a radio station, a concert, and a reel of tape. I would like to suggest, however, that the particulars of the story were anything but random; instead, I believe they were firmly embedded in a cultural context broadly, and inaccurately, known as "The Sixties."

Consider the factors which came together. Norman Blake was a musician from a traditional background – but with an awareness of musical culture made possible by the technology of sound reproduction and the reissuing of earlier material on LP recordings, which began in the 1950s and gathered force in the 1960s. He was also a man whose creative directions were shaped by the musical world around him and, in the Sixties, that was an eclectic world indeed. Blake's extended explorations of fiddle tunes on flat-picked guitar owed more to the improvisational style of San Francisco rock bands such as the Grateful Dead than it did to tradition; such things were simply not done in the old-time or even the bluegrass world, although the latter paved the way.

KDNA was similarly embedded in its time; in a way, the station embodied it. Community radio may have begun with hard-edged politicos in the 1940s, but this generation of community radio, although it certainly included politics, had far more of the free-flowing "hippie ethos" than its predecessors. (You knew I'd say "hippie" sooner or later!) It shared with the times an extraordinary informality, whether it manifested itself in unorthodox stylistic juxtapositions, ocean-wave recordings, or program hosts doing station identifications while chewing on a sandwich. That informality was crucial: it gave the station an environment open enough that a musician could walk in unannounced and be put on the air.

Another context in which this story is embedded is technological: it was the first era in which many people owned tape recorders. These had been exotic devices in previous decades, mostly found in recording studios and radio stations, but companies like Sony and Roberts had created a consumer market, and prices had dropped to the point where even young people who weren't particularly well-off could afford them. The underground tape-swapping network of this period was a fairly new phenomenon, and it certainly contributed to the impact these events had on the scene.

Finally, without wanting to psychoanalyze an old buddy, I think it likely that the humanistic impulses which prompted Barry Bergey, like so many in that time, to become a conscientious objector were the same ones that led to his interest in musical forms and styles of a populist nature.

The folk revival changed many people in many places and St. Louis was certainly no exception. It led some to careers in folklore or musical programming and others to performing, for pay or for love. It gave us that most precious of human commodities: connection – with our culture, our times, and each other. It was a gift of the time in which it arose and the people who made it possible, and for this gift we are deeply thankful.

The cover of influential guitarist Norman Blake's first album, released in 1972
(http://www.allmusic.com/album/back-home-in-sulphur-springs-mw0000311981; acc. 6/6/15)

Radio station KDHX, from which author Paul Stamler has broadcast his show *No Time to Tarry Here* every week since 1987
(http://en.wikipedia.org/wiki/KDHX; acc. 6/6/15)

To learn more about…

Folk Music in St. Louis

Everts-Boehm, Dana. "'You'll Never Get Ireland in America': Irish Traditional Music and Dance in St. Louis, Missouri," Missouri Folk Arts Program (http://mofolkarts.missouri.edu/docs/irish.pdf; acc. 6/6/15).

FolkFire – The Folk and Ethnic Dance and Music Resource for St. Louis and the Central States [articles are available online from all 1996-98 issues and some 1994-95 and 1999-2001 issues] (http://www.folkfire.org; acc. 6/6/15).

"The History of the Focal Point," The Focal Point Arts Center (http://www.thefocalpoint.org/history.html; acc. 6/6/15).

Music Folk (http://www.musicfolk.com; acc. 6/6/15).
[Click on "About Us" for access to some good articles.]

The Folk Revival in North America

"American Folk Music Revival," *Wikipedia* (http://en.wikipedia.org/wiki/American_folk_music_revival; acc. 6/6/15).

Cantwell, Robert. *When We Were Good: The Folk Revival* (Harvard, 1996).

Cohen, Ronald D. *A History of Folk Music Festivals in the United States* (Scarecrow Press, 2008).

Cohen, Ronald D. *Rainbow Quest: The Folk Music Revival and American Society, 1940-1970* (University of Massachusetts Press, 2002).

Cohen, Ronald D. *"Wasn't That a Time!": Accounts of the Folk Music Revival* (Scarecrow, 1995).

Cohen, Ronald D. and Rachel Donaldson. *Roots of the Revival: American and British Folk Music in the 1950s* (University of Illinois Press, 2014).

Coltman, Bob. *Paul Clayton and the Folksong Revival* (Scarecrow, 2008).

Dunaway, David King and Molly Beer. *Singing Out: An Oral History of America's Folk Music Revivals* (New York: Oxford University Press, 2010).

Filene, Benjamin. *Romancing the Folk: Public Memory and American Roots Music* (University of North Carolina Press, 2000).

Gottesman, Stephen. "Tom Dooley's Children: An Overview of the Folk Music Revival, 1958-1965," *Popular Music & Society*, 5 #5 (1977): 61-78.

Gruning, Thomas. *Millennium Folk: American Folk Music since the Sixties* (University of Georgia Press, 2006).

Jabbour, Alan. "The Flowering of the Folk Revival" in *American Roots Music* (Abrams, 2001): 56-83.

Kristofferson, Kris. *Folk Revival* (America's Music 3; VHS; Turner, 1996).

Mitchell, Gillian. *The North American Folk Music Revival: Nation and Identity in the United States and Canada, 1945-1980* (Ashgate, 2007).

Rosenberg, Neil V. *Transforming Tradition: Folk Music Revivals Examined* (University of Illinois Press, 1993).

Santelli, Robert; Holly George-Warren, and Jim Brown, eds. *American Roots Music* (Abrams, 2001).

Weissman, Dick. *Which Side Are You On?: An Inside History of the Folk Music Revival in America* (Continuum, 2005).

Selected Writings by Paul J. Stamler

"Arthel Lane 'Doc' Watson (1923-2012)" [obituary]
Folk Music Journal, 10 #3 (2013): 423-426.

audioXpress [online magazine]
(http://audioamateur.com/ax-supplementary-material, "Stamler"; acc. 6/6/15).

"Frontier Folklife Festival: Photo Essay," *M.F.F.A.*, 6 #1 (Spring 1979): 8-9.

"'Just the Thought of Going Home': Sheila Kay Adams and the Singers of Madison County, N.C.," *Sing Out!* 46 #2 (Summer 2002): 60-65, 67-69.

"Janet Boyer, 1927-2008" [obituary], *Sing Out!* 52#3 (Fall 2008): 169+.

"Passing of Multitalented St. Louis Musician Steve Mote" [obituary]
Sing Out! 46 #3 (Fall 2002): 25.

Recording [magazine] (http://www.recordingmag.com/issues/archives.html, search "Stamler" for a list of Paul's articles; acc. 6/6/15).

"Phønix: Rejuvenating Danish Folk," *Sing Out!* 47 #4 (Winter 2004): 57+.

"Reviews," *FolkFire* (http://www.folkfire.org, find "Stamler; acc. 6/6/15).

"Robert Winslow Gordon" (pp. 171-189) and "Commodification and Revival" (pp. 207-221) in *The Ballad Collectors of North America: How Gathering Folksongs Transformed Academic Thought and American Identity*, ed. by Scott B. Spencer (Lanham, MD: Scarecrow Press, 2012).

"Sam Hinton: Master of the Solo Diatonic Harmonica" [recording review, "Off the Beaten Track" column], *Sing Out!* 49 #3 (Fall 2005): 134+.

About Paul: Hyland, Deborah. "KDHX Deejay Paul Stamler," *FolkFire*, Jan./Feb. 2000 (http://www.folkfire.org/rev7n1.htm; acc. 6/6/15).

Paul Stamler (photo by Rebecca Taylor; courtesy of the author)

Introduction – "Nancy Dill"

An Ozark native investigates a song handed down in his family

The next article is Jim Vandergriff's story of his personal quest for the history of a song he heard his mother sing to his daughter in the early 1980s. Jim, a Missourian born and bred and a long-time MFS member, lets us join him as he follows a crooked path through the byways of folk song books and the new folk song resources on the Internet to discover where his mother learned the song and how it might have descended through both sides of her family. He journeys back through the centuries to his ancestors' home in the British Isles, taking us on fascinating side trips along the way.

Dr. James H. Vandergriff
(Courtesy of the author)

Only four generations removed from his ancestors who helped settle the Ozarks, Jim was born in rural Laclede County, near Stoutland, Missouri. He grew up there and in Pulaski and Phelps counties. He got his BS and MA degrees in English from Central Missouri State University in Warrensburg and later his PhD in Teacher Education from the University of Arizona. During his early years as a teacher, he survived a couple of stints at high schools (including McCluer North in Florissant, Missouri, only blocks from where Lyn Wolz, one of the editors of this issue, grew up!). Until he retired in 2010, Jim was assistant professor of educational studies at Knox College in Galesburg, Illinois, where he taught a mixture of literature, composition, education, and folklore courses. He taught the same types of courses earlier at Central Missouri State, the University of Missouri, Southwest Missouri State, Drury College, Emporia State University, and the University of Oregon.

Besides the articles Jim has written and edited for scholarly publications (some of which are included in the selected bibliography of his works on page 69), he has written more than thirty-five book reviews, many of them for this journal. He has also written poetry that appeared in literary periodicals such as *Pleiades* and *Encore*.

Jim's extensive work with MFS publications has included serving as the General Editor of this journal for several years and as a periodic editor of, and contributor to, the Society's newsletter. He also led a project to digitize the back issues of this journal and the MFS newsletter for their eventual presentation on the MFS website. [Update: The Society's board has signed a contract with non-profit organization Hathi Trust to take over that work for the Society. Soon, nearly thirty years' worth of back issues will be available on the Internet.] In addition, for almost twenty years now, Jim has been the Book Review Editor for this journal and, with the help of his wife Donna Jurich (who served as the editor of the MFS newsletter for several years), has been staffing the exhibit room at the MFS annual meeting for many years.

One of the dwindling number of charter members who attended the first meeting of the revived Missouri Folklore Society in Columbia in 1977, Jim has served on the MFS Board of Directors for nearly four decades. He is also a past president of the Society, having organized the annual meeting in Hannibal in 1990. (He also served as president of the Ozarks Folklore Society for two years in the early 1990s.) Volunteering for these and other jobs that needed doing, Jim has made many substantial and much appreciated contributions to the society, to academia, and to the field of folklore over the past thirty-plus years. He's one of the rocks upon which the Missouri Folklore Society stands and for all of these and other reasons, we thank him for his devoted service.

In addition to his work for the folklore society, Jim has been active in other organizations, mainly in the area of education. He chaired the Commission on American Indian Education for the national Association for Teacher Education for several years and served a term as president of the Illinois Association of Teacher Educators, a group for which he is currently serving as consulting editor. He also has articles on his CV about both education in general and education for Native Americans in particular, a population in which he has long had a special interest.

Jim is currently enjoying the retired life in Tucson, spending a lot of his time with his four grandchildren since his daughter's family moved from Columbia, Missouri, to the Tucson area last year.

So, without further ado, let's embark on our next journey, with Jim acting as our guide, leading us through the twists and turns of his family history and the transatlantic travels of a song his mother sang.

"NANCY DILL"
SEARCHING FOR A SONG MY MOTHER SANG

Jim Vandergriff

Mary Ella Vandergriff Myers neé Perkins (1920-1999), the author's mother
(Photo taken in 1936; courtesy of the author)

In 1982, I chanced to hear my mother singing my three-year-old daughter Amy to sleep. The song sounded like a folk song to me, so I grabbed my tape recorder and asked Mom to start again. Afterwards, I interviewed her about how she had learned the song. My mother's mother died in 1929, when Mom was nine, so Mom and her infant brother were raised by their grandparents. Mom said she learned the song by listening to her grandmother sing it as a lullaby to Barney, my mother's infant brother. Mom's great-grandfather, John W. Armstrong (1848-1884), had been a Confederate soldier serving for most of the war in Company K, 16th Missouri Infantry, and was also the son-in-law of a slaveholder.[1] Because of this family history, I thought I was on the trail of an authentic Southern folk song handed down orally through the generations and, because of the lyrics, probably a song of African-American origin. (See my mother's lyrics on page 54.)

Harl and Lizzie Armstrong Gibson, the author's maternal great-grandparents
(Photo ca. 1905; courtesy of the author)

I'm a real novice at tracking down music, so for the next few years my sporadic efforts to find information about my mother's song were not very fruitful. However, in 1989 or 90, Dr. Jim Jones of Southwest Missouri State University (now Missouri State University) sent me photocopies of two versions of a song called "Nancy Till" from the WPA collection in the Alderman Library at the University of Virginia. The singers were Flora Smith of Waterfall, Virginia (recorded by Susan Morton in 1941) and Etta Kilgore of Wise, Virginia (recorded by Emory Hamilton in 1939). (See the lyrics for these two versions of the song in the Appendix, pages 55 and 56.) Interestingly, the Morton manuscript contains a note that says "this was sung over seventy-five years ago by a man who learned it as a boy on the James River." That note particularly intrigued me because my Armstrong ancestors – my aforementioned great-grandmother's progenitors – first settled in North America on the James River in Virginia about 1740. In 2001, I began to find what became a virtual avalanche of information about the song, shattering some of what I believed about its origins; for example, I learned that William Sidney Mount, the noted early 19th-century African-American painter, makes mention of a song—that may be the same one—as early as 1838.[2] Lacking any

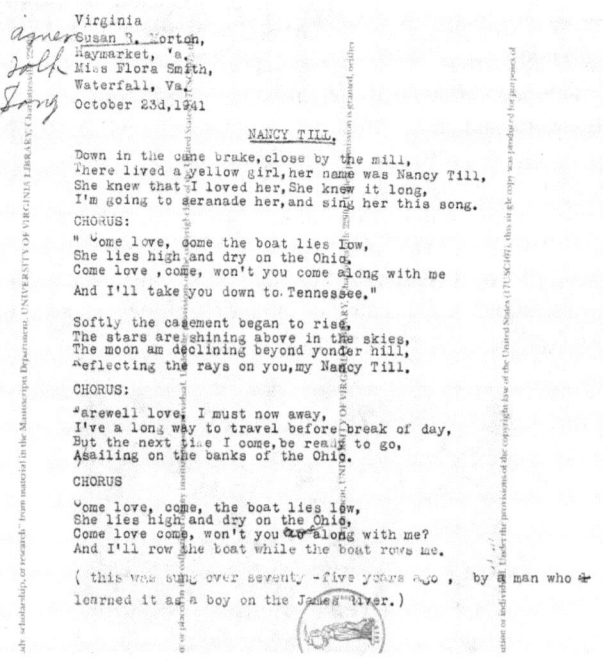

An example of the song "Nancy Till" from a field collection
(WPA Collection, Alderman Library, University of Virginia)

concrete evidence, however, I concluded that my grandmother's version was an old Southern folk song handed down from her Virginia ancestors, though I now think I was wrong about that. This paper is an attempt to determine, by analyzing several versions of the song, whether it is truly a *folk* song, and to provide a clearer picture of how it was transmitted and how it has evolved.

Before I go into what I've learned about my mother's song, though, I need to make a couple of points about what constitutes *folk* music. According to folklore scholar (and MFS member) Jan Brunvand, there are two elements that must be present for a piece to be *folk* music. First, it must be transmitted by the folk process; i.e. one person learns it from another – what is generally referred to as oral transmission. Second, the piece must exist in variants.[3] We generally associate true folk music with anonymous originators as well, though that is not a critical characteristic. Many folk songs have been, or could be, traced to an identifiable composer, as folklorist Barre Toelken points out:

> Because the song's ability to trigger a group's feelings is more important than the practical matter of who the composer was, a folksong usually loses its direct connection with its maker and becomes the ward of those who sing it. It becomes a folksong not simply because a lot of people like it or because thousands have listened to it, but because some have persisted in singing it among themselves, and in their own way.[4]

Likewise, many things we associate with folk style – the ballad form, for instance – are not critical characteristics. Neither is there a particular set of instruments that must be used, nor a set of particular occasions on which the music may be performed, and so on. What *really* matters is how it survives – oral transmission and variants. As Brunvand says, "Only the production of variants via communal re-creation, as a song remains for a time in the possession of a definite group, can justify the label 'folksong.'"[5]

When I interviewed my mother about her song "Nancy Dill," she volunteered to me that she had changed some of the lyrics. For instance, she substituted "pretty little girl" for "colored girl" and "little baby" for "pickaninny," because, as she said, "You can't say those things these days," meaning she didn't want my daughter to learn racist language. Her alteration to the lyrics was quite in line with how folk variations occur: such changes generally occur either intentionally, as was the case with my mother, or because someone has forgotten the original lyrics and makes up some that fit the melody, as was apparently the case with Eleazar Tillet's version collected by Anne and Frank Warner in North Carolina in 1951.

My research pretty quickly led me to believe that my mother's song was not the old plantation folk song that I had thought it to be. I discovered that the score was copyrighted by Firth, Pond & Co. in New York City in 1851. The song was, according to the sheet music, "written for and sung by White's Serenaders," a well-known and very popular group of blackface minstrels who toured extensively in Europe and America in the 1850s.[6] (See lyrics on p. 57.)

However, I later found out that, according to art and music critic Alfred Frankenstein, biographer of artist and fiddler William Sidney Mount, Mount wrote down a song called "Nancy Gill" in 1838, and might have collected versions that he noted in his "fiddler's book" even earlier.[7] This means that the song might well have been in the oral tradition and then collected and printed by Firth, Pond & Co., or rewritten by a "hack" songwriter and sold to the publisher, processes that often happened throughout the history of broadside and sheet music publishing.

Whatever its origin, the song was so popular over the decades that it was subsequently arranged for piano, fiddle, mandolin, guitar, dulcimer, banjo, and Scottish small-pipes, as well as being parodied in a song called "Uncle Bill."[8] (See lyrics on page 58.) There was even a version of it for the Autophone, also called the "Roller Organ," which was something like a hand-cranked player piano or music box.[9]

This is a Gem Roller Organ, one of the novelty instruments for which versions of "Nancy Till" were arranged in the early 20th century; it uses a different "cob" to play each song

(Courtesy of Bob Brooke, Antiques Almanac [http://theantiquesalmanac.com/rollerorgan.htm]; photo originally appeared on The Roller Organ website [http://www.rollerorgans.com]. Both sites acc. 6/6/15)

If the number of sheet music appearances of "Nancy Dill" is any indication, some variation of the song seems to have remained somewhat popular for more than seventy-five years. I've found many examples of sheet music, broadsides, and songsters containing the words and music for this song on the Internet. These include nine appearances under the title "Nancy Till" on the Bodleian Library broadside ballads website, the songs all dated between 1858 and 1885 and all published in England. Six versions appear under that title in the Library of Congress's "American Memory" collection, while the Lester S. Levy Collection of Sheet Music has only one. The George Boswell Collection of folk songs from middle Tennessee includes two versions, while the Digital Tradition database has lyrics for a version called "Nancy Gill" collected in Vernon, British Columbia, in 1915, as well as several other versions under different titles. In short, the Internet has made it quite easy to find printed versions of both the music notation and the lyrics of this song.[10]

Sheet music for "Nancy Till" as sung by White's Serenaders (1851)
(See end note #6 for publishing information and online address)

Beginning in the 1920s, many versions of the song appeared in books and on recordings, in addition to its appearances in sheet music. For example, Frank Crumit, who was a radio superstar in the 1920s, recorded a version in 1928 that he called "Down in de Cane Brake."[11] (See the lyrics on page 61.) In 1927, Charles Finger published a set of the lyrics in his *Frontier Ballads* with the title "Come, Love, Come."[12] (See page 62.) In 1942, Carl Carmer published the lyrics and tune in his *Songs of the Rivers of America*. (Carmer's version is interesting to me because it specifies that the music is to be played "with pastoral tenderness," hinting strongly of its connection to a plantation work song, though his version is pretty obviously the White's Serenaders' version.)[13] Frank Crumit's version, on the other hand, while it does employ the pseudo-dialect that was in the White's Serenaders' lyrics, survived in none of the other recordings I've been able to locate, though several versions use his title or some variant of it. Smiley Burnette, for instance, recorded a version of the song in 1938, calling it "Down in the Cane Brake."[14] (See page 63.) This version is interesting because, though it certainly has a western flavor to it, it also employs a muted trumpet reminiscent of Crumit's version, making it likely that Burnette was influenced by Crumit.[15]

In 1951, Frank Warner, a student of folklorist Frank C. Brown, made a field recording of the song Brown had himself recorded from informant Charles "Tink" Tillet in 1938. When Warner returned in 1951 to record it from Tink, he found that Tink had passed on, so he persuaded Tink's wife Eleazar to sing it for him. She called her version "Come, Love, Come" and she combined it with another song – Dan Emmett's "Boatman's Dance."[16] (Her husband's version did not include the Emmett lyrics, so it seems evident that she introduced them.)

Eleazar Tillet's version is particularly interesting because its lyrics have become the dominant contemporary version. In 1987, Jeff Warner (the son of folk song collectors Anne and Frank Warner) and his friend and fellow singer Jeff Davis recorded their rendition of the song, taken—as they acknowledge—from Frank Warner's tapes of his recording of Martha Etheridge singing it; Martha was Eleazar Tillet's sister. Jeff Warner said, "My parents...got 'Nancy Till' from sisters Eleazar Tillitt [sic] and Martha Ethridge [sic] (born ca. 1880) in 1951 in the Outer Banks of North Carolina, in the town of Wanchese..." He goes on to say, though, that the blending of the two songs comes from Tillet's version. Warner and Davis call their version "Come, Love, Come." (See page 64.) I asked Jeff what changes he made to the song and he told me that he started with Eleazar Tillet's fragment, which contains a verse from "Boatman's Dance," then added other verses from "Boatman's Dance" that he liked. He says, "I took what I liked from the Emmett text to fill out the version of 'Come Love Come' that I sing."[17]

In 1997, a duo calling itself Shanghaied on the Willamette recorded the song and Jonathan Lay, one of the duo, told me in an e-mail that they had taken their version directly from the Warner/Davis version.[18] More recently, a group calling itself The Johnson Girls recorded an *a cappella* version of the Warner/Davis song on a CD called *Sea Chanteys and Maritime Music*. They used Warner's title, so I e-mailed the group about their source and received a reply from one of them saying she didn't remember where they got it. However, Sandy Paton of Folk Legacy Records, who produced the CD for them, told me that he thought their version was from Warner's, which seems very likely to me, since it uses the same lyrics as Jeff Warner's and is much more a chantey than a minstrel song.[19]

These are the versions readily available on the folk music market today, which I think says more about the contemporary folk scene and how the artists build repertoire than anything else because there are many other versions available with a little digging. For example, I found reference to another recording of the song—by Sandy and Caroline Paton—on a Folkways Records CD entitled *The Folk Next Door* and their version is also based on the Warner/Davis recording.[20] The Sons of the Pioneers released their own version in the 1950s, though they used the title "Nancy Till"[21] (see page 65), and I found another version on a 1960s collection of "campfire songs" sung by Ken Carson, who was a member of the Sons of the Pioneers.[22] (See page 66.) Merle Travis recorded a version for Capitol Records in the 1940s. (See page 67.) He used the title "Nancy Till" and it remains fairly close to the White's Serenaders' version (minus the pseudo-dialect).[23] The Mountain Rangers recorded a version of "Nancy Till" for the Renfro Valley Barn Dance in Kentucky in the 1930s or '40s; their version has lyrics that are, as far as I can tell, also those of the White's Serenaders' version.[24] (See page 57.) This is just a selection of the many recordings of this fairly well-known song that are either available online or in historic formats.

Thus far, my research had uncovered five basic title variants: "Nancy Dill," "Nancy Till," "Nancy Gill," "Down in de Cane Brake," and "Come, Love, Come." This variety of titles alone makes a sufficient case that the song exists in multiple variants, especially when one recalls, as I mentioned earlier, that there are lots of variations in the lyrics as well, including Frank Crumit's use of pseudo-dialect. In pursuing my leads further, however, I found still more evidence of variants—one such example being that the song exists in an arrangement for small-pipes (the traditional bagpipe of the "Borders" area between England and Scotland) that appeared in *The Northumbrian Pipers' Second Tune Book*.[25] In hopes of learning more, I contacted the Northumbrian Pipers' Society and the secretary had this to say:

> It is a generally known tune in English traditional music circles, usually as "Nancy Dill", and in its American form as "The Cane Brake." I would think it quite likely that this last picked up words in the [nineteenth century], but I don't have copies of them. It is not necessarily a pipe tune, more probably a fiddle tune played by pipers, which is why it's been put in the book. I think it became "Nancy Till" in Northumberland because there is a River Till in the north of the county.[26]

According to Hans Nathan's history of minstrelsy,[27] American minstrel groups were extremely popular in England throughout the 19th century and often toured there. In an email to me, Jeff Warner seconded that observation and addressed how popular the songs were in the British Isles—"There are many instances of American minstrel songs being found in UK oral tradition. It's possible the Northumberland tune is post-1850 and came from the US."[28] The Bodleian Library collection and the Roud indexes attest to the popularity of such music in the UK,[29] so it seems likely to me that the song must have crossed the Atlantic that way.

An additional intriguing piece of evidence concerning how the tune was traded back and forth "across the pond" is that in 1954, English folklorist Peter Kennedy collected a fiddle version of "Nancy Till" performed by piper Jack Armstrong, the man who had been elected chair of the Northumbrian Pipers' Society in 1937.[30] It seems to me that Armstrong could have learned the song from someone who learned it from the minstrels who toured in the late 1800s. On the other hand, he could have learned it from any number of other sources, including the Crumit broadcasts from the 1920s, Smiley Burnette's 1930s recording, the version the Beverly Hill Billies performed in the 1938 Tex Ritter movie *Rollin' Plains*, the Sons of the Pioneers' radio broadcasts of the 1930s-'f'50s, or the recording Merle Travis made in the 1950s.[31] Since Armstrong's fiddle version is a schottische, and since Firth, Pond & Co. published the sheet music for a schottische version of the song in 1853,[32] I opt for him having learned it through oral transmission from the minstrel tours…but regardless of how he learned it, the tune seems now to be what Sir Walter Scott referred to as "minstrelsy of the Scottish border;" that is, music Scots consider their own.

I have acquired one other non-commercial version besides my mother's that doesn't follow the Warners' version of the lyrics. It was collected from Olive Kelly Smith by Gertrude Edens, a student in a folklore course taught by Joan O'Bryant in Kansas in the 1950s. Smith called her version "Down in the Canebrake."[33] (See page 68.)

By the way, at this point in my quest, I ventured onto the threads of the Mudcat Café Forum[34] where I found out that there are many people who know, or know of, the song. The Internet allowed me to discover that the song is much better known than I had thought these past many years.

So far in my search, I had noted two fairly different versions of the lyrics – one based in the White's Serenaders' lyrics and one based on the song from the Warners' collection. In fact, as I found through further research, there actually seem to be three major variations of the lyrics, as well as some less common ones. One variant, of course, is the Warner version which is a direct descendant of the Eleazar Tillet song Frank and Anne Warner recorded. The second set of lyrics is quite widespread, too, though mainly in versions from earlier times – the 1930s and back. The third version, which I think of as the Crumit version, is the one I think my mother's lyrics are based on, as I believe are Olive Kelly Smith's and the numerous cowboy versions from the 1930s and 1940s. Furthermore, I think Crumit's version is probably based on the version in the Prewett Collection, which apparently predates Crumit by about thirteen years.[35] However, since my mother and most of the more recent singers don't use the pseudo-dialect, perhaps they are basing their version on Smiley Burnette's, though his is ten years later than Crumit's. Burnette's lyrics are very similar to Crumit's, but without the pseudo-dialect and, as I've mentioned before, Burnette employs the muted trumpet so prominent in Crumit's rendition, which I have found in none of the other versions. Since Burnette was a very well-known radio performer, his version might well have influenced many singers.

To reiterate, the three major variant strands and numerous smaller ones indicate that "Nancy Dill" is indeed a folk song with considerable variation in the lyrics across both time and place. One issue concerning the lyrics is that of dialect. The "original" White's Serenaders' version is written in the stylized Black dialect so popular among minstrels – pseudo-dialect, I prefer to call it, as it was a made-up language that had no actual existence outside of the minstrelsy and literature of its day. Thus:

> Down in de cane-brake, close by de mill,
> Dar lib'd a yaller gal, her name was Nancy Till.
> She know'd dat I lub'd her, she know'd it long.
> I'm gwine to serenade her and I'll sing dis song.
>
> Come, love, come, de boat lies low,
> She lies high and dry on de Ohio.
> Come, love, come, won't you go along with me;
> I'll take you down to Tennessee.

Dialect versions survived right up through the late 1920s in Frank Crumit's very popular radio version, though his lyrics vary somewhat from the White's version. (See page 61.) Since the 1920s, however, I have found no extant dialect versions, with the exception of the Travis instance I mentioned above.

How many and which verses are included in the song is the second major area of variation. Many of the early versions have the set of verses popularized in the Firth, Pond & Co. publications. My mother's version, though, has a couple of verses not included in the Firth, Pond & Co. White's Serenaders' version. She included:

> There will be a cabin and a trundle bed,
> And there'll be a pickaninny all because I said,
> "Come, my love, come; won't you come along with me
> And I'll take you down to Tennessee."

Her version also eliminates several of the verses from the Firth, Pond & Co. version. She did not, for example, sing:

> Open de window, love O do,
> And listen to de music I'se playin' for you.
> De whis'prings ob love, so soft and low,
> Harmonise my voice wid de old banjo.
>
> Softly de casement begin for to rise.
> De stars am a-shining above in de skies.
> De moon am declining behind yonder hill,
> Reflecting its rays on you, my Nancy Till.
>
> Farewell, love, I must now away,
> I've a long way to trabel afore de broke ob day,
> But de next time I come, be ready for to go
> A-sailing on de banks ob de Ohio.

In fact, my mother's version reflects a successful romance, whereas the White's Serenaders' version reflects just the opposite. Of course, that isn't unusual in folk songs and tales, but worth noting here. My mother's lyrics, in fact, are much closer to those in the version sung by Charles Edward Prewett, though I really can't imagine that my great-grandmother would have come into contact with that version, unless it would have been while she and her husband were living in the California logging woods, which might have been about the time that the Canadian Prewett was living and working in the U.S.

However, Frank Crumit recorded his version in 1928, with lyrics that are very close to the Prewett lyrics, though not an exact match. When I interviewed my mother about the song, she said that she had probably learned it in 1930. As I pointed out at the beginning of this article, Mom's mother died in 1929, at which time Mom and her infant brother Barney, who was just nine months old, went to live with their grandmother – Lizzie Gibson. Mom said that Grandma sang the song as a lullaby to my Uncle Barney.[36] My surmise is that Grandma probably learned it from Crumit's broadcast version, which he may have taken from the Prewett minstrel version. However, Mom's lyrics also vary a little from Crumit's. For instance, she doesn't use the pseudo-dialect and her final verse is considerably different, as is her second verse. Though I did not ask her at the time I interviewed her, and cannot do so now, my interpretation is that she had forgotten some of the lyrics and filled in with words and phrases that worked with the music and the story. Also, as I noted elsewhere, she replaced the word "pickaninny" with "little baby" when she sang the song to my daughter and "yellow gal" with "colored girl." (Those same variations occur in other singers' lyrics as well.) Looked at overall, I believe her variations were examples of the folk process at work.

Another version of the song also seems to be based in Crumit's. Olive Kelly Smith's rendition, which I found in the Joan O'Bryant collection at the Wichita State University library, has only slight variation from the Crumit version. (See page 68 for Smith's lyrics.) She renders the last two lines as:

> We'll meet St. Peter there;
> He'll give us both a table for us to share.[37]

A second major variation of lyrics comes from another genre wherein this song had a rather lively existence…cowboy music. Most of these versions have similar lyrics, the ones I associate with the Sons of the Pioneers. Whether the Sons of the Pioneers were the first cowboy group to record this song, I'm unable to determine. However, the connection of several of the versions to the Sons of the Pioneers is pretty clear – Smiley Burnette was at one time a member of that group, as were Merle Travis and Ken Carson, though Carson's solo performance lyrics vary quite a bit from those he sang with the group. I'm less sure whether there is a connection between the Sons of the Pioneers and Tex Ritter, though he would undoubtedly have heard them sing. In any event, his lyrics (that is, those of the Beverly Hill Billies) are the same as the lyrics sung by the Sons of the Pioneers.

The other major strand of the three major sets of lyric variations is that based on the song from the Anne and Frank Warner collection, which as we've seen was adapted by their son Jeff, whose version is widely known and has been recorded by Shanghaied on the Willamette, Sandy and Caroline Paton, and the Johnson Girls, among others – all of whom acknowledge that they sing Jeff's version.

A fourth, and less widely distributed, set of lyrics occurs in Finger's *Frontier Ballads*. While these lyrics share much with other versions of the song, they too vary considerably, again suggesting to me that a faulty memory might account for the differences. One of the things I find most interesting about Finger's version is what he says about it: "…these two ['Come, Love, Come' and 'Bluetail Fly'] must be quoted in no contracted fashion, because they were potent in an artistic way as making for the gaiety of nations. For they were learnt and copied, sung and passed on; were taken to Tierra del Fuego, and to Australia, and to New Zealand."[38] It would have been helpful if Finger had been more specific about where and when he heard the song. However, all he gives us in that vein is "once upon a time the *Seatoller* was wrecked down near Cape Horn, so we gathered together cutters, a schooner, a whale boat or two, and sailed down south. On Staten Island we found our men, not the familiar Staten Island but the lesser known one, which is, or was, an Argentine convict settlement."[39] As to the singer, he says only this: "There was a party in one part of the rooms which centered about a Negro who was doing a breakdown. . . . As for his orchestration, it was his voice."[40]

Another dimension of the song that needs more discussion than I am able to give it here is the music itself. I regret that I lack the technical knowledge of music theory to talk about it, but I do want to point out that the style of the music varies widely. Crumit's version – and the White's Serenaders' version – sound like minstrel songs.[41] Other versions of the song, sung by the Sons of the Pioneers, Merle Travis, Tex Ritter, Roy Rogers, Gene Autry, and others, have melodies and rhythms in which we can almost hear the clop of horses' hooves; therefore, in my estimation, it is also a cowboy song. My mother's version was a plaintive love song. Jeff Warner's version is a river ballad and the Johnson Girls' version is done as a sea chantey, while Jack Armstrong's version is played as a schottishe.

In fact, such variations of both lyrics and tune continue today. In the tradition of folk singers through the ages, a performer named Jerry Ernst told me that he wrote his own tune for the lyrics to "Come, Love, Come."

> [The lyrics come from] the *Jack Morgan Songster*, published by Branson and Farrar, 1864. It's a neat collection in many ways, and the cover claims it was written by 'A captain in Lee's army.'
>
> The music is a bit off from the original, because the songster was words only. I just sort of made up the music to sing the words to...When I finally found a copy of the sheet music, I freaked out for a moment...it is very close to what I made up for it![42]

His music is very "folk" sounding. What sounds like a banjo to me dominates, with spoons in the background. I hear no other instruments, so even the musical accompaniment varies, further proof that this really has become a living piece of folk music.

One other point needs to be made before I close – the song has also had a bit of a life in other areas of popular culture besides the music scene. For instance, Willa Cather, in her novel *Sapphira and the Slave Girl*, has a character named Nancy, whom she describes, through Sapphira, as a "smart yellow girl," and also mentions Nancy's mother, whose name is Till.[43] Cather scholar Ann Romines points out that Cather mentions in one of her letters an "Aunt Till," probably Matilda Jefferson, who had been a slave of Cather's Siebert great-grandparents. She then muses that perhaps Matilda was the prototype of the fictional Till and Matilda's own daughter – a mulatto girl – was the fictional Till's daughter Nancy.[44] That Cather at least associated those names with the song is supported by the fact that in *Sapphira*, Martin – the mistresses' son – looking for Nancy, sings what Cather calls "that old darky song," the first two lines of "Nancy Till":

> Down by de cane-brake, close by de mill,
> Dar lived a yaller gal, her name was Nancy Till.[45]

The central focus of Romines' article is the autobiographical basis of the novel, so the mention of the song suggests, perhaps, that it was alive in Virginia in Cather's youth,[46] but also suggests a connection with African-American roots, at least in Cather's mind.

Another area of popular culture that has exploited and added to the lifespan of the song is the cinema. As noted above, the Beverly Hill Billies sing it in Tex Ritter's 1938 *Rollin' Plains*. One of my favorite contemporary renditions of the song is from the anti-war movie *Hell in the Pacific*,[47] starring Lee Marvin (as an American Marine) and Toshiro Mifune (as an Imperial Japanese soldier). Stranded together on a small Pacific island during WWII, the two enemies eventually learn to cooperate instead of trying to kill each other. Ultimately, they work together to build a raft to take them off the island. As they sail away and the sun sets into the ocean, Lee Marvin on first tiller watch sings "Down in the canebrake, down by the mill..." as the screen fades.

What all this adds up to is, quite simply, that because it exists in so many variants, because it is passed on by the oral method, because it is redefined to suit different groups' needs, because it lives and has lived in so many times and so many places, no matter what its origins, "Nancy Dill" or "Nancy Gill" or "Nancy Till" or "Down in the Canebrake" or "Come, Love, Come" is truly a *folk* song. It no longer really matters whether the *Ur* version was composed for Firth, Pond & Co. in 1851 or whether it initially had its origin among the folk (though I still want to know). It is now a *folk* song in the truest sense of the term, a song that belongs to the people. In short, this song I chanced to hear my mother singing in 1982 is a folk song, despite the fact that it has (maybe) a known author and (maybe) a known composition date, and despite the fact that the Warner version seems to have become frozen as *the* contemporary version. Folk versions of the song currently exist in both the U.S. and the U.K. It exists in multiple versions and multiple genres, has multiple titles, and is still being handed down via the oral transmission process. And, though Vance Randolph, H. M. Belden, and Max Hunter did not happen to collect it, it has some claim, via my mother and great-grandmother, to being an Ozark folk song.[48]

The tune as played by "The Wedderburn Oldtimers," an Australian band
(Transcribed by band member Peter Ellis; courtesy of the author)

Notes

[1] For additional information about John Armstrong, see my article "The Legend of Joe's Cave: Murder, Medicine, Counterfeiting and Vigilantism" which appeared in the *Missouri Folklore Society Journal* (Vols. 15-16, 1993-1994) on pages 29-50.

[2] As yet, I have not been able to acquire copies of Mount's notes, which are housed in the Museums at Stony Brook, New York; the museum staff has offered me access as soon as the items I want to look at are available.

[3] Jan Brunvand. *The Study of American Folklore: An Introduction*, 4th ed. (New York: Norton, 1998, 1968): 270.

[4] Barre Toelken. "Chapter 7: Ballads and Folksongs" in *Folk Groups and Folklore Genres: An Introduction*, ed. by Elliott Oring (Logan: Utah State University Press, 1986): 147.

[5] Brunvand, 270.

[6] "Nancy Till" [sheet music] (New York: Firth, Pond & Co., 1851; above the title on the cover – "The favorite Ethiopian melody;" at the top of the first page – "Written for and sung by White's Serenaders." Found online in the Library of Congress American Memory Project titled *Music for a Nation: American Sheet Music, 1820-1860* (http://www.loc.gov/item/sm1851.491730; acc. 6/6/15).

[7] Frankenstein says that "... huge quantities of the music Mount played on his fiddle survive in the library of the Museums at Stony Brook. Most of it is written in [Mount's] own hand on individual sheets of staff paper..." One page in the collection contains three different versions of 'Nancy Gill,' the third version dated May 10th, 1838. Mount had written at the bottom of the page 'Nancy Gill has hard work to get up hill.'"

Frankenstein's information on Mount's papers can be found in the liner notes he wrote for the Smithsonian Folkways recording *The Cradle of Harmony: William Sidney Mount's Violin and Fiddle Music* (Folkways Records, FW 32379, 1976; http://folkways.si.edu, search "William Sidney Mount," acc. 6/6/15). Additional information can be found in Frankenstein's exhibition catalog, *Painter of Rural America: William Sidney Mount, 1807-1868* (printed by H. K. Press, 1968).

[8] Sung by J. W. Thompson at the "Kossuth Exchange" (published by J. Andrews, No. 38 Chatham Street, N. Y. [n. d.]; ca. 1850s; http://bluegrass messengers.com/nancy-till--version-3-parody-uncle-bill.aspx; acc. 6/6/15).

Also published by Harris, Printer, S. E. corner Fourth and Vine Streets (Philadelphia, Pennsylvania [n. d.]; http://memory.loc.gov; search "Uncle Bill," acc. 6/6/15).

[9] The organs were manufactured by the Autophone Co. between about 1887 and 1920 in large numbers. Over the years the Gem Roller Organ was manufactured, over 1000 different tunes were available for it and tune cards with lyrics for individual songs came with the rollers.

Bob Brooke. "A Gem of a Roller Organ" (http://theantiquesalmanac.com/rollerorgan.htm; acc. 6/6/15).

"Honor Rolls" (http://www.honorrolls.net; acc. 6/6/15).

"Todd Augsburger's Roller Organ Website" (http://www.rollerorgans.com; acc. 6/6/15); also, email from Todd Augsburger, 1/11/03.

[10] *Bodleian Library Broadside Ballads*, Bodleian Library, Oxford University (http://www.bodley.ox.ac.uk/ballads; acc. 6/6/15).

Music for the Nation: American Sheet Music, 1820-1885; Library of Congress, Music Division, American Memory (acc. 6/15; http://www.loc.gov/collections/american-sheet-music-1820-to-1860/about-this-collection).

Lester S. Levy Collection of Sheet Music, Milton S. Eisenhower Library, Johns Hopkins University (http://levysheetmusic.mse.jhu.edu; acc. 6/6/15).

Folk Songs of Middle Tennessee: The George Boswell Collection, Special Collections Library, Vanderbilt University (http://www.library.vanderbilt.edu/speccol/exhibits/boswell_george.shtml; acc. 6/6/15).

The Digital Tradition (http://www.mudcat.org; acc. 6/6/15).

The Roud Folk Song Index, Vaughan Williams Memorial Library, English Folk Dance and Song Society (http://www.vwml.org/search/search-roud-indexes; acc. 6/6/15).

The Traditional Ballad Index, hosted by California State Univ. at Fresno (http://www.fresnostate.edu/folklore/BalladSearch.html; acc. 6/6/15).

Folk Music: An Index to Recorded and Print Resources by Jane Keefer (http://www.ibiblio.org/folkindex; acc. 6/6/15).

[11] *Frank Crumit #2* (MC Productions, CD 111; originally released in 1928, Victor 21340).

[12] Charles J. Finger. *Frontier Ballads* (New York: Doubleday, Page & Co., 1927): 165-166.

[13] Carl L. Carmer. *Songs of the Rivers of America* (New York: Farrar and Rinehart, 1942): 166.

[14] Lester Alvin ("Smiley") Burnette. "Down in the Cane Brake," *Smiley Burnette: Gentle Genius of Country Music, 1934-1947* (Cattle Compact Mono, CCD 203, 1998); originally released as Decca 5633, 1938). [Info obtained from *Country Music Records: A Discography, 1921-1942* by Tony Russell and Bob Pinson (Oxford University Press, 2004): 145.]

[15] A few other examples I've found of recordings of this song:

Frank Luther. "Down in de Canebrake" (Vocalion 5227, 1928).

Hartford City Trio. "Down in the Cane Break" (Gennette, 1929).

Pickard Family. "Down in the Cane Break" (Conqueror 7574, 1930).

[16] Eleazar Tillett. "Come, Love, Come" on *Her Bright Smile Haunts Me Still: The Warner Collection, Volume 1*, collected by Anne and Frank Warner (Appleseed Records, APR CD 1035, 2000). This CD contains field recordings made along the Eastern Seaboard between 1940 and 1966. The information given about Eleazar Tillett was found in the liner notes that accompany this CD.

[17] Jeff Warner and Jeff Davis. *Wilder Joy* (Flying Fish, 2002, 1986): notes.

E-mail, Jeff Warner to Jim Vandergriff, 2/20/03.

[18] Shanghaied on the Willamette. *Weighing Anchor* (Jonathan Lay and Gordy Euler, SOW-CD101, 1997).

Email, Jonathan Lay to Jim Vandergriff, 2/3/03.

[19] The Johnson Girls. *Sea Chanteys and Maritime Music* (Folk Legacy, CD 5102, 2000).

[20] Sandy and Caroline Paton. "Come, Love, Come" on *The Folk Next Door 1* (WWUH Radio, The Folk Next Door Concerts, University of Hartford, West Hartford, CT., 1991). I am grateful to Sandy and Caroline for providing me with a copy of their version.

21 "Nancy Till" by Sons of the Pioneers appears on/in:

> *Songs of the Hills and Plains* (LP; AFM-731, 1982).
>
> *Songs of the Prairie* (5-CD set; Bear Family Records, 15710, 1998); taken from broadcast transcripts.
>
> *Lucky U Ranch* (transcript recordings of the radio show—broadcasts from 1951 and 1952; TR-154 > TR-157, TR-228 > TR-231, and TR-324 > TR-327; Eugene Earle Collection [20376] and Sons of the Pioneers Transcription Discs Collection [20400], Southern Folklife Collection, Wilson Library, University of North Carolina, Chapel Hill).
>
> Interestingly, even though Ken Carson was a member of the Sons of the Pioneers, his version varies from those on the Lucky U transcripts.

22 Ken Carson. "Nancy Till," *Campfire Songs* (The Longines Symphonette Recording Society, no date).

23 The Coonhunters featuring Merle Travis. "Nancy Till," *The Coonhunters* (Bear Family Records, CDD042, 2002; radio transcriptions originally issued on Capitol Records). This album is also available under the same title from the British Archive of Country Music (CDD042). The lyrics in the appendix below were transcribed by the author from the BACM CD.

24 The Mountain Rangers. "Nancy Till," *The Fun and Frolic of 60 Years in the Valley Where Time Stands Still* (Rockcastle Records, audio cassette); originally sung on the Renfro Valley Barn Dance show that originated from Renfro Valley, Kentucky, and was broadcast on radio station WLW out of Cincinnati. Also available on *Welcome to Renfro Valley* (CD/DVD set available at the Kentucky Music Hall of Fame).

25 *The Northumbrian Pipers' Second Tune Book*, 2nd ed. (Newcastle upon Tyne: Northumbrian Pipers' Society, 1991; 1981).

26 Email, Julia Say to Jim Vandergriff, 2/14/03.

27 Hans Nathan. *Dan Emmett and the Rise of Early Negro Minstrelsy* (Norman: University of Oklahoma Press, 1977, 1962).

28 Email, Jeff Warner to Jim Vandergriff, 2/20/03.

[29] The Bodleian ballad collection contains nine images of broadside publications of the song, while Steve Roud's broadside and folk song indexes contain citations to 81 versions of it (either noted by collectors or printed on broadsides in the British Isles); there is no overlap between these two counts, which means that at least 90 appearances of the song are documented in the U.K. from these two sources alone.

[30] Email, Peter Kennedy to Jim Vandergriff, 11/2/03.

Armstrong's version of the tune appears in Peter Kennedy's *Fiddler's Tune Book* (N.Y.: Hargail Music Press, 1951; originally published by the English Folk Dance and Song Society): 22. This information was found on the website—*The Fiddler's Companion* (http://ceolas.org/ceolas.html; acc. 6/6/15) under both titles – "The Cane Break" and "Nancy Dill."

Jack Armstrong and Peg Jennings. *The Northumbrian Small Pipes* (Newcastle upon Tyne: Mortonsound, LP MTN 3074, 1969).

Emails, Mrs. Robyn Park (New Zealand) to Jim Vandergriff, several between 3/12/03 and 12/30/03; she sent me a cassette with a recording of Armstrong's performance of "Nancy Till."

[31] Beverly Hill Billies. "Nancy Till," *Ezra and His Beverly Hill Billies* (Dover: British Archive of Country Music, BACM CD D 147; from transcriptions produced by the MacGregor Transcription Company, recorded c. 1939-1940.) For an interesting history of the group, who were extremely popular in the 1930s and also served as the artistic model for the Sons of the Pioneers, see http://www.hensteeth.com/e_discog/hillbill.html; acc. 6/6/15.

Rollin' Plains (Grand National Pictures, 1938; directed by Albert Herman and produced by Edward F. Finney.) Between them, the Beverley Hill Billies and Tex Ritter (in various combinations) sing at least four songs in the film.

See citations for the following performers in these notes (above):
    Crumit – #11
    Burnette – #14
    Sons of the Pioneers – #21
    Travis – #23

[32] "Nancy Till Schottisch," [sheet music] Arranged by Henry Chadwick (New York: Firth, Pond & Co., 1853). Found online in: Library of Congress, American Memory Project, *Music for a Nation: American Sheet Music, 1820-1885* (http://www.loc.gov/resource/sm1853.210140; acc. 6/6/15).

³³ Joan O'Bryant Kansas Folklore Collection, MS 2002-12, Box 36, FF1; Wichita State University Library.

³⁴ Mudcat Café (http://www.mudcat.org; acc. 6/6/15). This website includes both the *Digital Tradition* database of song lyrics and a searchable archive of emails that concern all aspects of folk music in English.

³⁵ The only references I have found to the Prewett Collection are on the Bluegrass Messengers and *Digital Tradition* (*DT*) websites.

The song "Come, My Love, Come" ("Nancy Till") appears in the *Digital Tradition* database with the following note:

"Collected from the songs of Charles Edward Prewett, British Columbia Light Horse, minstrel shows, Vernon, British Columbia, Canada (ca. 1915)." I cannot find out where this information comes from because the *DT* only identifies contributors of songs by initials, in this case, "MC."

There is more information about Prewett in the Mudcat Café Forum. Prewett's grandson, identified in the forum only as "Metchosin," said:

"I am seeking help in trying to trace the movements of my grandfather, Charles Edward Prewett, during the 15 years he spent in the U.S., in the late 1800s and early 1900s, prior to settling in British Columbia. He was an incredible banjo player and had two songs…in his repertoire that I [have] never heard anyone else play or sing…I was hoping there might be someone here who may have heard [this song] before or know of someone else who might have [it] in a family repertoire."

³⁶ Though she was actually my great-grandmother, I always called her Grandma because she filled that role in my life. (One of my earliest memories is of listening to the radio at Grandma's house prior to Grandpa's death in 1947.)

³⁷ I need to caution readers that the O'Bryant recording is of very poor quality; it's sometimes difficult to understand exactly what Smith is saying, so I'm quite uncertain about parts of these last two lines.

³⁸ Finger, 165.

It's interesting that "Nancy Till" still has some currency in Australia and New Zealand. I recently received a transcribed copy of the song from Peter Ellis, a member of the Wedderburn Oldtimers, a Bush band from Victoria, Australia (tune on p. 45 above). See the *Musical Traditions* website for more information about the group (http://www.mustrad.org.uk/articles/o_timers.htm#music; acc. 6/6/15).

[39] Finger, 153.

[40] Finger, 162-63.

We know from the information about Finger on the University of Arkansas website that he was in South America – including Chile and Tierra del Fuego – in the early 1890s, and that, in 1944, the Maritime Commission posthumously named a freighter after him (http://libinfo.uark.edu/special collections/findingaids/finger.html; acc. 6/6/15).

[41] At one point, I said this to Jeff Warner in an e-mail and he responded "Do you know something about how minstrel songs were rendered that I don't?" I don't! What I'm referring to is the honeyed, homely, maudlin tone of songs like "Swanee River."

[42] Email, Jerry Ernst to Jim Vandergriff, 2/28/05. Ernst performs his version of "Nancy Till" on *In Love & War* (CD, 2000). Ernst got his lyrics from:

The Jack Morgan Songster. Compiled by a captain in Gen. Lee's army. (Raleigh: Branson & Farrar, 1864). Found in the Harris Index, No. 3360. *Harris Collection of American Poetry and Plays* (microfilm).

[43] Willa Cather. *Sapphira and the Slave Girl* (New York: Random House, 1975; reprint of the edition originally published in 1940 by Alfred A. Knopf, Inc.): 8-9.

[44] Ann Romines. "Finding Till: An Editor's Romance," *Willa Cather Newsletter and Review* (Fall 2004): 34-35.

[45] Cather, 179.

[46] Cather was born, and lived for nine years, in Back Creek, Virginia, where the novel is set.

[47] *Hell in the Pacific* (directed by John Boorman, Selmur Pictures, 1968; DVD, Anchor Bay Entertainment, 1999).

[48] My great-grandmother, Elizabeth Armstrong, was born in 1878 in Wet Glaize, Camden County, Missouri. She lived most of her life in Camden, Laclede, and Pulaski counties in Missouri and died in 1974 in Richland, Pulaski County, Missouri. Her father immigrated to Missouri in the late 1850s, first settling in Elston Station on the Missouri River, but later moving to Camden County. Her grandfather William Dodson settled in Glaize City, Camden County, Missouri in 1832. And I'd say, that's about as native as you can get!

Appendix
(arranged in order of their appearance in the article)

"Nancy Dill"	Mary Myers (author's mother; MO, 1982)
"Nancy Till"	Flora Smith (VA, 1941)
"Nancy Till"	Etta Kilgore (VA, 1939)
"Nancy Till"	Firth, Pond & Co. (published in 1851)
"Uncle Bill"	Parody (NY/Philadelphia, ca. 1850s)
"Nancy Till"	George Boswell (TN, 1953-54)
"Come, My Love, Come"	Charles Prewett (late 1800s, Canada)
"Down in de Cane Brake"	Frank Crumit (recorded in 1928)
"Come, Love, Come"	Charles Finger (book published in 1927)
"Down in the Cane Brake"	Smiley Burnette (recorded in 1938)
"Come, Love, Come"	Jeff Warner/Jeff Davis (recorded in 1986)
"Nancy Till"	Sons of the Pioneers (radio, 1951-52)
"Nancy Till"	Ken Carson (recorded in the 1960s)
"Nancy Till"	Merle Travis (recorded in the 1940s)
"Down in the Canebrake"	Olive Kelly Smith (KS, 1950s)

"Nancy Dill"

Down in the canebrake, close beside the mill,
There lived a pretty little gal, her name was Nancy Dill.
We're gonna marry; and it won't be long.
I'll serenade her and this'll be my song.

> Come, my love, come, the boat lies low.
> It lies high and dry on the Ohio.
> Come, my love, come; won't you come along with me,
> And I'll take you down to Tennessee.

Down in the canebrake some happy day,
There'll be a cabin and this is what I'll say:

> Come, my love, come, the boat lies low.
> It lies high and dry on the Ohio.
> Come, my love, come; won't you come along with me,
> And I'll take you down to Tennessee.

There in the cabin will be a trundle bed
And a little baby, all because I said:

> Come, my love, come, my boat lies low.
> It lies high and dry on the Ohio.
> Come, my love, come; won't you come along with me,
> And I'll take you down to Tennessee.

Down in the canebrake, that's where I'll stay,
Close beside my Nancy until I'm laid away.

> Come, my love, come, my boat lies low.
> It lies high and dry on the Ohio.
> Come, my love, come; won't you come along with me,
> And I'll take you down to Tennessee.

Recorded and transcribed by Jim Vandergriff from his mother,
Mary Vandergriff Myers neé Perkins (1920-1999);
Richland, Missouri; 10/3/1982

"Nancy Till"

Virginia
Susan R. Morton,
Haymarket, Va.
Miss Flora Smith,
Waterfall, Va.
October 23d, 1941

NANCY TILL.

Down in the cane brake, close by the mill,
There lived a yellow girl, her name was Nancy Till,
She knew that I loved her, She knew it long,
I'm going to serenade her, and sing her this song.

CHORUS:

" Come love, come the boat lies low,
She lies high and dry on the Ohio.
Come love, come, won't you come along with me
And I'll take you down to Tennessee."

Softly the casement began to rise,
The stars are shining above in the skies,
The moon am declining beyond yonder hill,
Reflecting the rays on you, my Nancy Till.

CHORUS:

Farewell love, I must now away,
I've a long way to travel before break of day,
But the next time I come, be ready to go,
Asailing on the banks of the Ohio.

CHORUS

Come love, come, the boat lies low,
She lies high and dry on the Ohio,
Come love come, won't you come along with me?
And I'll row the boat while the boat rows me.

(this was sung over seventy-five years ago, by a man who
learned it as a boy on the James River.)

Collected from singer Flora Smith by Susan Morton in 1941
WPA Collection, Alderman Library, University of Virginia

"Nancy Till"

Emory L. Hamilton
Wise, Virginia

Here is one of the few old negro songs that I have been able to uncover. This is from Etta Kilgore, March 6th. Today this one is not very widely known in this section.

NANCY TILL

Down in the cane-brake, close by the mill,
    There lived a yellow girl, her name was Nancy Till; *Pretty*
She knew that I loved her, she knew it long,
    I'm going to serenade her, and I'll sing this song:

Chorus:
Come, love, come, the boat lies low,
    She lies high and dry on the Ohio;
Come, love, come, won't you go along with me?
    I'll take you down to Tennessee.

Open the window, love, oh, do,
    And listen to the music I'm playing for you;
The whisp'rings of love, so soft and so low,
    Harmonize my voice with the old banjo.

Softly the casement begins for to rise,
    The stars are a-shining above in the skies;
The moon is declining behind yonder hill,
    Reflecting it's rays on you, my Nancy Till.

Farewell, love, I must now away,
    I've a long way to travel before the break of day,
But the next time I come, be ready, love, to go,
    A-sailing on the banks of the Ohio.

Collected from singer Etta Kilgore by Emory L. Hamilton in 1939
WPA Collection, Alderman Library, University of Virginia

"Nancy Till"

Down in de cane-brake, close by de mill,
Dar lib'd a yaller gal, her name was Nancy Till.
She know'd dat I lub'd her, she know'd it long.
I'm gwine to serenade her and I'll sing dis song.

    Come, love, come, de boat lies low,
    She lies high and dry on de Ohio.
    Come, love, come, won't you go along with me?
    I'll take you down to Tennessee.

Open de window, love O do,
And listen to de music I'se playin' for you.
De whis'prings ob love, so soft and low,
Harmonise my voice wid de old banjo.

Chorus

Softly de casement begin for to rise.
De stars am a-shining above in de skies.
De moon am declining behind yonder hill,
Reflecting its rays on you, my Nancy Till.

Chorus

Farewell, love, I must now away,
I've a long way to trabel afore de broke ob day,
But de next time I come, be ready for to go
A-sailing on de banks ob de Ohio.

Chorus

(New York: Firth, Pond & Co., 1851)
Found online in *Music for a Nation: American Sheet Music, 1820-1885*
American Memory, Library of Congress
(http://www.loc.gov/resource/sm1851.491730, acc. 6/6/15)

"Uncle Bill"
(A Parody of "Nancy Till")

Way up town near the top of the hill,
There I met a toper and his name was Uncle Bill;
He knows he's a toper, he knows known it very well,
And if he keeps a drinking they will put him in a cell

      Come, Bill, come, your funds are low,
      As you sit dry near the Park fountain, O;
      Come, Bill, come, just you go along with me,
      I'll pay the way as we go on a spree.

I come from the Island, to-day they set me free,
So come along, my chum, we will have a jolly spree;
Like a fish you must drink, till your funny old nose
Will turn to the hue of a full-blown rose.

Chorus

Slowly the tumbler begins for to rise,
His lips touch the glass as he winks both his eyes;
The landlord he laughs with a right hearty will,
As he sees all the capers of old Uncle Bill.

Chorus

Open your mouth, Bill, drink till you're blue,
Drink to my health, while I'm paying for you;
I have got lots o' rocks, so drink to your fill,
O! see how it glides down the throat of Uncle Bill.

Chorus

Sung by J. W. Thompson at the "Kossuth Exchange," lyrics by John L. Zieber (Published by J. Andrews, No. 38 Chatham Street, N. Y. [n. d.]; ca. 1850s (http://www.bluegrassmessengers.com/nancy-till--version-3-parody-uncle-bill.aspx; acc. 6/6/15)

"Nancy Till"

NANCY TILL

1. Down in the ~~cane~~ cane brake close by the mill
   There lived a gal, and her name was Nancy Till.
   She knowed that I loved her, she knowed it along.
   I am going to ~~serenade~~ serenade her and I'll sing this song.

Cho. Come love, come, the boat lies low,
   She lies high and dry on the Ohio.
   Come love, come, won't you go along with me?
   I'll row the boat while the boat rows me.

2. Open the window, love, oh, do,
   And listen to the music I'm playing for you.
   The whispering of love so soft and low,
   Harmonize my voice with the old banjo.

3. ← Softly the casement began for to rise,
   The stars as a-shining above in the skies.
   The moon is declining behind yonder hill,
   Reflecting its rays on you, my Nancy Till.   *Refrain*

4. Farewell love, I now must away,
   I've a long way to travel before the break of day.
   But the time I come be ready for to go
   A-sailing on the banks of the Ohio.

Manuscript from Frances Trew of Tennessee Wesleyan, Athens, secured in 1953 by Professor E. G. Rogers. I have three occurrences in my collection and Duncan, p. 295 has one. The present one is as good as any I have seen. This tune was sung by Mrs. Annie Stevenson in Clarksville January 26, 1954, probably learned from her father.
  See NCIII 491 and Carmer p. 166, who traces it to 1851.

George Boswell Collection, Vanderbilt University Library,
Special Collections and University Archives (acc. 6/6/15;
http://library.vanderbilt.edu/speccol/exhibits/Boswell/boswell_nancytill.jpg)

"Come, My Love, Come"

Down in d' canebrake, close by the mill,
There lives a colored girl, her name is Nancy Gill.
I told her I loved her, I loved her very long.
I'm gonna serenade her and this'll be my song:

>Come, my love, come; my boat lies low,
>She lies high and dry on the O-hi-o,
>Come, my love, come, won't you come along with me?
>And I'll take you down to Tennessee.

Down in d' canebrake some happy day,
You'll hear the wedding bells a-ringin' mighty gay.
There's gonna be a cabin and a little trundle bed.
There'll be a pickaninny and all because I said:

Chorus

Down in d' canebrake, that's where I'll stay,
'Long side my Nancy Gill till we are laid away,
And when I get to heaven and Peter lets us in,
I'll start my wings a-flappin' and sing to her again:

Chorus

Credited "as sung by Charles Edward Prewett" (Vernon, British Columbia, Canada; ca. 1915) in the *Digital Tradition* database; further information in the Mudcat Forum (http://mudcat.org/@displaysong.cfm?SongID=9064; acc.6/15)

"Down in de Cane Brake"

Down in de canebrake, close by de mill
Dere lived a colored gal her name was Nancy Dill.
I told her dat I loved her, I loved her very long.
I'm gonna serenade her, this will be my song

    Come, my love, come, my boat lies low,
    She lies high and dry on the Ohio.
    Come, my love, come, won't you come along with me,
    And I'll take you down to Tennessee.

Down in de canebrake, dahs where I'll go,
Down where de yella moon is hangin' mighty low.
I know dat she'll be waitin' beside de cabin door.
She'll be mighty happy when I tell her once more.

Chorus

Down in de canebrake, some happy day
You'll hear de weddin' bells a ringin' mighty gay.
There's gonna be a cabin and in the trundle bed
There'll be a pickaninny and all because I said:

Chorus

Down in de canebrake, dahs where I'll stay
'Long side a Nancy Dill until we're laid away.
And when we get to Heaven and Peter lets us in,
I'll start my wings a-flappin' and sing to her again

Chorus

Frank Crumit. *Frank Crumit #2* (MC Productions, CD 111; originally released in 1928, Victor 21340)

"Come, Love, Come"

Down in the cane brake, close to the mill,
There lives a yeller girl whose name is Nancy Till.
She knowed that I loved her, she knowed it long,
I'm gwine to serenade her and I'll sing her this song.

> Come, love, come, the boat lies low.
> She lies high and dry on the Ohio,
> Come, love, come, won't you come along with me,
> I'll take you down to Tennessee.

Softly the casement 'gins for to rise,
Stars am a shinin', love, above us in the skies.
The moon is declinin' behind the hill,
Reflectin' its pale rays on you, my Nancy Till.

Chorus

Farewell, my love, I must now away,
I've long to travel, love, before the break of day.
Next time I come, love, I hope you'll go,
A-sailin' with me, love, upon the Ohio.

Chorus

Charles J. Finger. *Frontier Ballads* (Garden City, NY: Doubleday, Page & Company, 1927): 165-166

"Down in the Cane Brake"

Down in the canebrake, close by the mill
There live a colored gal and her name was Nancy Dill.
I told her that I loved her and I'd love her very long.
I'm gonna serenade her and this will be my song.

    Come, my love, come, my boat lies low,
    She lies high and dry on the Ohio.
    Come along love, won't you come along with me,
    And I'll take you don to Tennessee.

Down in the canebrake, that's where I'll go,
Down where the yella moon is hangin' might low.
I know she'll be waitin' beside her cabin door
And she'll be might happy when I tell her once more.

Chorus

Down in the canebrake, some happy day
You'll hear the weddin' bells just a-ringin' mighty gay.
There's gonna be a cabin and in the trundle bed
There'll be a little pickaninny all because I said:

Chorus

Down in the canebrake, that's where I'm gonna stay,
'Long side a Nancy Dill until we's laid away.
And when we get to Haven and Peter lets us in
I'll start my wings a flappin' and sing to her again

Smiley Burnette. "Down in the Cane Brake," *Smiley Burnette: Gentle Genius of Country Music* (Cattle Compact Mono, CCD 203; originally recorded on the Decca label in 1938)

"Come, Love, Come"

Down by the canebrake, close by the mill,
Lived a pretty little girl, her name of 'Nessa Field.
1 knew that she love me, and I knew it was wrong.
Now I serenade her and I sing her a song:

> Come, love, come. The boat rides low,
> Rides high and dry on the Ohio.
> Come, love, come, and go with me.
> We'll go down to Tennessee.

I never mat a pretty gal in all my life
But that she was some boatman's wife.
Boatman dance and boatman sing
And boatman do most anything.   (Chorus)

Boatman dance and boatman sing
And boatman do most anything.
When the boatman go on shore,
Spend his cash and he work for more.   (Chorus)

When you go to the Boatman's Ball,
You dance with my wife or you won't dance at all.
Sky-blue jacket and tarpaulin hat,
Look out, boys, for the nine-tailed cat.   (Chorus)

I've come this way and I won't come no more.
Let me by and I'll go on shore.
There I'll turn my passions loose,
And they'll cram me in the caleboose.   (Chorus)

Jeff Warner and Jeff Davis, *Wilder Joy* (LP; Flying Fish Records, FF 431, 1986); lyrics at http://www.bluegrassmessengers.com/nancy-till--version-5-jeff-davis-and-jeff-warner.aspx; acc. 6/6/15

"Nancy Till"

Down in the canebrake, close by the mill,
There lived a yella gal; her name was Nancy Till;
She knew that I loved her; she knew it long.
I'm gonna serenade her and I'll sing this song.

> Come, my love, come, the boat lies low;
> She lies high and dry on the Ohio.
> Come, my love, come, won't you go along with me?
> And I'll take you down to Tennessee.

Open up the windows, love, oh do.
Listen to the music I'm a-playing for you,
The whisperings of love, soft and low,
Harmonize my voice with my old banjo.

Chorus

Softly the casement begins to rise –
The stars are a shining up above in the skies;
The moon is declinin' down behind the hill,
Reflecting all its rays on you, my Nancy Till.

Chorus

Farewell, love; I must now away;
I've a long way to go before the break of day.
But the next time I come, be ready for to go
Sailing on the banks of the Ohio.

Chorus

Sons of the Pioneers. *Lucky U Ranch*. Eugene Earle Collection (20376), Southern Folklife Collection, University of North Carolina at Chapel Hill. Transcripts TR-154 through TR-157, TR-228 through TR-231, and TR-324 through TR-327, 1951-52; 1951-52 (http://www2.lib.unc.edu/mss/inv/s/Sons_of_the_Pioneers.html; acc. 6/6/15)

"Nancy Till"

Down in the canebrake, close by the mill,
There lived a little gal and her name was Nancy Till;
She knew that I loved her and she knew it all along.
Listen to my story and I'll sing my little song.

> Come, my love, come, the boat lies low;
> She lies high and dry on the Ohio.
> Come, my love, come, won't you come along with me?
> And I'll take you down to Tennessee.

Open the window, Oh, my love, do,
And listen to the music I'm a-playing for you,
The whisperings of love, so soft and so low,
Harmonize my voice with my old banjo.

Chorus

Softly the casement begins for to rise –
The stars are a shining above in the skies;
The moon is descending behind yonder hill,
Reflecting its ray on my Nancy Till.

Chorus

Farewell, love; I must now away;
I've a long way to travel before the break of day.
The next time I come, be ready for to go
Sailing on the banks of the Ohio.

Chorus

Ken Carson. "Nancy Till," *Ken Carson Singing Your Favorite Campfire Songs* (The Longines Symphonette Recording Society, LW 149, [1960s])

"Nancy Till"

Down in the canebrake, over by the mill,
There lives a little gal and her name is Nancy Till;
She knows that I love her; she's knowed it all along.
I'm gonna serenade her and sing her this song.

>Come, my love, come, the boat lies low;
>She rides high and dry on the Ohio.
>Come, my love, come, won't you come along with me?
>I'll take you down to Tennessee.

Open up your window, love, please do,
Listen to the music I'm a-playing for you,
Whispering love songs soft and low,
Harmonize my voice with my old banjo.

Chorus

Softly the casement begins to rise –
Stars am a twinkling up in the sky;
The moon am declining way beyond the hill,
Reflecting its light upon my Nancy Till.

Chorus

Fare thee well, love; I must now away;
Got a long way to travel before the break of day.
The next time I come, be ready for to go
Sailing down the middle of the Ohio.

Chorus

Merle Travis' lyrics, transcribed by the author of this article from *The Coonhunters* featuring Merle Travis (Bear Family Records, CDD042, 2002) [The radio transcriptions were originally issued on Capitol Records. This recording is also available from the British Archive of Country Music.]

"Down in the Canebrake"

Down in the canebrake, close by the mill
There lived a colored girl her name was Nancy Dill.
I told her that I loved her, I loved her very long.
I'm gonna serenade her, this will be my song

> Come, my love, come, my boat lies low,
> She lies high and dry on the Ohio.
> Come, my love, come, won't you come along with me,
> And I'll take you down to Tennessee.

Down in the canebrake, there's where I'll go,
Down where the yellow moon is hanging mighty low.
I know that she'll be waiting beside de cabin door.
She'll be mighty happy when I tell her once more

Chorus

Down in the canebrake, some happy day
You'll hear the wedding bells a ringing mighty gay.
There's gonna be a cabin and in the trundle bed
There'll be a pickaninny and all because I said

Chorus

Down in the canebrake, there's where I'll stay
Along side of Nancy Dill until we're laid away.
And when we get to Heaven, we'll meet St. Peter there
He'll give us both a table for us to share.

Chorus

Olive Kelly Smith's lyrics; recorded by student Gertrude Edens for Joan O'Bryant's folklore class in Kansas in the 1950s. Transcribed by the author of this article from the Joan O'Bryant Kansas Folklore Collection (MS 2002-12, Box 36 FF1), held by the Wichita State University Library

Selected Publications by Jim Vandergriff

"Culturally Appropriate and Place-Based Practices" [co-author Donna Jurich], *Success in High-Need Schools*, 4 #2 (2007); www.acifund.org/aci-center.

"An Eskimo-English Dialect," *USF Language Quarterly* [University of Southern Florida], 18 (Spring-Summer 1980): 36-38.

Editor, *Heritage of Kansas* (1972-1975) [Emporia State, folklore quarterly].

Editor, *Hertzler Heritage* by Edith Coe (Emporia State Press, 1975).

Editor, *The Indians of Kansas* (Emporia: Teachers' College Press, 1973).

"Kotzebue English" in *Essays in Native American English*, Guillermo Bartelt, et al., eds. (San Antonio: Trinity University Press, 1982): 121-156.

"The Legend of Joe's Cave," *MFS Journal*, 15-16 (1993-1994): 29-50.

"Native American Teachers Needed," *Teachers College Record* [invited commentary] (Dec. 21, 2006); www.tcrecord.org.

"Reflections on History: Violence in Ozark Folklore" [invited article], *Bentley House Beacon* [Springfield, MO: Museum of the Ozarks] (Spring 1990): 3-4.

"Terrible Swift Sword: Justice in Ozark Folklore," *MFS Journal*, 26 (2004): 66-78.

"Update on The Legend of Joe's Cave," *MFS Journal*, 17 (1995): 117-122.

"What Standards Leave Behind" [co-authored with Donna Jurich] in *No Child Left Behind*, proceedings, Midwest Association of Teacher Educators, 18th Annual Spring Conference, March 25-26, 2004 (Urbana: 2005).

Jim taught at Knox College in Illinois before leaving the Midwest
(Photo courtesy of the author)

Introduction – "The Dawg Song War"

The Ozark "Dawg Song"
(*San Francisco Chronicle*, March 17, 1912)

Luckily, a war of words instead of blows....

Some of our readers will already be familiar with MFS member Sue Attalla and her extensive research on "The Dawg Song." Her first article on the topic appeared in the 2002 issue of this journal under the title "'An Orphan Ditty': In Search of the Ozark Houn' Dawg." This time around, Sue uncovers further historical information about the origin of "The Dawg Song" and the "war" held in newspapers in the early 20th century over its authorship. Sue has single-mindedly pursued trails of evidence through newspapers and documents from all over the state of Missouri, as well as from other states such as Arkansas and Texas, where local "lights" claimed authorship. Such devotion to scholarship is admirable, especially considering the sacrifice of eyesight involved in spending so many hours reading scratchy microfilm and dusty old newspapers!

Sue's self-penned "About the Authors" blurb in the 2002 issue informs us that she is "perhaps the only MFS member to have lived on three sides of Missouri, but never within its borders." She grew up in Des Moines and earned her BA and MA in English from the University of Northern Iowa. She earned her PhD in English from Rice University in Texas and she taught English for four years at Pittsburg State University in Kansas, barely five miles west of the Missouri state line. Sue recently retired from Tulsa Community College in Oklahoma (another of Missouri's western border neighbors), though she's still teaching classes, this time online.

Sue is a fine storyteller who has enthralled numerous groups with her "Dawg" stories at the Scott Joplin Ragtime Festival in Sedalia, the Ozarks Studies Symposium at Missouri State University in West Plains, and at five MFS annual meetings. Her future book on the topic is destined to be the definitive source of information about "The Hound Dawg Song." We're all looking forward to seeing the finished product!

THE DAWG SONG WAR

Susan C. Attalla

During Speaker of the House Champ Clark's 1912 bid for the Democratic presidential nomination, the ballad of a much maligned houn' dawg achieved national fame. However, prior to the song's adoption by the Clark campaign, it had already become phenomenally popular in Missouri and nearby states. Members of the Springfield Commercial Club first learned the dawg song during a "booster" train trip to Mammoth Spring, Arkansas, in September, 1911. They then began its rapid spread across the state as they sang the infectious song from Mountain Grove to Mammoth Spring and back to Springfield, stopping in many communities along their route.[1]

Boisterously performed from town to town, the dog song quickly spread throughout the state. With the song's popularity came curiosity about its origin. Three and a half months after Springfield businessmen had introduced the kicked dawg to an eager public, the *St. Louis Republic* published a letter to the editor recounting the song's alleged history:

> The truth is this song is one of the oldest in the country. It is a folk song of the Virginia, Kentucky and Tennessee mountains and came to Missouri with the drift of the earliest settlers.
> Daniel Boone and his home-spun cronies sang it in the woods of the lower Missouri. The old-time dance callers sang it in the Ozark hills to the rhythm of the corn fiddle and the shuffle of cowhide boots on puncheon floors. The freighters on the old Boone's Lick road and the Santa Fe trail sang it at night around their camp fires.

"Daniel Boone and His Hound"
(Portrait by Alonzo Chappel; from *National Portrait Gallery of Eminent Americans, Vol. 1*
[N.Y.: Johnson, Fry & Company, 1861])

And the original Missouri pioneers carried it with them over the plains and through the Rockies to the Western Ocean. I first heard it on the lips of Thad Bass, an exiled Missourian from Columbia punching cows on the staked plains of New Mexico. He used it to lull to rest many a herd of longhorns on the trail to Cheyenne.

> Chaw de meat and save de bone,
> De Blue Neck lives on Tallyhone;
> Makes no difference if he is a houn',
> You gotta quit kickin' my dog aroun'.

The immortal 'Sally Goodin,' 'Sugar in de Gourd,' 'Old Tom Willson [*sic*],' 'Turkey in the Straw' and 'Quit Dat Kickin' My Dawg Aroun'' are the folk songs of the hill people. If you are a Missourian, or have Missouri blood in your veins, all these tunes find an echo in your being and your voice and feet swing naturally into their rhythm.

Words are nothing. Tune plays a small part in a song of the people. That nameless something which is at once a call to battle and an order to march must be found in any song which moves the people collectively.

The 'Hound Dog' song is the Ozark Booster song, and as such, has, in my humble opinion, come to stay. The Ozark region has been kicked around long enough. The hill people have spoken: 'You gotta quit kickin' my dog aroun'.'[2]

The letter writer was John H. Curran, candidate for Railroad and Warehouse Commissioner and former Missouri Commissioner of Immigration, whose job it had been to attract new residents to the state.

Could Curran have realized the lasting impact of his words? Three days later, the *New York Herald* helped preserve and spread his story: "A correspondent of the *St. Louis Republic* says the dog song was sung by Daniel Boone."[3] A myth was born that has been perpetuated over the years.

Roughly three weeks after Curran's letter, Columbia's *Missouri Herald* revealed that the dog song had also caught the attention of the Missouri Folklore Society and its leader, Professor Henry M. Belden:

> The casual reader who might imagine it to be a production originating in the brain of some lover of the animal will probably be surprised to know that this song or a longer one of which this is only a fragment was sung by Daniel Boone and his companions in pioneer days. This statement was recently made in a newspaper. A contributor writes that he heard the verse sung in the California gold fields in the forties by Thad Bass of Columbia, Mo. The Missouri Folk-Lore Society, which is collecting all such stray fragments of verse that have at some time been popularly sung in the state, would like to know more of the origin of the song. If anyone in Columbia knows more words or has heard the music to which the words were sung, the society would like to hear from him. Dr. H. M. Belden has charge of the work.[4]

DANIEL BOONE SANG DOG SONG

"Stop Kickin' " Used In California In 40's by Columbian.

The Daniel Boone claim—a boost for the Missouri side!
(*Columbia Missouri Herald*, January 19, 1912)

How Columbia's Thad Bass got from his cow-punching job in New Mexico to California gold country is not explained. Perhaps Bass had been working his way west, or perhaps the story had grown in the retelling. For some reason, Belden did not include the hound dog song in *Ballads and Songs Collected by the Missouri Folklore Society*, but Curran's connection of the song with Daniel Boone continued to interest writers and researchers.

In *Our Times* (1930), Mark Sullivan expressed his belief in the song's Blue Ridge/Appalachian origins and spoke authoritatively about its spread to Missouri:

> The song was very old; for generations it had expressed occasional emotions entertained by mountaineers in Virginia, Kentucky, and Tennessee. After Daniel Boone and other early settlers carried it across the Mississippi, it came to be thought of as essentially a Missouri song; and 'They gotta quit kickin' my dawg aroun'' was supposed to express a characteristic Missouri state of mind.[5]

As author of a popular newspaper column nearly twenty years earlier at the height of the dog song's popularity, Sullivan may have made these remarks from memory of what he had read in 1912 newspapers. He provided no details or source citations to substantiate his claims.

Subsequent scholars questioned this Daniel Boone connection. For instance, in *Tall Tales from Arkansas*, James R. Masterson mentioned Sullivan's comments but added, "We hesitate, however, to believe that the song could have existed from the time of Boone (who died in 1820) until 1912 without leaving any printed trace."[6] Aside from the song's chorus, which Masterson accepted as old, he, instead, proposed that the verses arose in the Ozarks of either Missouri or Arkansas around the time of Champ Clark's bid for the presidential nomination.

A few years later, Vance Randolph summarized Sullivan's and Masterson's comments and quoted a fragment of a letter from Aaron Weatherman, Swan Post Office, Taney County, Missouri. Writing to the *Springfield Republican,* Weatherman explained how the abuse of a hound dog owned by young Zeke Parrish before the Civil War had inspired the song. Although Randolph dated Weatherman's letter to December 28, 1911, he was not working from Weatherman's full letter. He credited the story to a February 28, 1937 letter sent by May Kennedy McCord to the *Springfield News and Leader*. Randolph also wrote that McCord had quoted Weatherman's letter "with apparent approval."[7]

Randolph seems to have tried to verify Weatherman's claim as quoted in McCord's letter. He turned to Ozarks poet Mary Elizabeth Mahnkey as support for his belief that the song originated more recently. "Our folks located near Forsyth in '79," said Mahnkey; "We were all interested in songs. If there had been a 'Hound Dog' song in the Civil War era, surely an echo would have lingered, and I would have caught it." Mahnkey believed that the song did not predate 1910.[8]

William K. McNeil, late director of the Ozark Folk Center in Mountain View, Arkansas, also doubted the Daniel Boone and Zeke Parrish stories. The Boone origin lacks supporting evidence, McNeil argued, observing that Randolph's account of the Zeke Parrish story "sounds too good to be true."[9]

Because no one had reprinted Aaron Weatherman's full original letter, it was necessary to search the *Springfield Republican*. The letter was located a week after the authorship date cited in the 1937 *Springfield News and Leader*, later cited by Randolph and McNeil:

> Swan P.O. Dec. 28, 1911
> Mr. McJimpsy
>
> I seen by the papers that a hull lot of talk is a goin roun bout a Booster song. The paper says that this here song was writ by sum land agent. It aint no such a thing a tall, so I set down an got my dauter Selina Aun's little gurl to rite you this letter. I disrember the yeer I hearn thet song the furst time, but it were long before the War. I wuz livin about 3 mile north of Forsyth, an my paw and grandpa Slater wuz fratin goods from Forsyth to Springfield.
>
> In them days they wuz no ralerode and they brung the goods from St. Louis by bote down the Mississippi an then up the White River to Forsyth on a little stern wheel bote thet were named Rosie Bell. When the goods wuz uploded Grandpaw Slater an Dad tuk em to Springfield. They wuz other fraters, too. One of them wuz Pursley Parish and he had a boy named Zeke, who used ter help him frate. Zeke wuz rite smart of a hunter an always had a houn dog. Every time Zeke an his paw cum to Forsyth he brung his dog. He were a good houn, all rite, but Zeke he only fed him wen he thunk about it an thet wuz about wunst a week. When the houn cum along to town he wuz a-rustlin grub evry minute en he warnt perticklar whoose grub it were. So everbody node the houn, being he was steelin grub frum evry back door, houses an stores alike and the folks got such a gruge agin the houn, thet they wood kick him when they seed him on the square. One day a big feller about 18 kicked the houn and Zeke seen him do it an lit inter the feller an shore changed his looks sum. The sherif cum along an rested both the boys and Zeke bein a country boy wuz skeered and blubbring. Jest when the sherif wuz takin the boys into Squire Johnson's office, Zekes Paw seed him an he hollered to

> Zeke what wuz the matter. Zeke wuz a-cryin an so when he hollered back to his Paw, 'Every time I cum to town, the boys all kick my dog around. I don't care if he is a houn, they gotta quit kicken my dog around.' It sounded jest like a song and all the fellers around Forsyth sung the song for a rite smart time, till the war broke out and they wuznt time to sing. Thets when that song started fer I were there an knowed Zeke an his Paw an the houn.
>
> Aaron Weatherman[10]

Seeing Weatherman's complete letter, purportedly dictated by an illiterate who claims to have followed the hound dog song accounts in the newspapers, one must agree with McNeil's assessment that it is "too good to be true."

An additional reason exists to doubt Weatherman's story. Newspapers abounded with conflicting accounts of the dog song's origin and these accounts quickly escalated into a lively competition for the right to be known as the dog song's composer. Claimant after claimant set forth a new version of the song's history as each aspirant attempted to sway public opinion in his favor. Weatherman, or whoever wrote the Weatherman letter, was most likely just one among many purporting to know the story behind the Ozark dog song.

The authorship conflict began in Springfield on a local scale when the *Springfield Republican* announced a plan set forth by Senator F. M. McDavid, President of the Springfield Club. McDavid had announced that "he would at once appoint a committee to investigate the origin and status of the hymn."[11] The newspaper added that committee chairman W. W. Naylor would build a team of investigators to examine readers' claims to "the honor of having started the words and tune which have set the whole state singing."

On the heels of this announcement, Aaron Weatherman's claim had reached the *Springfield Republican*'s editor, E. E. E. McJimpsey. The authorship controversy spread from Springfield to St. Louis, perhaps with the aid of Senator McDavid's curiosity, which could have increased statewide interest in the search. Among the earliest claimants to contact the *St. Louis Republic* was Professor Skid Snively, poet laureate of the suspicious-sounding and unlocated town of Teaserville, Missouri. Snively claimed to have composed the tune accidentally in 1893 while fiddling and later to have added words to commemorate a local incident in which a Teaserville dog had been abused.[12] Professor Snively was described as a man with great empathy for animals. In fact, he was said to be capable of "soul transmigration," resulting in his special ability to impersonate "horse, mule or jackass, whose characters he could assume at will for the entertainment of visitors at the livery stable" where he had begun his career. His one failing was that, unlike his four-legged counterparts, "he couldn't be driven to work." As a result, Snively was forced to leave the livery stable and to pursue "political, educational, and purely literary paths," which led to his composing the Ozark dog song.[13]

A reader named Ed Fonzer contested Professor Snively's claim:

> They never was a man in Teaserville on eather side of the river that could tell the truth on Oth no more than this here fello Pro Snively can on a stack of Bibals. . . . What's more Snively ain't a profesor he caint fiddle er play a jews-harp er pat Juba even but I made up that houn' peace mysef, I played it fer dances and barn warming around hear back of 1892, you ask any of the Dawson boys or Hon. Con Roach.[14]

The *St. Louis Republic* requested the government's help finding Ed Fonzer, who had not provided a return address: "If the Secretary of State can locate and identify his constituent we should be grateful for the information."

With accusations flying concerning the song's authorship and Secretary of State Cornelius Roach now named by Ed Fonzer as a witness who might settle the primacy dispute, the *St. Louis Republic* announced that the dog ditty had been running around "like a stray cur for weeks" and would soon "have more authors than Homer had birthplaces."[15] The *Republic* took the next logical step—it launched a contest to discover the origin and authorship of the Ozark dog song. On February 1, 1912, the newspaper pleaded, "We ask only that such claimants as may develop, and their partisans, shall refrain from too bitter and violent abuse and recriminations. We have not approved of Fonzer's applying the short and ugly term [of liar] to Prof. Snively, yet we must have the *truth* at any reasonable cost to personal feelings in order that the prize may be awarded justly." The *Republic* further stated, "Yet we would not appeal to any Missourian's love of mendacity. If there are any liars . . . we ask them to keep out of this contest."[16] The prize was to be a much-coveted fiddle and bow and the battle had begun.

The contest will end with the awarding of the victor's laurels
(T. E. Powers, *New York American*, March 24, 1912)

On February 3rd, Secretary of State Roach wrote to the *St. Louis Republic*.[17] Declaring his eagerness to supply the truth and to aid folklore research, Roach supported Ed Fonzer's claim. Not only did Roach attest to his constituent's truthfulness and moral character, he displayed his own grasp of history—or penchant for tall tales—by arguing that the ancient Ozark mountains had provided a landing place for Noah's Ark. Noah's "sea dogs" then evolved into the hound dogs of which the now-famous dawg was, according to the Secretary of State, "a perfect specimen." Despite Professor Snively's ambition, Roach expressed his confidence that a visit to Taney County, with its "surroundings conducive to the birth of a lyric of this character," would convince Snively that no other place "could have given birth to the dog song."

Many readers were closely following the *St. Louis Republic*'s contest. In a letter to the editor dated February 10, 1912, an author, who signed himself only "J.A.B." of Salem, Missouri, wanted to set the record straight. Although he did not claim authorship, he insisted that he had heard the dog song before the Civil War and that he knew the author, a young country dance fiddler:

> Being very much interested in the arguments for or against the authorship of the houn' dawg song, I would like to add my testimony in favor of one whom all lovers of homespun music in St. Louis have heard of and that is Col. Thomas Benton Moss of Hillsboro, ... Mo.
>
> Away back in 1860 I first heard the strains of that old houn' dawg song. Old Tommy Moss, who 'fit' Indians in earlier years, lived out on Sandy. He had eight boys, all of whom played the fiddle. Bent Moss, then a young fellow, played almost continually for dances all over old Jefferson County. It was at old Tom Moss' farmhouse that I heard Bent Moss play that old tune, and he said then that he made it up.
>
> Bent was a crack fiddler then and is yet. I never heard the tune again until I moved to the Ozarks, which is the original Garden of Eden. I think Col. Moss should have the fiddle and bow, rosin and strings, also a good leather case for same.[18]

But Colonel Moss wouldn't win the prize so easily.

On February 21st, the *St. Louis Republic* declared that the contest was widening and simultaneously published John T. Briskett's claim that he had "played it on the French harp at Cape Girardeau in steamboat days."[19] Later, still contending that he wrote the music and determined to win the prize fiddle, Briskett submitted what he claimed to be the original manuscript of the dog song. With the manuscript came further details of the song's origin. According to Briskett, he and a boyhood friend in Hannibal had been co-owners of a hound dog named Ring, and, indeed, the lyric was "the inspired work of no less a genius than Mark Twain," Briskett's young friend. With this, Briskett had gone a step too far because the *St. Louis Republic* began to doubt his claim:

> Expert examination of the manuscript (and it may be said that it bears the mellow tint of age and certain other earmarks of apparent genuineness) will determine the issue. Either the world and Mark Twain's publishers will have to thank Mr. Briskett for an enormous, a monumental contribution to American literature, or Mr. Briskett will be established as one of the most enormous and monumental falsifiers of the living age upon a pedestal of his own making.
>
> Either John T. Briskett will win our fiddle or we shall present him as a consolation prize another stringed instrument known from ancient times as the lyre.[20]

The same day that the *St. Louis Republic* voiced its doubts about John T. Briskett's honesty, the *Springfield Daily Leader* reported the sighting of the dog song's author in Walsenburg, Colorado.[21] If true, this account would credit the dog song to Ozark County, Missouri. Lige Spencer was said to have stopped by Walsenburg's Greenlight Saloon, declaring, "I'm it, the original houn' dawg man. I writ it and I'm running away." After pointing out the spotted hound sleeping by his Missouri mules and after drinking the whiskey that he said would "make a man from the Mountains of Missouri talk straight," Spencer told his story:

> Gentleman, it is like this: Down in our country there is three things that a man is proud of, his family, his stummick for squirrel whisky and his coon dawgs. Well, me and 'dawg' thar, in the last few years have become the most famous individuals in southern Missouri and northern Arkansas. Every dance, coon hunt or feud pulled off in that neck of the woods for years has ended up with tales of how me and 'dawg' there fit bars, coons and catamounts. After awhile every one got jealous of us....
>
> Then one day last spring a feller by the name of Lem Andrews, who runs a store down at the county seat, became so jealous of me and 'dawg' that he coaxed 'dawg' into his store and just about kicked the life out of him. Now 'dawg' is sure funny. He'll fight any varmint from a tree frog to a polar bear, but he just natcherly seems afraid of humans when they begin gettin' rough. Won't fight or anything, just duck his tail between his legs and howl.
>
> Everybody knowd about 'dawgs' failin' after that and the poor fellow was kicked by every dawg owner in Ozark country. I fit every man that I could get to, averaged five a week, but it wasn't no use. Why, even 'dawg' got discouraged and didn't want to hunt coons any more. I finally wrote to the governor about it; thought maybe he could make 'em stop kickin' my dawg around. I was feeling kind of blue and the rhyming part of the letter just came natcheral. That's all of how the song came to be writ. But after that it was worse than ever. Everybody got to singin' about me and 'dawg.' Then he got discouraged and so did I. About a month ago I just natcherly couldn't stand it any longer and I hitched up the mules, whistled to the dawg and struck out for Colorado. Told the wife and kids I'd locate and then come back for 'em. Now, B'Gad, gentlemen, I'm going out and set down on a piece of Uncle Sam's land, and this kickin' about of 'dawg' is going to stop.

Having finished his story and his whiskey, Spencer climbed aboard his wagon and headed toward the Spanish Peaks, followed by "dawg."

Signing himself "Truthful James," a contender writing from Portia, Arkansas, claimed the song for Washington County, Missouri.[22] He told of traveling with a friend along the ridge road from Black River to Potosi in 1863 and hearing a yelping dog as they approached a small mill:

> There seemed to be no person around. Standing over the meal box, with his head alternately in the box and his snout up the spout, stood a long, hungry-looking hound dog, who was eating up the meal as fast as the burrs ground it out. While watching the dog there entered a negro man from the rear of the mill. Going to the mill he hit the dog a couple of heavy kicks, which sent the dog howling out of the mill. As the dog went out the door, a half-grown boy hove in sight from out the sawmill part of the establishment.
>
> 'Say, you better stop kicking my dog around. If he is only a hound, you got to stop kicking him 'round,' he says.
>
> The negro man says, 'You got to keep that dog away from here. This is the second time I kotch him eaten out dat meal box.' The boy says, 'If you don't want him to eat up your meal, why don't you put a shutter on that door to keep dogs out? Any dog could eat up the meal faster than your old mill grinds it.'
>
> 'How long you spec he could do it?' says the miller.
>
> 'Until he starves himself barking up the spout,' says the boy.

According to Truthful James, he and his friend told this story that night at Potosi's Wisharp Hotel where Polly Ann Dogget, an employee who "could play on the fiddle, sing and whistle like a mockingbird," improvised the song. He attributed the song's "You gotta quit kicking my dog around," rather than "You got to quit," to Polly Ann's French parentage, which resulted in her not speaking "very plain English."

Soon after Truthful James' claim for Washington County, Boone County registered its claim in a Columbia paper. T. E. Britt of Appleton City related a childhood memory from his family's Boone County farm where he claimed that Sep Smith, a farm hand and country fiddler, had played the dog song along with "Sifting Sand," "Arkansas Traveler," and hornpipes. Britt recalled two verses that he said had appealed to his curiosity:

> Every time I cum to school,
> The teacher lams me with a rule,
> It makes no difference if I am a fool,
> He's gotta quit lamming me with a rule.
>
> When I feed my dawg on milk and soup,
> He come and jumped right thro' a hoop,
> It makes no difference if he is a houn',
> They got to quit kickin' my dawg around.

To add credibility to his claim, Britt added, "The Hart boys, Clem Griffin and Sid Grindstaff will remember this dawg song."[23]

A claim appeared in the *St. Louis Post-Dispatch* for Phelps County. "It was in Rolla, 'way along before the War," declared an unidentified resident. "There was a lot of boys kickin' a dog around the square, an' the young chap that owned the dog came up and hollered 'You quit a-kickin' my dog aroun'!' ... An' it weren't long after that, that I heard somebody singing a song about it, with the words just about like they are now."[24]

Although interest in the search had spread to other papers, the *St. Louis Republic*'s contest continued. M. W. Lowry's letter arrived from Washington, Missouri, in which he staked a claim for his boyhood home in Ray County:

> I have read these untruthful claims of the originator of the 'Houn' Dawg' song until I have at last become disgusted and will in a short time call at your office and prove to your satisfaction that there has been no foundation to *any* of the past claims. It is true that the song originated in Missouri, but, at Richmond, Mo.
>
> Twenty years ago, when I was a mere boy, my father lived on a farm near Richmond . . . and after our hound dog, 'Sport' by name, had died, my two sisters and myself were so grieved over his death that our father, in order to amuse us and drive away our sorrow, wrote the song entitled 'The Houn' Dawg' although the words have been changed considerably since that time. . . I have written to my sister for the words of the original song, which we still have in reserve in our family Bible.[25]

The verses purportedly preserved in the Lowry family Bible never appeared in the *St. Louis Republic*.

While some readers might have been eagerly awaiting those verses, the Kentucky Club of St. Louis sparked a debate during a meeting in which the organization celebrated Kentucky pioneers and spun a new tale about the origin of the dog song. The *St. Louis Republic* described plans for the club's impending meeting.[26] The club was to resurrect the "branch water man," a legendary class of poor Kentuckians, who made their home by the nearest stream or "branch," thus avoiding the need to dig a well. Although the branch water man typically had a large family, he was said to have cherished his hound above all else and to have crooned a song whenever the dog was abused by more industrious townsfolk who resented his laziness. The *Republic* went on to describe additional entertainment planned for the enjoyment of Kentuckians living in Missouri: "The musical programme will consist of the early Kentucky 'fiddle' music, such as 'Old Dan Tucker,' 'Zip Coon,' 'Soap Suds,' 'Great Big Tater in the Sandy Lan',' and 'Natchez Under the Hill.'"

The Kentucky claim—the truth lies in ancient stone cups!
(Jean Knott, *St. Louis Post-Dispatch*, March 29, 1912)

According to a follow-up article, the Kentucky Club had kept part of its plans a secret. During the meeting, club member Sam McChesney, disguised as a famous archaeologist in academic regalia and long white wig and beard, entertained his fellow members with a tall tale of how the dog song arose among Kentucky's Stone Age people, the Lithites, and made its way to the Ozarks. This "learned scholar" claimed to have discovered twenty-eight ancient stone cups in Russell Cave near Lexington, Kentucky. From the hieroglyphs on some of the cups, he had deciphered the words of the hound dog song. After pouring water into accompanying unmarked cups, he had discovered they gave off tones which, taken together, formed the tune of the dawg song. According to the visiting archaeologist, evidence indicated that one of the Lithites had been disliked for his habit of telling his friends ancient stories. Rather than punishing the man, they kicked his much loved dog. In protest, he composed the song and sang it so often that the other Lithites killed him, thus starting the first Kentucky feud which continued until all but one of the Lithites were killed.

As evidence that this lone survivor, an original branch water man, had moved to the Ozarks, McChesney told of discovering a stone image in the Ozarks—a hound with a stone tin can tied to its tail. Upon the stone can appeared the identical hieroglyphs previously seen on the ancient cups found in the Kentucky cave. According to the bogus archaeologist, a transcription of these hieroglyphs fell into the hands of a black hotel porter who had heard the archaeologist humming the tune and this was allegedly the cause of the dog song's recent revival.[27]

Although the *Republic*'s announcements of the former Kentuckians' meeting had been matter-of-fact and although the paper had committed to discovering the song's origin, the *Republic* expressed outrage at Kentucky's attempt to steal fiddle tunes, including Missouri's dog song:

> Claims to fiddle tunes ought to be asserted cautiously. It is a delicate matter to steal another State's music. 'Dan Tucker' and 'Zip Coon' no more belong to Kentucky than does 'Pop Goes the Weasel.' As for 'Soapsuds' and 'Taters in the Sandy Land' they do not amount to much anyhow, and Kentucky may take them; but when she boldly snatches 'Natchez Under the Hill' from Tennessee, Arkansas may well look to its famous Traveler and Missouri to its Houn' Dawg.
>
> We intend to keep the latter chained up nights while the Kentuckians are in session.[28]

With the dog song attracting attention in Missouri and engendering feuds long ago in Kentucky, should anyone be surprised that the dog song war had crossed Missouri's southern border into the Arkansas Ozarks? Fred W. Allsopp's *Folklore of Romantic Arkansas* (1931) reprints a stirring warning issued by Arkansas to Missouri:

> I know that Apollo swept such harmony from the lyre that the listening gods were charmed and the world acclaimed him deity of song. I know that Orpheus with magic strain led rocks and trees and beasts to follow him, and so enthralled the underworld that angels gazed thereon with envy. I know that David drew from his entrancing harp a concord that dispelled the gloom about the brow of Saul and flooded Israel's palaces with the laughter of music and the joy of song...I know that all of these combined into one gorgeous rhapsody, by a master greater than any who yet has lived, cannot equal the touching cadence and simple majesty of 'The Ozark Dog Song.' And, men, think of Missouri continuing her intimations that she is the parent of this famous and undying melody! No! Better perish Missouri by her own hand than allow this to drift along until the citizenship of the great State of Arkansas arises and violently wrings Missouri's neck.

Allsopp states that Attorney John H. Caldwell had issued this challenge, but provides no additional information about Caldwell other than saying that his words had been printed in the *St. Louis Post-Dispatch*. The rest of Allsopp's story provides an important clue, however. Also in Caldwell's words, Allsopp records the far-fetched tale of late night shenanigans in Mammoth Spring, Arkansas, which led to Arkansas' claim to the song:

> One recent morning at two, the lone one-armed Town Marshal at Mammoth Springs, Arkansas, was walking his weary beat from the blacksmith shop to the town pump and back. The night was warm and still. The moon floated like a pale lemon across the mild blue sky. Then suddenly, says one veracious chronicler who was on the scene, 'Great holes were torn in the atmosphere.' A crowd of Knight Templars, just relieved of 'fez' and 'buckle,' had emerged from their sanctuary, and with their advent into the street burst the dog song upon the night air.
>
> The vigilant Marshal was right on the job. He commanded silence, but before he could enforce his decree, the 'bunch' had taken refuge in the village drug store and defied him to do his worst. The roar of their 'Dog Song' rattled the plate glass windows. The intrepid Marshal dared the choir to walk out into the street and sing.[29]

The Dawg Song War 83

Still singing the dog song, the revelers are said to have risen to the challenge by joining hands "in a ring-around-a-rosy" formation with Mammoth Spring's marshal in the middle. Allsopp alludes to the dismissal of a court case against the perpetrators, when "testimony of an indubitable character" vouched that the dog song was native to the state and had been previously adopted by the Mammoth Spring Commercial Club.

What is the truth behind the tale? Who was Attorney Caldwell? What were the facts of this court case and its witness of "indubitable character"? Did Mammoth Spring's claim predate Missouri's as Caldwell claimed?

A search for the dog song in surviving issues of Mammoth Spring's *The Monitor* turned up advertisements for John H. Caldwell's legal practice,[30] so one can conclude that the man whose story Allsopp has preserved was a Mammoth Spring resident in 1911. Unfortunately, the sporadic available issues of *The Monitor* contain no account of the trial or mention of the song.

Fortunately, help is available in other sources. Thanks to John H. Caldwell's decades-long interest in Mammoth Spring's dog song incident, the State Historical Society of Missouri has preserved a fuller account of the tale quoted, in part, in Allsopp's *Folklore of Romantic Arkansas*. This account is spread throughout a series of letters and a five-page manuscript, the latter of which Caldwell retyped in 1953 from his original account sent to the *St. Louis Post-Dispatch*.[31] The most detailed account of the trial appears in the letters.

> News of the arrest of these members, bankers, preachers, doctors, lawyers, merchants, teachers and other leaders of the community, spread far and wide. All were taken before the Mayor who was not a Mason but a mighty good man. After a postponement or two the trial day came with reporters from Springfield, Kansas City, St. Louis and Memphis, and members of the Order from south Missouri and North Arkansas. It was a gala day and a tremendous crowd for a unique trial.
>
> The Mayor was a Presbyterian. F. W. Harris, one of the arrested 'criminals,' was a traveling salesman. He brought Isaac F. Stappleton from Ft. Smith whom he introduced at the trial as the pastor of the First Presbyterian church at Fort Smith, hoping for favorable reaction or impression on the Mayor. Stappleton testified that he always opened his church with this hymn. That settled it. The Mayor just couldn't believe such a song as would be used in opening church services could be offensive. All were acquitted. Stappleton graciously left town before the Mayor discovered that he was not a pastor of any church any where, lived at Harrison, and in fact was a revenue agent for the Government, and active Mason whom Harris had met years before. We all felt grateful to Harris for procuring such an able-bodied witness, at a time we all needed just that kind.[32]

Caldwell prefaces this description with a statement that the dog song was born "back in 1912 . . . full blown and without pedigree or malice toward anybody-----just born!" Such a comment may have resulted from faulty memory more than forty years later as he recounted the story in his letter to the State Historical Society of Missouri. However, it also appears to discredit his claim of Arkansas' primacy because the dog song had been introduced to Mammoth Spring in September 1911 during the Springfield Commercial Club's visit. A February 1912 article from Mountain Grove, near which the Springfielders first learned the song while riding the train to Mammoth Spring, alludes to the song's first performance in Mammoth Spring and to the later trial:

> At Mammoth Springs, where a fine banquet was prepared for the Boosters, they made the banquet hall ring with the music of the houn' song, and it seems that the song made such a hit in Mammoth Springs that a number of the best citizens of the town were arrested for singing it, but as soon as the officers learned the true merits of the song they were released with many compliments.[33]

The young Mammoth Spring attorney who appreciated perjury in the dog song trial remained willing to continue spinning his own tall tale about the dog song's origin four decades later as a Little Rock attorney and Arkansas Supreme Court librarian.[34]

Their court case won and the dog song now officially approved by Mammoth Spring's mayor, Caldwell had threatened dire consequences if Missouri persisted in claiming Mammoth Spring's—and his Arkansas'—song:

> It is currently rumored that Governor Donaghey has already promised to marshal the entire fighting force of the State Militia and send them to the Northern borders of our state at Mammoth Spring if necessary to spot this un-precedented act of vandalism until Congress relieves the situation by some Special Act indicated by the next message of the President. Oh, you Missouri! You may have discovered the Philosopher's stone for aught I know, and even the secret of future destinies-----but keep hands off our dog![35]

The Arkansas claim—the state prepares for war against Missouri!
(Folk Music Vertical Files, Missouri Historical Society Library [see note 31])

The threatened Arkansas-Missouri battle caught the attention of nearby Muskogee, Oklahoma, and a local paper suggested a means of averting the crisis: "The claim of Arkansas that the 'Missouri Dawg song' is not original might be settled in an old fiddlers' contest."[36] Although those on both sides of the Missouri-Arkansas border would surely have enjoyed such as amicable solution, the protests of one of Mammoth Spring's irate neighbors seemed destined to start a local feud: "Mammoth Spring is trying to get away with another Salem honor. It makes our blood boil to think how selfish and ungrateful some people can be."[37]

Perhaps Salem recognized that Attorney Caldwell's claim would not hold up under examination. Indicating that the local population might have known how the Springfielders learned the song in Mountain Grove during their train trip to Mammoth Spring, Salem concocted a story that explained how the houn' dawg, although not the song itself, arrived in Mountain Grove in the summer of 1911—a few months *before* Springfield's businessmen would learn the song there and subsequently introduce it to the world. Salem declared:

> Last summer the notorious canine followed Uncle Abe Hughes to West Plains. Abe didn't know he was being shadowed until he prepared for his suppertime lunch. When, lo and behold! There was Nero gnawing the last chicken bone with all the pensiveness of a Methodist circuit rider. Abe arose in his righteous wrath and exclaimed: 'You doggoned, confounded, dod danged, dod dratted, flea-bitten whelp, you'd steal a lunch from a gold fish.' Then he had taken a barrel stave and missed the dog. Not once did this noble Arkansas animal look back on the wicked city. He flew. Abe will swear that it would be impossible for him to have checked up before he reached Mountain Grove. This is the true story of the Ozark dog.[38]

By now the *Boston Globe* had declared the *St. Louis Republic* "the Houn' storm center," and the commotion resulting from the *Republic*'s authorship search was escalating and spreading. Unwilling to let Missouri's southern neighbor claim the booty, Illinois also entered the fray.[39] "I heard the hound dog song nearly 70 years ago...in the State of Illinois, and believe it originated in that State instead of the Ozarks...because at that time the Ozarks country was peopled by Indians and almost the only white men there were a few trappers and fur traders, and if the author is still alive he must be in the Methuselah class," declared one correspondent of the *Globe*.

Despite this refusal to consider the dog song's possible origin among the indigenous people of the Ozarks, Washington soon attributed authorship to a different Native American group. Chairman R. B. Milroy of the Yakima County Republican Central Committee explained that the song had been sung by the Kittitas and Yakima tribes "before the coming of the white man" and that in 1912 "several versions of the song [were] still to be found among the Indians."[40] In case readers might regard this as a Republican ploy to steal Democrat Champ Clark's campaign song, Mayor A. J. Splawn of North

Yakima, a Clark Democrat, supported Milroy's claim, adding that he did not want to hurt Clark's chances to win but that he felt it only fair to give credit to the Indians, whom he had lived among since 1861 and whom he remembers singing the dog song.

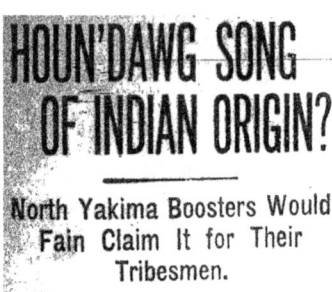

The Native American claim—the song came all the way from Washington state!
(*Oregon Daily Journal*, March 18, 1912)

In an effort to bring the Kittitas-Yakima song back to the Ozarks, a reader sent the *St. Louis Republic* this letter:

> I am not among the applicants for that fiddle and bow offered by the *Republic* to the author of the houn' dawg song. He will never be found. The lyric is too old. I have just returned from an archaeological expedition to the sand hills of Rice County, Kansas. There I discovered a cache containing a manuscript in Sixteenth Century Spanish. It purports to be an account of the expedition of Coronado to those parts, and embodies some translations of Indian songs. Among them is this 'del pais de las Oxarques,' which I translate 'from the Ozark country.'
>
> > Todas las veces que yo voy a la piazza,
> > Los muchachos non dejan acocear me perro.
> > A mi no me importa que esta ma cachorrillo
> > Necessita que cesaran acocear mi perro.[41]

Thus, the dog song was pronounced the first example of American lyric poetry, preserved by a Spanish explorer's translation from its original Ozarks Indian language!

In the face of intense competition, Texas had been making several attempts to tell it bigger and better. A Dallas-Fort Worth paper had claimed the song by mid-January 1912 in a report picked up by the *New York Herald*. According to the *Herald*, the original Texas lyric was the same as the version now sung in Missouri with the exception of Missouri's omission of an opening "O-oh." Despite the nearly identical lyric, changes in the tune were viewed as just cause for "a new War of Rebellion." Texans declared they had grown up with the tune and would not tolerate "that it shall be butchered."[42] The *Herald* then included a parody appropriately beginning with "O-oh":

> O-oh Texas folks are deep in scorn
> About that Ozark houn' dog song,
> Makes no diff'rence when it was born,
> You've gotta quit singin' that dog tune wrong.

Another page of the same day's *New York Herald* added to the discussion of the variant tune and voiced its tongue-in-cheek opinion of the conflicting claims of primacy: "The advocates of the original melody are up in arms against the Texas tune, which goes to the air 'There was an old geezer and he had a wooden leg.' This debate in the musical centres of the West will no doubt do as much to improve culture as to enforce the protection of the hound."[43]

Lone Star Minstrelsy Records "Houn'" Lay in Almost Identical Words, but the Time Varies Greatly from That of the "Show Me" State, and Guardians of the Traditions Arise in Protest.

The Texas claim—we won't take it lying down!
(*New York Herald*, January 14, 1912)

As the weeks passed, the Lone Star state's claim spread and expanded. Keokuk, Iowa's *Daily Gate City*, for instance, printed an alleged Texas parody and followed it with an allusion to the Kentucky and Illinois claims and a hint at the dog song author's ultimate fate:

Texas is at swords' point with Missouri as to the Houn's origin and in defense of her claims has advanced the following:

> Every time I come to town,
> The boys keep singin' my dawg song wrong.
> I don't care if it is a bum song,
> They gotta quit singin' my dawg song wrong.

Other claimants for the 'honor' of having originated the lines are Kentucky and Illinois. One thing is certain and that is that the author, whoever he is and wherever he lives, will have a lot to answer for on the last great day.[44]

Although originally said to be nearly identical to the words sung in Missouri, the Texas lyric changed as the weeks passed. Unwilling to take the booting endured by Missouri's dawg, the cowboy's hound was of "a sterner breed . . . [always] ready for a scrap." This new cowboy lyric began appearing in newspapers across the country and ran, in part, like this:

> When I ride in from the Lazy Z,
> Ol' Jim-dog trots along with me;
> It makes no difference if he is a houn',
> You bet the town boys don't kick him aroun'.
>
> One day a tenderfoot come in the door
> Of old Sam Peterson's general store.
> An' when he saw my lop-eared houn'
> He made a start to kick him aroun'.
>
> I jus' lit in and smoked him up,
> While Jim-dog chawed on the onery pup,
> 'Till the tenderfoot had to be made anew,
> When me and my ol' houn' got through.
>
> Every time I come to town,
> I bring along ol' Jim-dog houn';
> He trots along by my cayuse
> An' mixes in when hell breaks loose.[45]

Other verses were said to be "improvised to suit the time and occasion by the riders of the range."

With all this squabbling, what was the outcome of the *St. Louis Republic*'s quest for the dog song's composer? The prize went to Missourian J. Frank Neighbors, a Mountain Grove businessman, who appears to have concurred with Texas' opinion of the correct tune. According to a letter to the editor submitted on Neighbors' behalf by Mayor W. S. Chandler of Mountain

The Dawg Song War 89

Grove, Frank Neighbors had been appointed to escort the Springfield Commercial Club into town by joining them for part of the train ride on the Frisco. In high spirits during their journey toward Mammoth Spring, the Springfield boosters had been singing all along the route. Suddenly, there was a lull in the fun. They had run out of tunes. It was then that Frank Neighbors taught them the words he claimed to have fitted to the tune "Sallie Had a Wooden Leg" twenty years earlier after he and his family had been enticed to leave the Ozarks for newly opened territory in Western Oklahoma.[46] The *Mountain Grove Journal* reported, "Once [the song] started [on the train] there was no stopping, so it was sung all the way back to Springfield and could be heard on every corner of the square of the city of Springfield, as well as in every town along the line."[47] The *St. Louis Republic* explained its decision:

> Many in good faith, many misinformed, many imaginative ones, some amiable prevaricators and a few very able and dangerous liars have claimed the honor, but since the actual author must have been dead lo! these 10,000 years at least, we can but award the prize to the next best and worthiest among the living. Angels might do more, were the prize a harp and the original author accessible above, but down here on earth, in Missouri, this is the best we can do with our fiddle.[48]

And the winner of the victor's laurel is – J. Frank Neighbors of Missouri!
(*St. Louis Republic*, May 19, 1912)

If the hound dog song had a single author, we are unlikely to discover that person's identity. One fact that can be proven is that the song achieved local popularity in the fall of 1911. Another fact is that, in the spring of 1912, the dog song became the subject of an intense, if humorous, war over its authorship and the dog's ownership. Perhaps a Southern Oklahoma newspaper, the Ada *Evening News*, summed up the dog song war best:

> Makes no difference who wrote the rot,
> The infernal thing is on the trot,
> From the east to the west, we hear the sound,
> From north to south, it's the song of the hound.[49]

Notes

[1] See Susan C. Attalla. "An Orphan Ditty: In Search of the Ozark Houn' Dawg," *Missouri Folklore Society Journal*, 24 (2002): 1-19.

[2] John H. Curran. "The Morning Mail: One of the Oldest Songs" [letter to the editor], *St. Louis Republic* (December 30, 1911): 8.

[3] "All Missouri Is Chanting the Houn' Pup's Defence," *New York Herald* (January 2, 1912): 5.

[4] "Daniel Boone Sang Dog Song," *Missouri Herald* (January 19, 1912): 7.

[5] Mark Sullivan. *Our Times, 1900-1925* (New York: Scribner's, 1971, 1930): Vol. 3, 345.

[6] James R. Masterson. *Tall Tales of Arkansas* (Boston: Chapman & Grimes, 1942): 389, endnote 34.

[7] Vance Randolph. *Ozark Folksongs, Vol. 3* (Columbia: State Historical Society of Missouri, 1949): 278.

May Kennedy McCord (1880-1979) hosted *Hillbilly Heartbeats*, a KWTO radio program in Springfield, MO, for many years. She also wrote a column of the same name for the *Springfield Leader & Press* newspaper from 1932 to 1943. For further information on McCord see:

> "Queen of the Hillbillies Reigns No More," *Springfield Leader & Press* (February 22, 1979): B1-2.

> Susan Croce Kelly, "May Kennedy McCord: The First Lady of the Ozarks," 44 #6, *Midwest Motorist* (August 1973): 8-9.

[8] Randolph: 278.

For a biography of Mary Elizabeth Mahnkey, see Ellen Gray Massey's *A Candle Within Her Soul: Mary Elizabeth Mahnkey and Her Ozarks* (Lebanon, MO: Bittersweet, 1996).

[9] Bill McNeil. "The Origins of a Poor Hound Dog," *Ozarks Mountaineer*, 44 #4 (August 1996): 54.

[10] "True Tale of Dog Song," *Springfield Republican* (January 4, 1912): 8.

[11] "Dog Song Is Published Now As Souvenir," *Springfield Republican* (December 30, 1911): 8.

[12] "Who Did Write the Houn' Dog Song?" *St. Louis Republic* (February 1, 1912): 8.

[13] "Prof. Snively's Rival," *St. Louis Republic* (January 29, 1912): 8.

[14] "Who Did Write the Houn' Dog Song?": 8.

[15] *St. Louis Republic* (January 30, 1912): 8.

[16] "Who Did Write the Houn' Dog Song?": 8.

[17] "The Secretary of State Indorses Ed Fonzer," *St. Louis Republic* (February 5, 1912): 8.

[18] "Col. Moss' Claim," *St. Louis Republic* (February 14, 1912): 8.

[19] "Our Houn' Dawg Contest Widens," *St. Louis Republic* (February 21, 1912): 8.

[20] "Did Mark Twain Write the Houn' Dawg?" *St. Louis Republic* (March 11, 1912): 8.

[21] "Dawg Song Author Flees from State," *Springfield Daily Leader* (March 11, 1912): 5.

[22] "The Houn' Song Again," *St. Louis Republic* (March 19, 1912): 8.

[23] "Houn' Dawg Song an Old One," *Columbia Statesman* (Mar. 22, 1912): 1.

[24] "Quit Kickin' My Dog Aroun'," *St. Louis Post-Dispatch* (March 24, 1912; magazine section): 2.

25 "An Old Family Song," *St. Louis Republic* (April 1, 1912): 8.

26 "Kentucky Claims Houn' Dawg Song," *St. Louis Republic* (March 29, 1912): 14.

27 "Houn' Dog Traced by Kentuckian," *St. Louis Republic* (Mar. 30, 1912): 7.

28 "State Tunes," *St. Louis Republic* (April 1, 1912): 8.

29 Fred W. Allsopp. *Folklore of Romantic Arkansas*, Vol. 2 (New York: Grolier Society, 1931): 197.

30 *The Monitor* [Mammoth Spring, AR], (November 17, 1911): 12.

31 Folk Music Vertical Files, State Historical Society of Missouri Library, Ellis Library, University of Missouri-Columbia. In an undated letter, Caldwell states that his account of the Mammoth Spring events was published on page 21 of the February 4, 1912 issue of the *St. Louis Post-Dispatch*. Evidently having received no reply, he wrote again on December 20, 1947, referring to an earlier letter of December 8th—presumably the undated letter. Floyd Shoemaker, State Historical Society of Missouri secretary, replied on December 23, 1947, to say that the Society had failed to locate the article in its bound copy of the February 4th *St. Louis Post-Dispatch* Sunday edition. Furthermore, the Society had found no page 21 in that edition so had searched surrounding dates, also to no avail. My search of *Post-Dispatch* microfilms had the same result. Like Floyd Shoemaker, one can conclude that the page might not have survived.

32 Letter from John H. Caldwell, Little Rock, Arkansas, January 28, 1953, to the State Historical Society of Missouri. Folk Music Vertical Files, State Historical Society of Missouri Library, Ellis Library, University of Missouri, Columbia; other Caldwell letters to the State Historical Society of Missouri, dated Dec. 20, 1947 and April 28, 1948.

33 "The Hound Dog Song," *Mountain Grove Journal* (February 22, 1912): 1.

34 Letters from Caldwell (1947-1948) indicate that he was Supreme Court librarian in Little Rock, whereas his January 28, 1953 letterhead identifies him as "Attorney at Law." Folk Music Vertical Files (see note 32 for cite). "John H. Caldwell" is listed as the Supreme Court Librarian (1941-1959) in Jacqueline S. Wright, "The Supreme Court Library," *Arkansas Historical Quarterly* 47 (Summer 1988): 137-149 (https://courts.arkansas.gov/sites/default/files/tree/sclib_history2.pdf; acc. 6/6/15).

The Dawg Song War 93

[35] John H. Caldwell. [Typed manuscript], Folk Music Vertical Files, State Historical Society of Missouri, University of Missouri, Columbia.

[36] *Muskogee* [OK] *Daily Phoenix* (February 21, 1912): 4.

[37] "The Original Houn' Dawg: Famous Canine Lived in Salem, Arkansas, for Many Years," *Washington Post* (March 10, 1912): M4.

[38] "The Original Houn' Dawg": M4.

[39] *Boston Daily Globe* (March 5, 1912): 5.

[40] "Houn' Dawg Song of Indian Origin?" [Portland] *Oregon Daily Journal* (March 18, 1912): 2.

[41] "In Spanish," *St. Louis Republic* (April 4, 1912): 8.

[42] "'Gotta Quit Kickin' My Dog' Song Stirs Texans' Wrath Against Missouri Bards," *New York Herald* (January 14, 1912; section 2): 7.

[43] "Dogs and Music," *New York Herald* (January 14, 1912; section 1): 10.

[44] "That Houn' Dawg Song," *Daily Gate City* (March 3, 1912): 4.

[45] "'The Houn' Song' in Texas," *Kansas City Star* (March 17, 1912): 8A. Attributed to an unnamed Austin, Texas, newspaper.

[46] "The Man Who Forgot It," *St. Louis Republic* (February 13, 1912): 8.

[47] "The Hound Dog Song," *Mountain Grove Journal* (February 22, 1912): 1.

[48] "Mr. Neighbors Wins Our Fiddle," *St. Louis Republic* (April 25, 1912): 8.

[49] "Vengeance on the 'Houn Dawg' Man," *Evening News* [Ada, OK] (April 2, 1912): 4.

Some of the colorful characters who claimed authorship of "The Dawg Song"
(*St. Louis Post-Dispatch*, Jan. 4, 1912)

© Susan C. Attalla (2013)

> ## "They gotta quit kickin' my dawg aroun'"
>
> HAVE you heard this old time "Missouri houn' song" made famous by its association with the presidential boom of Champ Clark?
>
> Everybody is quoting it, but it takes a man like Byron G. Harlan of the Edison Record Making staff to sing it as they do in the Ozark region.
>
> It is one of the new Edison Records and there are 32 others including some notable revivals of the ballads of long ago, many sparkling musical comedy songs, several selections and now and then a grand opera composition.
>
> There is a rare treat for Edison Phonograph owners in this list of
>
> # EDISON
> ## RECORDS FOR JUNE

Advertisement for a recording of the "Missouri houn' song"
(*Collier's*, May 25, 1912)

Recordings of "The Dawg Song" you can listen to online...

"Hound Dog Song," Ollie Gilbert, Max Hunter Folk Song Collection, #284, 1970; (http://maxhunter.missouristate.edu/songinformation.aspx?ID=978).

"Hound Dog Song," *Golden Ring*, Folk Legacy Records, CD 16; appears in the Digital Tradition (http://mudcat.org/@displaysong.cfm?SongID=2723).

"They Gotta Quit Kickin' My Dawg Around (The Missouri Dawg Song)," Byron G. Harlan with the American Quartet (1912); available on the *78 RPMs* site (http://archive.org/details/ByronGHarlanwithAmericanQuartet).

"They Gotta Quit Kickin' My Dog Around," Bob Dylan and The Band, *The Basement Tapes*, 1967; (http://www.bobdylanroots.com/dog.html).

> Bob Dylan's likely source for this song, according to the website, is probably version #1 of song #158, "The Hound Dawg Song" in the Lomax's *Folk Songs of North America* (Garden City, NY: Doubleday, 1960]: 311). The Lomax's evidently got their version from Vance Randolph's *Ozark Folksongs* (Columbia: University of Missouri Press, 1946-1950): Volume 3, page 278.
>
> The Dylan website credits the song to James Bland, "born of free Negro parents in New York, musically well educated, a graduate of Howard University. He joined a Negro minstrel show company (of which there were not many) and wrote more than seven hundred songs for minstrel use, copyrighting only a few. Equaled perhaps only by Foster in his gift for melody, Bland turned out good songs by the score, many published under others' names. 'Carry Me Back to Old Virginny' (1878) alone was enough to place Bland with the popular immortals....'They Gotta Quit Kickin' My Dog Around,' was a comedy favorite for years. When Bland's troupe visited London in 1884, he stayed there to enjoy a highly successful career on the English stage. When he returned twenty years later, the minstrel shows were nearly gone and he could not write what vaudeville wanted. Like Foster, he died broke and alone in 1911." Russel Nye. *The Unembarrassed Muse: The Popular Arts in America* (New York: Dial Press, 1978): 314.

[Sue reports that her future book will discuss the almost certain inaccuracy of Nye's claim that Bland composed "The Hound Dawg Song." – Eds.]

[All URLs in this section were verified on 5/15/15.]

Author and former college teacher Sue Attalla
(Photo courtesy of the author)

Here's another article by Sue Attalla that might be of interest...

"William Christopher O'Hare: Shreveport's Father of Ragtime ... and More," *The Ragtime Ephemeralist*, Issue #3 (2002).

In this article, Sue shares her research into the life of her great-grandfather, William Christopher O'Hare, composer of some of the earliest ragtime pieces.

You can also listen to some of Mr. O'Hare's tunes online:

"Levee Revels" as performed by Sousa's Band in 1902 (http://adp.library.ucsb.edu/index.php/matrix/detail/2000000118/Prematrix_B-328-Levee_revels; acc. 6/6/15)

"Cottonfield Capers" from a 1901 Columbia 7" recording (http://www.youtube.com/watch?v=zmRo_guNayA; acc. 6/6/15)

**William C. O'Hare,
composer of early ragtime music and the author's great-grandfather**
(Photo c. 1910; courtesy of Sue Attalla)

Introduction – "John Henry and the Reverend Bayes"

A new look at the old story of "The Steel-Drivin' Man"

Most of us are familiar with the story of John Henry from our childhoods, having heard the tale of his life at a library story hour or perhaps seen the animated Disney version of the story, which was often shown with stories of other "larger than life" American characters Paul Bunyan, Pecos Bill, Mike Fink, and Casey Jones. Some of these characters were created by modern authors or even advertising agencies—Paul Bunyan, for example, was created by ad men and is the bit of "folklore" for which folklorist Alan Dundes created the term "fakelore." John Henry, on the other hand, was the subject of songs and tales that were documented as having been based on possible historical facts and disseminated through the folk process of oral transmission.

Dr. John Garst, a retired professor of chemistry (University of Georgia), is also a historian and a folklorist. He has spent many years researching the historical reality of John Henry and the steam engine he defeated. His passion for finding the real John Henry—the man and the true location of the contest—has carried him through more than a decade of research which we hope will soon culminate in the publication of a book.

At the John Henry Day Celebration in Leeds, Alabama, in 2007, Dr. Garst gave a presentation outlining the in-depth research he has pursued through original documentation in archives and libraries in several states. (See the text at: alabamafolklife.homestead.com/John_Henry_Garst_paper.pdf.) He began the project, as all good researchers do, by thoroughly reviewing the existing literature on the song, the possible models for John Henry, and the possible locations for the event. He then spent countless hours combing through obscure census, courthouse, and railroad records. During his travels, he also interviewed people who were related to, or worked with someone they thought was the model for, John Henry.

Versions and variants are part of the fascination of researching historic songs, especially a song that spent a good deal of time being passed on through oral transmission. While teasing the facts out from all the speculations, Dr. Garst's scientific worldview led him to wonder if anything could actually be said to be "proved" beyond a shadow of a doubt by historical research – i.e., what would qualify as a historical "fact"? That led him to write this article, which gives us an interesting peek into the worlds of science, mathematics, philosophy, and logic, as he applies the logic of evidence to the facts surrounding the question of who the legendary John Henry really was and which railroad tunnel was actually the site of his contest with a steam drill.

(Beth's Music Notes © 2013; bethsmusicnotes.blogspot.com/2013/07/john-henry.html; acc. 5/5/14)

States Duel Over the Historical Location of the John Henry Story

The town of Leeds, Alabama offers an annual John Henry Celebration and Folk Festival in September. Author John Garst champions this location. (http://madelinesalbum.blogspot.com/2010/09; scroll down)

The town of Talcott, West Virginia offers an annual John Henry Days festival in July. Authors Guy Johnson and Louis Chappell were the primary champions for this location.
(http://en.wikipedia.org/wiki/John_Henry (folklore); both sites accessed on 6/6/15)

JOHN HENRY AND THE REVEREND BAYES

John Garst

Fiddler Earl Murphy was born in Missouri in 1917 and raised on a farm near Sedalia.[1] From his youth there, he recalled "John Henry" ("The Steel Driving Man"), perhaps the most widely known American ballad,[2] which has been discussed in this journal previously.[3]

Using a sledgehammer, John Henry pounded steel drills into rock to make holes for explosives to blast the rock away. According to ballad and legend, he got into a contest with a steam-powered mechanical drill – "Before I'd let that steam drill beat me down / I'd die with the hammer in my hand." He won the contest, then collapsed and died.

Perhaps John Henry was a real person. Perhaps these events really happened. The information available in testimony, ballad, and tale constitutes a large body of evidence on John Henry's historicity, but there is so little consistency, and so much contradiction, that nothing can be relied on.

Scholars have nominated West Virginia,[4] Jamaica,[5] Alabama,[6] and Virginia[7] as John Henry's place. They cannot all be right. How can this problem be approached?

I saw a possible answer when reading Guy Johnson's book *John Henry: Tracking Down a Negro Legend* in about 1960. In the sea of incoherence presented there, there is an island of coherence—the testimony in three letters from people who put John Henry in Alabama in the 1880s.[8] Louis Chappell, in his book *John Henry: A Folk-Lore Study*, added an item to the Alabama evidence, but did not recognize it as such.[9]

Even so, both Johnson and Chappell concluded that the historical John Henry event probably occurred at Big Bend Tunnel in Summers County, West Virginia, during construction of the C & O (the Chesapeake & Ohio Railroad) between 1869 and 1872. In reaching their decisions, these authors gave considerable weight to tradition, which favors West Virginia. In about 40% of early versions of the ballad, Big Bend Tunnel, the C & O, or both are mentioned as John Henry's place. After Johnson failed to verify selected elements of the Alabama claims, both he and Chappell set them aside in favor of West Virginia.

My purpose here is narrow—to give a logical treatment of three items of evidence found in the Alabama claims and in a version of the ballad. These items are a day of the week, the name of a tunnel, and the name of a person. First, however, we must consider aspects of history and folklore.

History Is Theory

Has George W. Bush been President of the United States of America? This question gets right to the point. "Probably" is the only acceptable answer. From relevant evidence (such as memories, news articles, television, hearsay), we infer that Bush has been President, but logically we must recognize that our interpretation of this evidence could be wrong. Further, any or all of the evidence could be false, misleading, or fake.

Because the past cannot be examined, histories must be imagined. They are theories, but they are not mere guesses. Like scientific theories, histories are carefully constructed so that they explain, or are at least consistent with, relevant evidence. Evidence makes histories probable, to some degree. Some histories are nearly certain.

Transmission of Folklore with Mutation

Folklore is passed on through chains of transmission, each step of which allows mutation, i.e. alteration of information. Let the surname Dabney be original information. It could come from a historical event or it could be fiction. As it is passed along a chain of transmission, it might change to Tommy. Similarly, Tommy could become Johnny. Alternatively, Tommy might revert to Dabney. These cases are illustrated schematically in Figure 1.

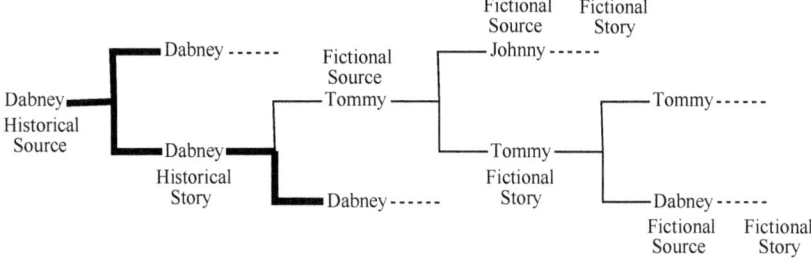

Flow of information ⟶

Figure 1
Schematic representation of mutations along branching chains of transmission among bearers of the tradition. Historical source: a historical event. Historical story: story derived accurately from a historical source (bold lines). Fictional source: source other than a historical event. Fictional story: story derived accurately from a fictional source. Dashed lines represent continuations of the stories. Bearers have the "same" story if their information traces backward, through accurate chains of transmission, to a common source. Two bearers with "Dabney" will not have the same story if the information from one traces back to a historical source and the other to a fictional source. Note: The original source, shown here as historical, could be fictional.

When accurate information about an original historical event is passed on, it becomes a "historical story." However, a mutation (Dabney becomes Tommy, for example) introduces a fictional source and initiates a "fictional story." Further mutations give rise to additional fictional sources and stories (Johnny and Dabney in Figure 1). The second Dabney story is fictional because it does not trace to a historical event through an accurate chain of transmission. Informants with the same information have the "same" story if that information traces accurately to a common source, historical or fictional.

A historical story might persist or it might be lost in transmission, depending on its attractiveness to bearers of the tradition. An informant who is closer to a historical source in proximity and time is more likely to bear a historical story.

A listener hearing someone sing "Dabney" could easily misunderstand it as the similar, and much more familiar, "Tommy." It is much less likely that Dabney would be heard as Jones or that Tommy would be heard as Dabney.

As in these examples, mutations tend away from the awkward and unfamiliar, toward the comfortable and familiar, and therefore more probable. The Second Law of Thermodynamics states that any change in an isolated system will result in an increase in entropy (a measure of the probability of the state of the system). Similarly, in folklore, the "probability" (familiarity, popularity, etc.) of information is expected to increase along a chain of transmission with mutation. Thus, Tommy is more "probable" (common) than Dabney.

Figure 2 below gives another example. It shows a plausible pathway of mutation from Margaret Dabney to Polly Ann. Margaret Dabney was the wife of Henry Dabney (census of 1870), a candidate for the historical John Henry, while Polly Ann is the name of John Henry's wife/woman found most commonly in the ballad.

$$\begin{pmatrix}\text{Margaret}\\ \text{Dabney}\end{pmatrix} \rightarrow \begin{pmatrix}\text{Maggie}\\ \text{D.}\end{pmatrix} \rightarrow \text{Maggadee} \rightarrow (\text{Magdalene}) \rightarrow \begin{matrix}\text{Mary}\\ \text{Magdalene}\end{matrix} \rightarrow \begin{matrix}\text{Mary}\\ \text{Ann}\end{matrix} \rightarrow \begin{matrix}\text{Polly}\\ \text{Ann}\end{matrix}$$

Figure 2. Plausible pathway of mutation from "Margaret Dabney" to "Polly Ann." Names not in parentheses have been recovered in the ballad. See text for rationales for the individual mutations.

Margaret Dabney could have been called Maggie D., which could have been heard as Maggadee.[10] Maggadee sounds like Magdalene, which implies Mary Magdalene.[11] Mary Ann is less cumbersome than Mary Magdalene and it provides a good rhyme: "Her name was Mary Ann … She would go and drive steel like a man."[12] Polly is both a common nickname for Mary and a favorite of ballad singers. Because Polly Ann is a familiar favorite that sings well and provides a good rhyme, it is probably a stable end point (maximum "entropy") of mutations of the name of John Henry's wife/woman.

The reverse sequence of mutations—from Polly Ann back to Maggadee, Maggie D., and Margaret Dabney—is very unlikely. The steps involved would be "upstream" from the less awkward to the more, from the more familiar to the less, from the more probable to the less, from a higher "entropy" to a lower. Just as Tommy will not mutate to Dabney, Polly Ann will not mutate to Maggie D.

Even though mutations are not random (being guided by sound, familiarity, rhyme schemes, and other factors), they tend toward items with higher probabilities as random choices. Earlier items in a chain of mutations tend to have lower random probabilities.

Some Evidence for John Henry in Alabama

In two letters to Johnson, C. C. Spencer (Salt Lake City, Utah) claimed to have been an eyewitness to John Henry's contest and death. Spencer wrote that the contest took place on September 20, 1882. John Henry had been "shipped to the Cruzee mountain tunnel, Alabama, to work." John Henry had a boss named "Dabner." "Cruzee" Mountain was near Red Mountain, Alabama, and "Risingforn" (Rising Fawn), Georgia.[13]

F. P. Barker (Birmingham, Alabama), another Johnson informant, claimed to have known John Henry. John Henry had worked at "Cursey Mountain tunnel" while Barker was driving steel at Red Mountain. John Henry died "about 45 years ago, somewhere about that time." That would have been around 1882.[14]

The uncle of a third Johnson informant, Glendora Cannon Cummings (Lansing, Michigan), was working with John Henry when he died. It was at Oak Mountain, Alabama, in 1887. John Henry had a boss named Dabney.[15]

Chappell received from C. S. Farquharson (Jamaica) the information that John Henry died during the building of the railroad between Bog Walk and Port Antonio, Jamaica, in 1894-1896.[16] One of John Henry's bosses was named "Dabner."

From Harvy Hicks of Evington, Virginia, Chappell recovered a ballad containing the line, "John Henry died on a Tuesday."[17]

Points of Agreement

Cummings appears most certain about the year John Henry died—1887. If Cummings got the year right, and if Spencer recalled the month and day correctly, then John Henry died on September 20, 1887. That day was a Tuesday, in agreement with Hicks's ballad.

"Cruzee" and "Cursey" are surely phonetic attempts to spell the same name, so Spencer and Barker agreed on the place. Cummings named Oak Mountain instead. I will explain this discrepancy later.

"Dabner" is really Dabney. "Dabner" is analogous to John F. Kennedy's "Cuber" (Cuba) and my wife's homefolks' "Edner" (Edna). Indeed, the 1870 Federal Census for Copiah County, Mississippi, enumerates Henry Dabney, but the 1880 census calls him Henry "Dabner" (same age, same wife, etc.) Hereinafter, I will use only Dabney.

Spencer, Cummings, and Farquharson agreed that John Henry worked for a Dabney.

Meanings of These Agreements

The agreement that John Henry died on a Tuesday implies that Spencer and the ballad told the same story.

Spencer and Barker told the same story about "Cruzee"/"Cursey" Mountain. Otherwise, the probability of agreement on "Cruzee"/"Cursey" would be vanishingly small.

Spencer, Cummings, and Farquharson told the same story about Dabney. Dabney is a rare surname and a very unlikely random choice.

Five informants told parts of the same story, in which John Henry worked for a Dabney at "Cruzee"/"Cursey" Mountain Tunnel, Alabama, and died in that vicinity on a Tuesday, probably September 20, 1887. It could be a historical story.

Johnson dismissed the "Alabama claims" because he chose to believe the testimony of C. S. "Neal" Miller, a self-proclaimed eyewitness who testified that he had watched John Henry's contest with a steam drill at Big Bend Tunnel in 1870.[18] Chappell also relied on Miller's testimony.[19]

Inductive Logic

Constructing a history uses inductive logic, the logic of evidence and explanation; that is, theory. Perhaps the most familiar use of inductive logic is in the courtroom, where lawyers try to convince juries or judges, one way or the other, by offering "theories of the case," explanations of the evidence. Like lawyers' stories, historians' stories are theories that explain the evidence.

Inductive and deductive logic differ.

> **Deductive arguments** are arguments in which it is thought that the premises provide a <u>guarantee</u> of the truth of the conclusion. In a deductive argument, the premises are intended to provide support for a conclusion that is so strong that, if the premises are true, it would be <u>impossible</u> for the conclusion to be false.
>
> **Inductive arguments** are arguments in which it is thought that the premises provide reasons supporting the <u>probable</u> truth of the conclusion. In an inductive argument, the premises are intended only to be so strong that, if they are true, then it is <u>unlikely</u> that the conclusion is false.[20]

One kind of logical statement takes the form – If (antecedent) then (consequent) – where the antecedent and consequent are statements that could be true or false.

In deductive logic, affirming the antecedent guarantees the truth of the consequent.

> If it is a bird, then it has wings.
> It is a bird.
> Therefore, it has wings. (guaranteed)

A history cannot be guaranteed. There is always the possibility that more than one history is consistent with the evidence. History cannot be established through deductive logic.

In deductive logic, affirming the consequent is a fallacy.

> If it is a bird, then it has wings.
> It has wings.
> Therefore, it is a bird. (fallacy)

Birds are not the only things with wings. "It" could be an airplane, a dragon, a pterodactyl, a seed, a building, a stage, etc.

Something like affirming the consequent can be good inductive logic.

> If it is a bird, then it has wings.
> It has wings.
> Therefore, the probability that it is a bird is increased.

The new information, "It has wings," eliminates some things that could have been "it." People are ruled out, along with dogs, refrigerators, streets, trees, hamburgers, etc., none of which have wings. Taking the new information into account shrinks the pool of possibilities for "it," increasing the probability that "it" is a bird.

When the consequent is affirmed cogently, the probability of the antecedent can become very high. It is 99+% probable that George W. Bush was President. The evidence is overwhelming. It is sensible to treat the Bush presidency as if it were a truth.

Bayesian Logic

Pigliucci gives an illustration of the logic of evidence as set forth in 1763 by the Reverend Thomas Bayes.[21]

> **The Sunny-Day Problem**
> A man goes fishing on 90% of sunny days, 50% of cloudy days, and 15% of rainy days. According to the weather forecast, a certain day has a 65% chance of being sunny, 25% cloudy, and 10% rainy. The day comes. We learn later that the man *did* go fishing. What is the probability that the day was sunny?

Consider the hypothesis that the day was sunny. The prior probability of the hypothesis – $P(S)$ – is 65% (weather forecast). It is "prior" because it precedes, taking into account the new information that the man went fishing.

After taking the new information into account, the "posterior" probability – $P(S \mid F)$ – applies ("F" for "fishing"). Read "$P(S \mid F)$" as "probability that it was a sunny day, given that the man went fishing." The problem asks for the value of $P(S \mid F)$.

To solve the problem, we construct a "Bayes table" headed "Sunny-Day Problem." There we include 1000 hypothetical instances of the day in question. This large number is chosen arbitrarily. The procedure described applies to any large number of instances and will always give the same result.

Table 1. The Sunny Day Problem

	Goes Fishing	Does Not Go Fishing	Total Days
Sunny Days	585	65	650
Cloudy Days	125	125	250
Rainy Days	15	85	100
Total Days	725	275	1000

The man went fishing; therefore, the posterior probability of a sunny day is $[P(S \mid F)] = 585/725 = 81\%$.

According to the weather forecast, there will be 650 sunny days (65% of 1000), 250 cloudy days (25%), and 100 rainy days (10%). The table has a row for each kind of weather and a column for each behavior (goes fishing or not). Since the man goes fishing on 90% of sunny days, the entry in the row "Sunny Days" and the column "Goes Fishing" is 585 (90% of 650). The other entries are reckoned similarly.

The entries in the body of the table represent prior information. The new information is that the man *did* go fishing.

When the new information is taken into account, the column "Does Not Go Fishing" becomes irrelevant. Of the 725 days on which the man goes fishing, 585 are sunny. Therefore, the posterior probability that the day was sunny – $P(S \mid F)$ – is $585/725 = 0.81 = 81\%$.

This reasoning is equivalent to Bayes' Rule.[22] The new information eliminates some of the old possibilities (those in the "Does Not Go Fishing" column), leaving a restricted set ("Goes Fishing") from which the posterior probability of the hypothesis is reckoned.

Two points merit particular attention. First, with the new information, the sunny-day probability increases from its prior value – $P(S)$ – of 65% to its posterior value – $P(S \mid F)$ – of 81%. In general, however, the change need not be an increase. For example, suppose that the new information were that the man did *not* go fishing. Then the sunny-day probability would have decreased from its prior value of 65% to a posterior value of 23% (65/280 – from the "Does Not Go Fishing" column).

Second, one item in the initial information is the probability that the man would go fishing, given that the day was sunny (90%). The quantity derived from the new information is the probability that it was a sunny day, given that the man went fishing (81%). Bayes' Rule relates a prior probability of the form $P(F \mid S)$ to a posterior probability of the form $P(S \mid F)$.

Bayes' Rule can be applied to instances of testimony and agreement about John Henry, thus formalizing common-sense arguments.

One Informant

An informant gives a name (Joe) and claims that it is historical. Let the prior information be that a name was given. The new information is that it is Joe. The hypothesis is that Joe is a historical, rather than fictional, story. Does the identity of the name affect its probability of being historical?

This is a test case for our logic. Because the informant is the only authority, we have nothing to test his testimony against. Consequently, the identity of the name cannot affect the probability that it is historical.

In a Bayesian treatment, let x be P(Historical), the prior probability that Joe is historical. Then, $(1-x)$ is the prior probability that Joe is fictional, a random choice.

Let ε be the probability of Joe as a random choice. Before the name was given, the probability that it would be Joe was ε for both a fictional story and a historical story.

The relevant Bayes table (below) is headed "One Informant." We must consider a large number of instances (N), but because N will be a factor of each term of each entry in the table, it will disappear by division (N/N = 1) from the final expression for P(Historical | Joe). The value of N is irrelevant. N is omitted from this table and those that follow.

Table 2. One Informant

	Joe	Not Joe	Sum
Historical	εx	$(1-\varepsilon)x$	x
Fictional	$\varepsilon(1-x)$	$(1-\varepsilon)(1-x)$	$(1-x)$
Sum	$\varepsilon x + \varepsilon(1-x) = \varepsilon$	$(1-\varepsilon)x + (1-\varepsilon)(1-x) = 1-\varepsilon$	1

Prior information: informant gave a name.

New information: the name given is "Joe."

P(Historical | Joe) = $\varepsilon x / [\varepsilon x + \varepsilon(1-x)] = x$, unchanged from the prior probability

The new information eliminates the column headed "Not Joe," leaving only the column headed "Joe." From that column, we reckon that P(Historical Story | Name) = $\varepsilon x / [\varepsilon x + \varepsilon(1-x)] = x$. The posterior probability of the hypothesis is the same as the prior probability, as it must be.

Two Informants

With two or more informants, there can be agreement or disagreement. Let the prior information be that each informant gives a name. The new information is that each gives the same name, Name (for example, Tuesday, Cruzee, or Dabney). Let ε be the probability of Name as a random choice.

Let the hypothesis be that the informants report the same story, as defined above. Let x be P(Same Story), the prior probability of the hypothesis—before it is taken into account that the informants agree on Name. Under the hypothesis, the probability that the informants would report the same name is one (otherwise they wouldn't be telling the same story) and the probability that that name would be Name is ε (random). Therefore, the prior probability that the informants report the same story (x), give the same name (1), Name (ε), is εx ($\varepsilon \times 1 \times x$).

The prior probability that the informants do not report the same story is $(1-x)$. In this case, both stories could be fictional or one could be historical and the other fictional.

When the informants report different stories, the prior probability that each reports Name is ε and the joint probability that both report Name is ε^2. The prior probability that the informants give different stories but nonetheless agree on Name is $\varepsilon^2(1-x)$.

The relevant Bayes table (below) is headed "Two Informants." "Other" includes both disagreement and agreement on a name other than Name.

Table 3. Two Informants

	Agree on Name	**Other**	**Sum**
Same Story	εx	$(1-\varepsilon)x$	x
Not Same Story	$\varepsilon^2(1-x)$	$(1-\varepsilon^2)(1-x)$	$(1-x)$
Sum	$\varepsilon x+\varepsilon^2(1-x)$	$(1-\varepsilon)x+(1-\varepsilon^2)(1-x)$	1

New information: informants agree on a name ("Cruzee" or "Dabney").
P(Same Story | Agree on Name) = $\varepsilon x/[\varepsilon x+\varepsilon^2(1-x)]$ = $x/[x+\varepsilon(1-x)]$ = $1/(1+\varepsilon[(1-x)/x])$

Equation 1 follows from the entries in the column headed "Agree on Name." It relates the posterior probability, P(Same Story | Agree on Name), to the prior probability, x, P(Same Story). (See Equation 1 below.)

$$\text{P(Same Story | Agree on Name)} = \frac{1}{1+\varepsilon\left(\frac{1-x}{x}\right)}$$

For Tuesday as the day John Henry died, the equation would be $\varepsilon = 1/7$, assuming that Tuesday is one of seven equally likely days. Equation 1 then becomes Equation 2 (below).

$$P(\text{Same Story} \mid \text{Agree on Tuesday}) = \frac{7x}{6x+1}$$

A plot of that function is given in Figure 3 (below).

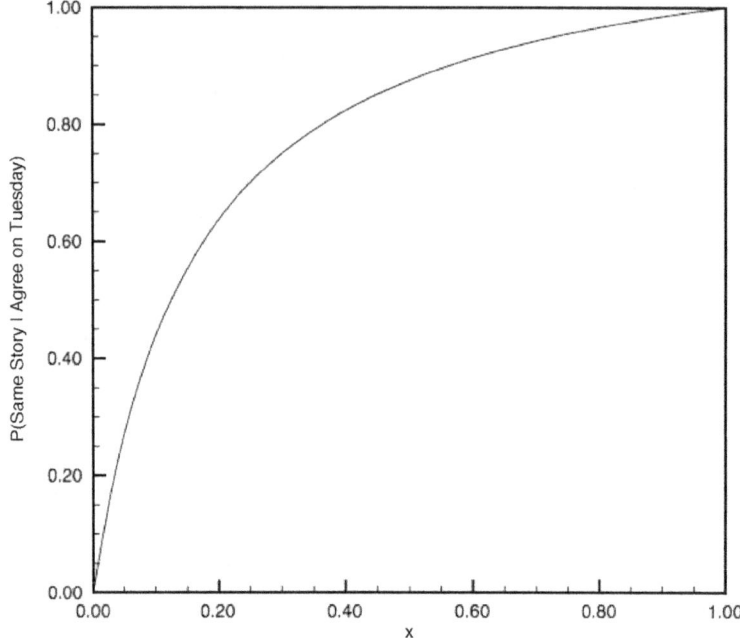

Figure 3. x: P(Same Story), prior probability that the informants give the same story about John Henry, not taking into account that they agree on Tuesday. P(Same Story | Agree on Tuesday): posterior probability that both informants give the same story, taking into account that they agree on Tuesday.

We need a value of the prior probability x. For those who consider it deeply, the estimation of prior probabilities is a complex and thorny problem.[23] Here, we simply make an educated guess based on knowledge of the situation concerning the two informants—Spencer and Hicks.

Even though he made several errors, Spencer was an incredibly good witness. It is clear from his testimony that he tried to be truthful and complete. A number of his details have been confirmed in documentation.[24] Spencer, born in December 1870, was sixteen years old when he witnessed John Henry's death.[25] His testimony came forty years later. How could he have recalled such detail?

The answer might lie in the excitement that must have been generated in him by witnessing the contest and John Henry's death. According to Maggie Jackson, "Emotion etches experiences into your memory because adrenaline and other stress hormones that accompany a moment of joy, fear, or other arousal amplify the chemical process of memory consolidation. (In medieval times, a child chosen as the official observer of an important event was afterward tossed into a river, a terrifying excursion that made him long remember the events of the day....)."[26] Spencer would have been like that medieval child, excited and frightened by what he witnessed.

It is hard to imagine that Spencer would have given a particular month and day if he were not confident of it. I think that the prior probabilities that he was reporting actual events and that he gave the September 20th date correctly are high. Even so, I am satisfied with the assumption that it is 50%.

Hicks's ballad line, "John Henry died on a Tuesday," is the only mention of John Henry's death day in the many (perhaps 150) versions of the ballad that I have examined. "Tuesday" is not in a rhyming position, nor is it an obviously more attractive day to sing than "Monday," "Friday," or any other day. I can think of no reason for bearers of tradition to have given a special preference to "Tuesday."

I believe that rare occurrences like this are often remnants from early ballad versions. Being closer to the original source, these remnants are more likely than later elements to reflect accurately the historical incident on which the ballad is based, if there is one. The remnants became rare because they were not particularly attractive to the singers who bore the tradition. We are fortunate that even one version naming a day survived. I estimate the probability that the ballad reports a historical event and gives the day correctly as 50%.

If the prior probability of a historical story for each informant is 50%, then the prior probability of that story for both is the joint probability, 50% × 50%, or 25%. This educated guess leads to a posterior same-story probability of 70% (see Figure 3 above). This is pretty good evidence, not compelling but not weak. It carries significant weight.

Now consider the testimony that John Henry was at "Cruzee"/"Cursey" Mountain. In this case, both men—Spencer and Barker—claimed to have been working in the Birmingham area and to have known John Henry. If true, this would make them bearers of a historical story. There must be a pretty good chance that their claims are legitimate, so the value of the prior probability that they told the same story, x in Equation 1, cannot be small; however, the value of ε must be tiny. "Cruzee"/"Cursey," whatever it really may be, is a very unusual name. Surely the chance that it would be picked randomly as the name of a mountain is no more than one in a thousand, 10^{-3}.

The coefficient of ε in Equation 1, $(1-x)/x$, will be of the order of one, which corresponds to x = 50%. If the value of $(1-x)/x$ is exactly one, P(Same Story | Agree on "Cruzee"/"Cursey") = $1/(1 + 10^{-3})$ = 99.90%. A larger value of x would make the same-story probability even larger. Even if x were as low as 10%, P(Same Story | Agree on "Cruzee"/"Cursey") would be 99.11%. I suppose that 10% is at the lower limit of reasonable values of x. Therefore, it is a near certainty that Spencer and Barker reported the same story.

In reporting that John Henry's boss was Dabney, Spencer claimed eyewitness knowledge, while Cummings said that she had heard it from her uncle, another eyewitness. Again, the prior probability x—that they reported on the same story—cannot be small.

We must also estimate the probability ε that someone would come up with Dabney randomly. I see nothing particularly attractive (euphonious, famous) about this name. Although some Dabney's have been prominent professionally, Dabney is very far from the first surname most people would think of.

Surely the probability of a surname as a random choice is related to its frequency in the American population. However, the most frequent surnames (Smith, Johnson, Williams, Jones, Brown, etc.) are not only common, but also well known as being common, so the probability that one of them would be a random choice may be greater than its frequency. If so, then the random probability of a rare name will be less than its frequency.

In the 1990 federal census, Dabney was number 4454 on the list of most frequent surnames.[27] The frequency of Dabney in the American population was 0.003%; that is, 3×10^{-5}. In 1920, Dabney reached a frequency as high as one in a thousand in Virginia and Iowa and one in two or three thousand in Pennsylvania and Illinois, but in all other states it was less than one in ten thousand. In 1880, Dabney had a frequency less that one in ten thousand in every state except Virginia, Alabama, and Arkansas, where it reached a frequency of one in two or three thousand.[28]

From these considerations, one in a thousand (10^{-3}) would be a generous estimate of the probability of Dabney as a randomly chosen name, with one in ten thousand (10^{-4}) being more likely. Taking $(1-x)/x = 1$ and $\varepsilon = 10^{-3}$ leads, by Equation 1, to P(Same Story | Agree on Dabney) = 99.90%. If $\varepsilon = 10^{-4}$ instead, then P(Same Story | Agree on Dabney) = 99.990%. It is a near certainty that Spencer and Cummings told the same story.

Three Informants

In his 1933 book, Chappell went a step further. Farquharson, a Jamaican, named "Dabner" (Dabney) as John Henry's boss.

With three agreeing informants (Spencer, Cummings, Farquharson), there are two possibilities in addition to that of completely random agreement. (1) Three reported the same story. (2) Two reported the same story and the third gave a random name. Following the previous procedure gives Equation 3 (see below), where x is the prior probability that three informants, and y the prior probability that two, reported the same story.

John Henry   111

$$P[\text{Same Story (from 2 or 3)} \mid \text{Agree on Dabney}] = \frac{1}{1+\varepsilon^2\left(\frac{1-x-y}{x+\varepsilon y}\right)}$$

The values of x and y cannot be very small. A reasonable estimate of the upper bound of $(1-x-y)/(x+\varepsilon y)$ is unity (1). For $(1-x-y)/(x+\varepsilon y) = 1$ and $\varepsilon = 10^{-3}$, P[Same Story (from 2 or 3) | Agree on Dabney] = 99.99990%. For $\varepsilon = 10^{-4}$, it is 99.9999990%.

With a value of ε^2 of 10^{-6} or 10^{-8}, it makes little difference what reasonable value of $(1-x-y)/(x+\varepsilon y)$ is assumed. As long as x is not very small, a value of $(1-x-y)/(x+\varepsilon y)$ that is larger than one can do no more than knock a "9" or two off the end of the string in the posterior probability that two or three of the informants told the same story.

The Alabama Claims and History

In the 1920s, there were circulating stories in which John Henry worked for Dabney at "Cruzee"/"Cursey" Mountain, Alabama. Are these stories historical or fictional? A historical origin is favored by the fact that three informants claimed to have been close to the event.

It should come as no surprise that a man named Dabney supervised the boring of a railroad tunnel through Coosa Mountain in the 1880s. He was Captain Frederick Yeamans Dabney, a civil engineer from Crystal Springs, Mississippi.[29] "Coosa" has been spelled and pronounced "Koosee."[30] You don't find this spelling much anymore, but you can still hear the pronunciation from old timers. Koosee (Coosa) is what Spencer and Barker meant by "Cruzee"/"Cursey."

Coosa Mountain is a southwest to northeast ridge, the southeastern border of the Dunnavant Valley, in which lies the community of Dunnavant, the site of a construction camp during the extension of the Columbus & Western Railway from Goodwater, Alabama, to Birmingham in 1887-1888. Dunnavant is about 3.5 miles south of downtown Leeds.[31]

Big Bend (WV) vs Coosa Mt (AL)

(http://www.rrpicturearchives.net; acc. 6/6/15)

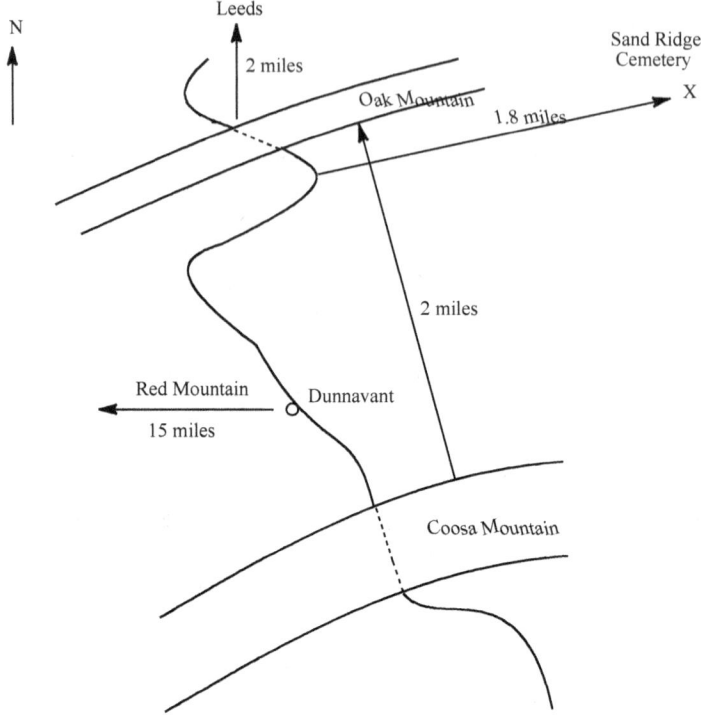

Figure 4. Schematic drawing (roughly to scale) of Oak and Coosa Mountains, their tunnels (dashed), and the C & W railroad line (solid with horizontal bars). Sand Ridge Cemetery, a possible burial site for John Henry, is 1.8 miles east of Oak Tunnel. Based on a USGS map from http://nationalmap.gov/historical/index.html (acc. 6/6/15).

The northwestern border of the Dunnavant Valley is Oak Mountain, a southwest to northeast ridge that lies almost exactly two miles north of Coosa Mountain. Tunnels were bored through Coosa and Oak Mountains in 1887-1888.[32]

The tunnels were made by the C & W, which was a wholly owned subsidiary of the Central Rail Road and Banking Company of Georgia, known by 1886 as the "Central of Georgia" (C of G), a name it assumed formally in 1895. The C & W (the Columbus & Western Railway Company) is now part of the Norfolk Southern network. Trains still run through the Coosa and Oak tunnels.

Dunnavant, on the C & W track between Coosa and Oak tunnels, is fifteen miles east of Red Mountain, a geologically rich ridge that runs from southwest of Birmingham to northeast. Along the way, Red Mountain is at Birmingham's southeastern edge.

Cummings gave Oak Mountain as the place of John Henry's contest with a steam drill. Local legends and those C of G employees agree, placing it outside the east portal of Oak Tunnel.[33] A steel drill, said to have been John Henry's last, once stuck up in the rock there.[34]

At 2438 feet, Coosa Tunnel is twice as long as Oak Tunnel, which is 1198 feet long.[35] Halfway through the boring of Coosa Tunnel, in the summer of 1887, the miners struck very hard rock, which delayed the opening of the line by six months.[36] Logically, John Henry would have worked on Coosa Tunnel, as stated by Spencer and Barker. The contest, however, could have been held at nearby Oak Tunnel, as legends say. It all makes sense.

Three important elements of the stories told by Johnson's and Chappell's informants—the names of two mountains (Coosa and Oak) and of the man who supervised the boring of tunnels through them (Dabney)—are documented. On these points, the informants reported history. Why should it be doubted that John Henry raced a steam drill and died there, as testified by the three informants who claimed a close connection to the event? The agreement of Spencer and Hicks that Tuesday was the day of John Henry's death also reinforces the case for Alabama.

There is additional evidence. By 1927, Leon R. Harris of Moline, Illinois, had rambled around the country, working in railroad camps and at other jobs for many years. He had heard the song "John Henry" everywhere, but he had heard it for the first time in Birmingham, Alabama, in 1904. The stanzas he provided to Johnson were also heard in 1909-1911 in West Virginia and Virginia. One of them is especially significant:

> John Henry's cap'n Tommy,
> V'ginny gave him birth;
> Loved John Henry like his only son,
> And Cap' Tommy was the whitest man on earth.[37]

As noted above, Tommy is among the expected mutations of Dabney. "V'ginny gave him birth" is historically accurate for Captain Dabney, who *was* born in Virginia.[38] His family had a reputation for kindness to slaves and for good relations with their ex-slaves. It is plausible that Captain Dabney "Loved John Henry like his only son."

The local John Henry tradition around Leeds, Dunnavant, and Vandiver, Alabama, is long and strong. It was documented in print in 1930,[39] and it is reported that it predates 1912.[40] It could easily date to the historical event of 1887.

Frequently, the ballad has John Henry "buried in the sand." Sand Ridge Cemetery is 1.8 miles east of Oak Tunnel (see Figure 4 above). John Henry could be buried there. According to a local story, a black man is buried at the edge of Sand Ridge Cemetery.[41]

The ballad also has people on locomotives coming by and saying, "There lies that steel driving man." Sand Ridge, at the cemetery location, is visible across a valley from an east-bound train emerging from Oak Tunnel.

In dry weather, the unpaved part of Sand Ridge Road is white with sand. This fits a line in the song about taking John Henry's body "on that long white road."[42]

Henry Dabney, black, appears as a farmer in Copiah County, Mississippi, in both the 1870 and 1880 Federal Census reports. Twenty years old in 1870 and thirty in 1880, he was probably born on Burleigh Plantation, a farm of nearly 4000 acres in Hinds County, Mississippi.[43] Burleigh belonged to Thomas Dabney, Captain Dabney's uncle. All of these facts make Henry Dabney a good candidate for the "steel driving man."

Both Charles C. Spencer and Glendora Cannon Cummings' uncle Gus were eyewitnesses to John Henry's contest and death, but two other eyewitnesses were known to Julius Moore (born in 1877)—Sam Angle and Hilliard Holly. Julius passed the story to his son Robert, who was eighty-six when I interviewed him in 2008.[44] Julius told Robert that John Henry had been brought from Mississippi to work at Dunnavant.

Two versions of the ballad place John Henry "'tween them mountains" or "between two mountains."[45] The place where the steel drill once stood in the rock, outside the east portal of Oak Tunnel, is between the ridges of Oak and Coosa Mountains. So is the community of Dunnavant, where John Henry might have lived in a construction camp.

Two other versions of the ballad have John Henry working for "the Georgia line" and the "Central of Georgia," owner of the C & W.[46]

In discussing the case for Big Bend Tunnel as the John Henry site, as presented by Johnson and Chappell, Leach wrote, "All the information about John Henry is from oral reports and it duplicates exactly the information in the songs."[47] Leach saw this as a great weakness of the evidence for Big Bend Tunnel.

The Alabama testimony gathered by Johnson and Chappell is *not* from the ballad. No known ballad mentions Dabney, Coosa Mountain, or Oak Mountain, and none states that John Henry was from Mississippi.

C. C. Spencer recalled singing, "John Brown was a little boy, sitting on his Mother's knee. He said 'The Big Ben tunnel on the C. & O. Road will sure be the death of me.'" This is obviously a variant of "John Henry," but Spencer did not make that connection. He did not associate it with John Henry or the events he had witnessed in the Dunnavant Valley.[48] The independence of the testimony of the Alabama informants from the ballad strengthens the case that they were telling historical stories.

The evidence that John Henry raced a steam drill and died near Dunnavant in 1887 is entirely circumstantial. Even so, I believe that it meets the level required for conviction in an American criminal court: "beyond reasonable doubt." To maintain otherwise would require that all the Alabama testimony and other evidence be explained somehow as fiction. No plausible explanation of this kind has occurred to me nor am I aware of one presented by anyone else.

What About Those Other Places?

Big Bend Tunnel is supported by tradition only; testimony from informants who were there during its construction is incoherent and contradictory.

Around Leeds, Oak Tunnel is the "little" tunnel and Coosa Tunnel is the "big" tunnel. Coosa Tunnel was the site of several serious accidents during its boring, costing more than a dozen lives.[49] It could have been called "that big, bad tunnel," which could have been heard by someone as "Big Bend Tunnel."

Folklorists speak of "localization," the assignment of a general story to a particular locale. "Relocalization" is the reassignment of locale. Localization and relocalization are very common in ballads and other folklore.[50] It is likely that a ballad about Coosa or Oak Tunnel and the C & W was relocalized to Big Bend Tunnel and the C & O. Big Bend Tunnel is much longer and better known than the Coosa or Oak tunnels and the C & O is much better known than the C & W.

The time frame is wrong for Jamaica. There is reliable testimony that the John Henry ballad was being sung by 1888,[51] several years before 1894-1896 when the incident in Jamaica would have occurred.[52] The John Henry tradition in that country is also very weak. Indeed, John Henry's contest is not present in the Jamaican tradition—he dies in an accident.

The Lewis Tunnel in Virginia is supported by: the name of convict John William Henry who was leased from the Virginia Penitentiary, a white workhouse at that penitentiary, an occasional ballad mention of taking John Henry to the white house for burial "in the sand," a mass grave on the penitentiary grounds containing sand, and a nearby railroad. According to an archeologist who examined the site, the soil in the mass grave at the Virginia Penitentiary was not sand.[53] There is no compelling evidence that the bodies of convicts who died at Lewis Tunnel were sent back to the penitentiary for burial, that John William Henry died at Lewis Tunnel, or, indeed, that he was ever there. There is no evidence that John William Henry was a steel driver or that there was a drilling contest at Lewis Tunnel. There is no tradition of John Henry there, no detailed testimony to that effect, and no other supporting documentation.

Logic militates against all three alternatives to Alabama. If it were not true that John Henry was in West Virginia, Jamaica, or Virginia, how easily could the data be explained? The answer is "Very easily indeed." The evidence for these places lacks substance, being deficient in particulars.

Alabama is the only location with a long, strong local tradition, coherent testimony, and documentation of significant elements of that testimony. If it were not true that John Henry was in Alabama, it would be difficult to explain how the data placing him there arose.

Johnson and Chappell, Theories and Facts

Johnson wrote, "Here is a neat problem in the weighing of evidence and the discovery of truth. In view of the absence of any sort of objective evidence to support these Alabama claims, they must be dismissed as unproved."[54] Also, "... the Big Bend Tunnel was built at least ten years before the alleged date of construction of the Cruzee or Cursey Mountain Tunnel in Alabama. It therefore has priority rights."[55]

Chappell wrote, "They [the Alabama claims] will probably deserve more attention as authentic records when the place where the alleged contest occurred is found in Alabama. At all events, the construction of the Chesapeake and Ohio Railway in West Virginia has priority claims, and the obvious leaning of the tradition would seem to promise more in that state."[56]

Neither Johnson nor Chappell appreciated the logical force of the testimony about Coosa Mountain and Dabney. Johnson located an Oak Mountain in Alabama. It is "just to the southeast of Birmingham, but my informant could not say whether this is the right place or not. There may be any number of hills in Alabama known locally as Oak Mountain."[57] Even though Johnson and Chappell had clues that the locale was near Birmingham (Red Mountain, Oak Mountain), they failed to verify the Alabama claims.

If either had examined the 15' U.S. Geological Survey quadrangle maps of the area east of Birmingham and Red Mountain, he would have found his targets. These maps had been available since 1905-1906.[58] They show the C of G going through Oak Mountain by means of an unnamed tunnel at Thompson's Gap and through Coosa Mountain by means of Coosa Tunnel. The Leeds Quadrangle map also shows much of Red Mountain and the Vandiver Quadrangle map shows Double Mountain, Double Oak Mountain, and Little Oak Ridge, as well as Oak Mountain. These are prominent features – it seems unlikely that Johnson or Chappell would have missed them.

In 1927-1929, both scholars were in the midst of their investigations of John Henry. This was only forty years after Oak and Coosa Tunnels were bored. Had they visited the area around Leeds, Dunnavant, and Vandiver, they would have found many informants who would have claimed to have known something about John Henry's contest and death. Perhaps they would have been able to examine C & W records that no longer exist. Perhaps they would have learned that Captain Dabney had lived in Crystal Springs, where they could have conducted fruitful interviews. Their failure to pursue the Alabama claims resulted in the general dissemination of the theory that John Henry died at Big Bend Tunnel, resulting in a great loss of accurate information.

Johnson wrote, "One man against a mountain of negative evidence! ... Perhaps the wisest thing would be to suspend judgment on the question ...."[59] The "one man" was C. S. "Neal" Miller, who claimed to have settled in the Big Bend area in 1869 and to have witnessed John Henry's contest with a steam drill there in 1870. The census contradicts this testimony. In 1870 Miller was eight years old, lived about twenty-five miles from Big Bend Tunnel, and attended school. In a face-to-face interview, his apparent honesty and sincerity convinced Johnson of his story, which we now know to have been fabricated.

Chappell wrote, "In the failure of documentary sources, therefore, the case for John Henry and his drilling-contest must rest on testimony, which of course the reader will take or leave."[60] Chappell, too, accepted Neal Miller's story.

In the long run, it does not matter that Johnson and Chappell picked the wrong theory. History and science are littered with trashed theories. Lasting contributions lay in facts. Johnson and Chappell gathered a treasure in facts, enough to allow the nut to be cracked. Without them, the historical John Henry might never have been revealed.

Acknowledgements

In 2007, members of BALLAD-L (a ballad scholars' listserv) objected strongly to some fuzzy thinking about probabilities that I had posted. Nathan Rose put his finger on my error, pointed out a possible treatment, and mentioned Bayes. Mathematician John Hollingsworth emphasized to me that probability problems can be simplified conceptually by reducing them to counting. Fish ecologist Gary Grossman assured me that it would be foolish overkill to apply Bayes' Rule to the same-story-about-Dabney hypothesis because it is so obviously correct by common sense. I did it anyhow, for its instructive value and its quantitation, however approximate, and because neither Johnson nor Chappell reached the "obviously correct" conclusion. I am grateful to all.

Author John Garst
(http://www.alabamafolklife.org/content/evidence-john-henry-alabama; acc. 11/22/13)

Notes

[1] "Earl Murphy [obituary]," *Athens Banner-Herald* (March 17, 2011). Murphy died on March 12 in Athens, Georgia.

Art Rosenbaum. "The North Georgia Folk Festival Shows a Powerful Lineup," *Flagpole* (http://flagpole.com/News/Features/TheNorthGeorgia FolkFestivalShowsAPowerfulLineup/2002-10-02; acc. 10/5/08).

[2] Earl Murphy. "John Henry" (personal interview, Athens, GA, Sept. 2008).

Norm Cohen. *Long Steel Rail: The Railroad in American Folksong*, 2d ed. (Urbana: University of Illinois Press, 2000): xxi-xxv, 61-89.

Brett Williams. *John Henry: A Bio-Bibliography* (Westport, CT: Greenwood Press, 1983): xi.

[3] Mary Ann Fitzwilson. "With Hammers of Their Own Design: Scholarly Treatment of the John Henry Tradition," *Missouri Folklore Society Journal* 17 (1995): 33-54.

[4] Guy B. Johnson. *John Henry: Tracking Down a Negro Legend* (Chapel Hill: University of North Carolina Press, 1929): 54.

Louis W. Chappell. *John Henry: A Folk-Lore Study* (Jena: Frommannsche Verlag, W. Biedermann, 1933): 92.

[5] MacEdward Leach. "John Henry" in *Folklore and Society: Essays in Honor of Benjamin A. Botkin*, ed. by Bruce Jackson (Hatboro, PA: Folklore Associates, 1966): 93-106.

[6] John Garst. "Chasing John Henry in Alabama and Mississippi: A Personal Memoir of Work in Progress," *Tributaries: Journal of the Alabama Folklife Association*, #5 (2002): 92-129.

[7] Scott Reynolds Nelson. *Steel Drivin' Man: John Henry, the Untold Story of an American Legend* (NY: Oxford University Press, 2006): 38-39.

[8] Johnson, 19-23.

[9] Chappell, 42.

[10] Neal Pattman. "John Henry" [performance] (Athens, GA: State Botanical Garden of Georgia; Aug. 13, 2002).

Neal Pattman. "Maggadee" [interview] (Athens, GA: State Botanical Garden of Georgia; Sept. 2003).

[11] Johnson, 108.

[12] Johnson, 130.

[13] Johnson, 19-22.

[14] Johnson, 22.

[15] Johnson, 22-23.

[16] Chappell, 41-42.

[17] Chappell, 105-106.

[18] Johnson, 40-42.

[19] Chappell, 16-18, 46-49.

[20] "Deductive and Inductive Arguments," *Internet Encyclopedia of Philosophy,* ed. by James Fieser and Bradley Dowden (Computer Center, University of Tennessee at Martin; http://www.iep.utm.edu/ded-ind; acc. 6/6/15).

[21] Massimo Pigliucci. *Denying Evolution: Creationism, Scientism, and the Nature of Science* (Sunderland, MA: Sinauer Associates, 2002): 135-137.

[22] James Joyce. "Bayes' Theorem," *Stanford Encyclopedia of Philosophy*, (online, first published in 2003; http://seop.illc.uva.nl/entries/bayes-theorem; acc. 6/6/15).

[23] James Hawthorne. "Inductive Logic: Posterior Probabilities and Prior Probabilities," *Stanford Encyclopedia of Philosophy* (http://seop.illc.uva.nl/entries/logic-inductive/#3.2; acc. 6/6/15).

[24] Garst, 115-117.

[25] Charles C. Spencer. Gravestone (Salt Lake City, Utah; 2000; photo located on the "Find a Grave" website—http://www.findagrave.com, acc. 11/13; site no longer free, 6/6/15). Photograph added by Judy Latshaw.

[26] Maggie Jackson. *Distracted: The Erosion of Attention and the Coming Dark Age* (Amherst, NY: Prometheus, 2008): 203.

27 U.S. Census Bureau. "Frequently Occurring First Names and Surnames from the 1990 Census" (http://census.gov/genealogy/names; acc. 10/7/08; site no longer available, 11/22/13; instead use U.S. Census Bureau. "Frequently Occurring Surnames from the 1990 Census," http://www.census.gov/topics/population/genealogy/data/1990_census.html; acc. 6/6/15). [Editors' note: Though the new title seems to indicate that it includes only surnames, it actually includes data on male and female first names as well.]

28 "U.S. Surname Distribution" (http://www.hamrick.com/names; acc. 10/7/08; URL no longer valid, 11/22/13. Same data available at http://www2.census.gov/topics/genealogy/1990surnames/dist.all.last; acc. 6/15).

29 Garst, 105-109.

30 U.S. Geological Service. "Geographic Names Information System" (http://geonames.usgs.gov/apex/f?p=136:2:0::NO:RP:: ; acc. 6/6/15).

31 Mark Turner. "Alabama: U.S.G.S. Topo Quadrangle Maps," 2007. (http://www.markturner.com/usgs/alabama.htm; acc. 11/13; not avail. 6/15).

32 "Railway Projects: Columbus and Western," *Railway World*, 14 #16 (April 21, 1888): 375. [Found in Google Books]

"The Savannah and Western Railroad Company and the Columbus and Western Railway Company," *The Right Way* (Dec. 20, 1958): 16-17, 25.

33 Warren Musgrove. "Alabama's John Henry Country," *Birmingham News Magazine* (Sunday, Sept. 11, 1955): 10-11.

34 "Old Negro Folk Song Commemorates Colored Spike-Driver on Our Line," *Central of Georgia Magazine* (Oct. 1930): 8-9.

Garst, 111.

35 Garst, 107.

36 Garst, 115.

37 Johnson, 92.

38 Garst, 108.

39 *Central of Georgia Magazine* (Oct. 1930), 8-9.

40 Jerry Voyles. *The Legend of John Henry* (River Oak Films, 2002).

41 Margie Isbell. "Gravesite." [personal interview] (Sand Ridge Cemetery near Dunnavant, Alabama; 2/3/07).

42 Chappell, 117.

43 Johnson, 19-21

Susan Dabney Smedes. *Memorials of a Southern Planter* (Baltimore: Cushings & Bailey, 1887); reprint – Fletcher M. Green, editor (New York: Alfred A. Knopf, 1965): 48. Online at http://docsouth.unc.edu/fpn/smedes/smedes.html as part of "Documenting the American South," University Library, University of North Carolina, Chapel Hill: 61.

Kay Amick, et al. "Burleigh Plantation" (http://milleralbum.com/wp-content/uploads/links/Burleigh/index.php; acc. 6/6/15). This site links to overlays of a map of Burleigh Plantation on Google Earth.

44 Robert Moore. "John Henry." [telephone interview] (Athens, GA, and Birmingham, AL; Oct. 14, 2008).

45 *Negro Folk Music of Alabama, Vol. III*. Rich Amerson, 1; notes by Harold Courlander [LP recording] (Ethnic Folkways Library, FE 4471, 1956): side 1, band 3.

John Jacob Niles. "John Henry," *More Songs of the Hill-Folk*, Schirmer's American Folk-Song Series, Set 17 (New York: G. Schirmer, Inc., 1936).

46 Johnson, 124.

Central of Georgia Magazine (Oct. 1930): 8-9.

47 Leach, 95.

48 Johnson, 21-22.

49 *Atlanta Constitution* (May 5, 1887): 1.

Atlanta Constitution (June 8, 1887): 5.

50 Roger D. Abrahams and George Foss. *Anglo-American Folksong Style* (N.J.: Prentice-Hall, 1968): 29-31.

D. K. Wilgus. *Anglo-American Folksong Scholarship Since 1898* (New Brunswick, N.J.: Rutgers University Press, 1959): 289.

Leach, 95.

51 Chappell, 31. Testimony of R. H. Pope.

52 Chappell, 41-42.

Leach, 101.

[53] Katherine Beidleman Thompson. [personal interview] (Richmond, VA; July 19, 2010).

[54] Johnson, 25.

[55] Johnson, 26.

[56] Chappell, 42.

[57] Johnson, 24.

[58] "Alabama: Leeds Quadrangle" [15' topographic map] (U.S. Geological Survey, 1905).

"Alabama: Vandiver Quadrangle [15' topographic map] (U.S. Geological Survey, 1906).

[59] Johnson, 53-54.

[60] Chappell, 60.

This statue of John Henry can be seen near Talcott, West Virginia
(Photo by Michael Keller, courtesy of *Goldenseal* magazine;
http://www.wvencyclopedia.org/print/ExhibitHall/12; acc. 6/6/15)

To learn more about John Henry – the ballad and the man

Chappell, Louis W. *John Henry: A Folk-Lore Study* (Frommannsche, 1933).

Cohen, Norm. *Long Steel Rail: The Railroad in American Folksong*, 2d ed. (Urbana: University of Illinois Press, 2000): xxi-xxv, 61-89.

Fitzwilson, Mary Ann. "With Hammers of Their Own Design: Scholarly Treatment of the John Henry Tradition," *Missouri Folklore Society Journal*, 17 (1995): 33-54.

Frede, Ari. "John Henry as History: Transform Students into Historians with the Legends, Tall Tales, and Songs About This Fascinating, Larger-Than-Life Folk Hero," *Booklist* (Jan. 1, 2013): S32+.

Garst, John. "Chasing John Henry in Alabama and Mississippi," *Tributaries: Journal of the Alabama Folklife Association*, 5 (2002): 92–129.

Garst, John. "Evidence for John Henry in Alabama" (lecture), John Henry Day Celebration, Leeds, Alabama, 9/15/07 (http://alabamafolklife.homestead.com/John_Henry_Garst_paper.pdf; acc. 6/6/15).

Garst, John. "On the Trail of the Real John Henry," *History News Network* (George Mason University; http://hnn.us/articles/31137.html; acc. 6/6/15).

Hempel, Carlene. "The Man: Facts, Fiction, and Themes," *John Henry: The Steel-Driving Man* (http://www.ibiblio.org/john_henry/analysis.html; 6/6/15).

"John Henry" (http://en.wikipedia.org/wiki/John_Henry_(folklore); acc. 6/15).

"John Henry," *e-WV: The West Virginia Encyclopedia* (http://www.wv encyclopedia.org/exhibits/12; acc. 6/6/15).

Johnson, Guy B. *John Henry: Tracking Down a Negro Legend* (Chapel Hill: University of North Carolina Press, 1929).

Leach, MacEdward. "John Henry" in *Folklore and Society*, ed. by Bruce Jackson (Hatboro, PA: Folklore Associates, 1966): 93-106.

Nelson, Scott Reynolds with Marc Aronson. *Ain't Nothing But a Man: My Quest to Find the Real John Henry* (Nat'l. Geo. Children's Books, 2007).

Nelson, Scott Reynolds. *Steel Drivin' Man: John Henry* (O.U.P., 2006).

Wade, Stephen. "John Henry," *NPR*, 9-2-02 (http://npr.org/templates/story/story.php?storyId=1149349; acc. 6/6/15).

Williams, Brett. *John Henry: A Bio-Bibliography* (Greenwood Press, 1983).

Introduction – "Pretty Polly"

A music teacher explores the history of a well-known folk song

In this article, Beth Brooks presents her insights into the history of a popular murder ballad usually titled "Pretty Polly" in America. She traces some of the variants the song developed over the almost 300 years we've had records of it and through its travels from the British Isles to North America. Demonstrating ways to explore one song in depth, her extensive knowledge of music adds a facet to ballad study that early scholars, at least in America, seldom pursued, in contrast to the British scholars who tended to concentrate on the music, considering the lyrics to be of secondary importance.

Ms. Brooks holds a master's degree in music technology from Indiana University-Purdue University Indianapolis (IUPUI) and a bachelor's degree in music education from Indiana University in Bloomington. She teaches in the Indianapolis public schools at the elementary level, but also serves as an adjunct professor of music at IUPUI. In addition to her regular music teaching duties, she is an opera buff who not only teaches 5th and 6th grade students to appreciate opera, but at one time also helped them to write and produce their own operas! Her other passions include using the Kodaly Method to teach music to young children and using technology to provide opportunities for students who would not otherwise be able to experience musical instruction.

A note from Lyn: Beth learned about this volume of the *MFSJ* from the Ballad-L listserv, where I had previously found Paul Stamler, whose article appears in the first section of this issue. Such listservs function as online communities of scholars—in this case, an international group of professionals and dedicated amateurs who love to share information about traditional ballads and songs. The members are generous to a fault and will help anyone with a sincere desire to learn. In fact, as the note at the end of John Garst's article earlier in this issue indicates, many people have reason to be grateful to the "Ballad-L'ers." If you're interested in folk songs, you would do well to join Ballad-L. (Send an e-mail to: list@list.indiana.edu with "subscribe ballad-l" in the subject line.)

Author and music teacher Beth Brooks
(http://music.iupui.edu/people/faculty.shtml, acc. 6/6/15; courtesy of the author)

"PRETTY POLLY"
A HISTORY OF A FOLK SONG

Beth S. H. Brooks

The murder ballad usually known as "Pretty Polly" in this country is one of the most popular and widely collected folk ballads in English-speaking countries around the world. Also called "The Cruel Ship's Carpenter," "Love and Murder," and " "Polly's Love," among other titles, the accepted theory on the origin of this ballad is that it is based on an English broadside ballad called "The Gosport Tragedy," which, as far as we can tell, first appeared in print around 1720.[1] However, we must also keep in mind the fact that printers of broadsides often pulled plots and characters from existing folk tales or songs to write "to the tune of" hack poetry to sell on the streets; that scenario could have been the case here, thus possibly pushing the timeline—for some of the plot elements, at least—even further back, perhaps as early as the 17th century.

My goal in researching the history of this song was to create a selection of its versions and variants so that teachers could use it to show how and why a song changes over time. I also wanted to include a survey of the tunes usually used for "Pretty Polly" because in studying ballads, the tune is just as important as the lyrics, though re-creating the original musical experience is nearly impossible in many cases because collectors often wrote down only the lyrics; this was usually because either they did not have the technical knowledge to put the tune into musical notation or because they collected ballads primarily to study them as folk poetry. Examples of this song also may not have been included in some collections due to its "racy" themes; that is, many of the early collectors regularly ignored, or collected but never published, songs that were perceived to be "immoral" in nature. As 19th-century Scottish folk song collector William Christie noted: "Only a few verses of the Ballad are given…the whole being unsuited..."[2]

The story this ballad tells is one of romantic love gone tragically wrong. The plot elements in most American versions of this song include a man (usually called Willie) who convinces his lover/fiancée (usually Polly, sometimes Molly or Mary) to go along with him on the pretense of seeing some friends or "some pleasure" before their wedding. While they ride along, Polly begins to fear for her life. Willie confirms her fears by showing her the newly dug grave that he has prepared for her. After she begs for her life, he murders her (usually by stabbing her in the heart), throws a little dirt over her, and leaves "nothing behind but the wild birds to mourn." Often, no reason is given for the murder, leaving the listener to wonder why Willie killed Polly. As ballad expert W.K. McNeil theorized:

> In most versions of 'Pretty Polly,' the reason for the murder is unstated, a situation that is often explained as being due to religious reasons. Possibly a religious conservatism that finds unwed pregnancies improper for public mention may be the reason for the omission, but it is not the only probable

explanation. It could simply represent a loss of detail in the process of oral transmission. There is also the possibility of intentional or unintentional editing to make 'The Gosport Tragedy,' a thirty-five quatrain ballad, into a shorter, more direct song.[3]

(In some variants, there is a moral at the end of the song—that Willie has a "debt to the devil" to pay for the murder—though in other variants, there is no stated moral.)

The broadside version of the story is considerably longer than the folk ballad version. In "The Gosport Tragedy" (subtitled "The Perjured Ship Carpenter"), William/Willie has asked Molly/Mary to be his wife, but she refuses on the grounds that she is too young and that being a sailor's wife would be a sorrowful and troublesome existence. His "cunning" soon gets the better of her judgment and she shows up again several months later bearing his child. He agrees to marry her, but later has a change of heart, stabs her, throws her in the grave, and hurries off to sea. Her ghost (sometimes with a baby in her arms) appears to the captain of the ship and one of his shipmates and, fearful that the voyage is doomed by the presence of the ghost of a woman murdered by one of his crew, the captain extracts a confession from William, who, "raving, distracted, died the same night." Although certainly full of powerful emotional content, the story is told in 34 or 35 stanzas, a length that, as McNeil observed, makes it a likely candidate for shortening.

If "Pretty Polly" is indeed based on the "Gosport Tragedy" broadside, the plot might be, at least in some part, based on historical fact. David Fowler, in an article he wrote for the *Southern Folklore Quarterly* in 1979, traced the historical elements contained in the broadside, investigating the possibility that it was based on an actual murder.[4] The ship cited in the broadside was the H.M.S. Bedford, with Charles Stewart as officer and John Billson listed in the captain's logs as the "ship carpenter" who died onboard the ship while it was at sea. The story for the broadside may have originally come from Charles Stewart, who makes an appearance in the text:

> Charles Stewart, a man of courage so bold,
> One night as he was descending the hold,
> A beautiful creature to him did appear,
> And she in her arms held a baby so fair.[5]

Stewart, as part of his regular duties, evidently had the task of trying to entice men to become sailors at meetings called "rondies" (from *rendezvous)*, which were held at taverns. It is Fowler's assertion that the original engraver of "The Gosport Tragedy" heard the story from Stewart at a "rondy," wrote it up in rhyming form, and printed it on broadside "penny" sheets to be sold in the street by ballad sellers. While it is difficult to prove the historical accuracy of this theory, it definitely provides a plausible origin and path of development for the plot and details of the British and early American versions of the song.

Pretty Polly

When tracing the history of a folk song, one must compare many variants and versions in order to see how the words and music changed over time. Using the examples I had available up to this point, I developed the following chart showing my reconstruction of the major changes this song experienced in both lyrics and tune over its nearly 300 years of documented existence.

Possible Family Tree for "The Gosport Tragedy" and Its Descendants

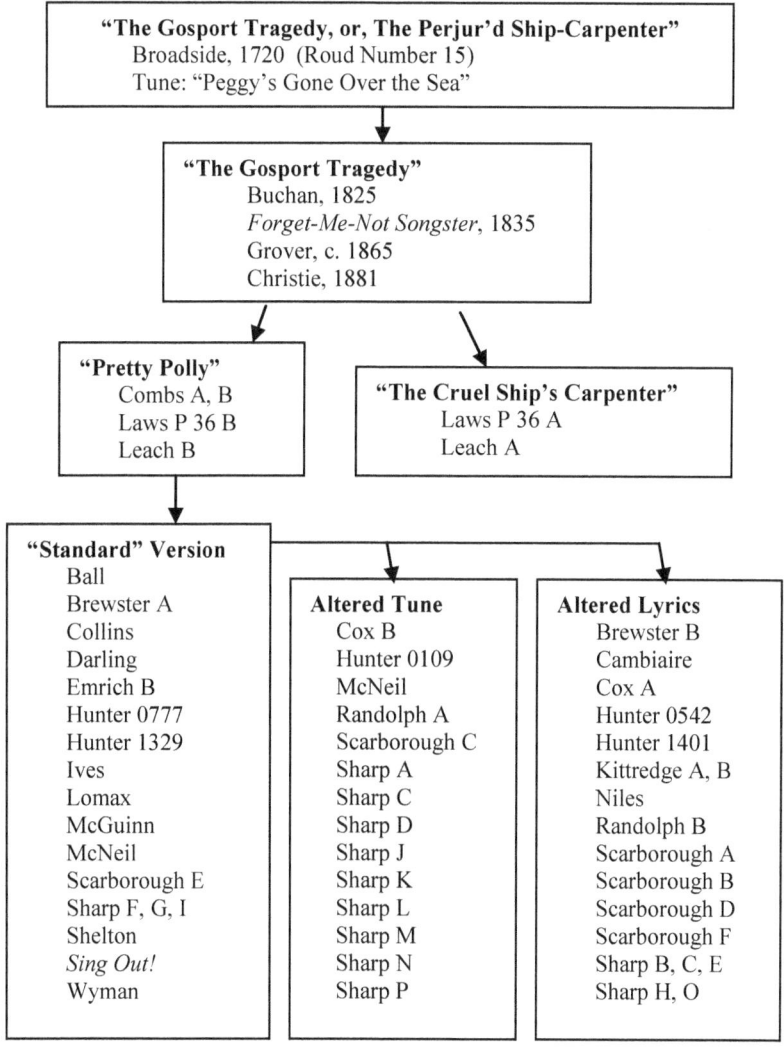

© Beth Brooks, 2003
[Citations to the sources above are listed on pages 140-142 below.]

Though the lyrics and tune of a song often change simultaneously, comparisons are clearer when we look at lyric and tune variations separately, so let's tackle lyrics first. We have examples of "The Gosport Tragedy" from broadsides, songsters, and folk song collections printed in the British Isles and America between circa 1720 through the mid-20th century. Versions of the ballad in America can be traced through broadsides printed here between 1798 and 1835, most of which have texts very similar to those of the earlier English broadsides,[6] as well as through later versions collected and printed in books as late as the mid-1900s. These American versions demonstrate a gradually reduced number of verses as the song underwent the process of oral transmission. For example, a version of "The Gosport Tragedy" printed in the early 1800s (held at the Library of Congress[7]) has 27 stanzas rather than the original 34 or 35 appearing in most of the earliest British and American broadsides. An 1865 version has 19 verses, while several versions collected around 1917 have either 10 or 7 verses. In other words, many versions of the song have been pared down to their "emotional core," some of them even becoming lyric songs without plots, rather than ballads.

One of the earliest American examples of "The Gosport Tragedy" we have that does not come to us through a broadside or a songster appears in Carrie Grover's book *Heritage of Songs*. Containing 19 stanzas, it is very similar in text and tune to one of the broadsides published in 1835. Grover tells us that her grandmother sang the song for "a party of soldiers [who] came along while she was singing the song…and the captain gave her a piece of gold to sing [it] again."[8] This event was thought to have happened during the Civil War, which dates this version to sometime in the early 1860s.

Carrie Grover's version of "The Gosport Tragedy"
(*A Heritage of Songs*, Norwood Editions, 1973: 43-45)

In 1907, George Lyman Kittredge, writing in the *Journal of American Folklore*, provided us with the first print source that uses the title "Pretty Polly" for this ballad.[9] He calls the first of his variants "much corrupted"; the text involves Willie shooting Polly with a revolver, Polly bearing "an infant of mine" in her arms as a ghost, and Willie returning to sea on a ship which sinks and kills him. The themes of this variant appear in some of the subsequently collected variants as well—Sharp A and Scarborough D and F, for example—while Kittredge's second variant is a more standard one.[10]

Chronologically, the next major set of "Pretty Polly" lyric variants to be collected in America appear in Cecil Sharp's book of Anglo-American folk songs collected during his travels in central Appalachia in 1916 and 1918.[11] His book includes 21 variants of "The Cruel Ship's Carpenter," of which only the first three have complete sets of verses—the "A" and "C" variants both have seven verses, while the "B" variant has ten. Although Sharp gives these three variants the title "The Cruel Ship's Carpenter," a common British title, they are most closely linked with the versions usually called "Pretty Polly" in America. Sharp's collection also contains two notable lyric variants—Sharp "C" and Sharp "Q." Sharp "Q" begins exactly like the broadside: "In fair Gosport town a young damsel did dwell/for wit and for beauty few did her excel." It is the Sharp variant that bears the closest resemblance to the broadside versions because the ghost of Polly has an infant in her arms and Willie's ship sinks. The "C" variant, however, seems to be a more modern version of the song because a revolver is used as the murder weapon.

Mellinger Henry's variant, collected in 1925 in Rominger, North Carolina, is worth noting, both for its similarity to other variants and its unusual humorous ending.[12] There are fifteen verses in couplet form—Polly appears as a "girl in London" (similar to Sharp B, Wyman and Brockway, and Scarborough A) and the ship, which Willie boards after stabbing Polly, sinks, presumably killing Willie, a theme also seen in Kittredge A, Sharp A and C, Scarborough C, D, and F, and Max Hunter 0109.[13]

In the version of the song recorded by banjo player and singer B. F. Shelton at the "Victor Sessions" in Bristol, Tennessee in 1927, the number of verses is pruned again and Polly speaks after she is stabbed, though this plot element is dropped in subsequent renditions of the song.[14]

Célestin Pierre Cambiaire collected a very different text version in the central Appalachian mountains and published it in 1934.[15] In his transcription, Polly's 'reputation is trouble to me' so Willie shoots her with a revolver and goes to "the old Frankfort jail," where his father bails him out, after which Willie goes to sea on a ship that strikes a rock and sinks.

Dorothy Scarborough collected variants of "Pretty Polly" in North Carolina and Virginia in the 1930s and transcribed them in her book *A Songcatcher in Southern Mountains*, which was published in 1937.[16] Her variants range from three verses (Scarborough B) to twelve (Scarborough D), variant A beginning with Polly being from "London fair city," a phrase that is also found in Sharp B, Wyman and Brockway, Henry, and Leach A.[17] In Scarborough's "A" variant, Willie's stated aim is to rob Polly, which appears in few other versions. The "A" version continues by explaining that Polly is the daughter of an "Asheville mason" and is to be wed to a ship carpenter (similar to Sharp E and U) and ends with Willie stabbing her with a sword—the sole variant to use this murder weapon. In Scarborough's variants D and F, the first line starts "one morning in May" and in both Willie shoots Polly with a revolver and then gets on a ship that strikes a rock and sinks.[18]

Both of Josiah Combs' versions of the song—collected in Kentucky and published in 1939—have the same text, which contains 12 verses and the ending where the ship strikes a rock and sinks, presumably killing the crew.[19]

MacEdward Leach lists two Canadian variants in his book, the "A" variant being most like the broadside version, but condensed to 11 verses. In this version, however, the action takes place in "fair Worcester city" and the ghost of Molly is vengeful: "she stript him and tore him, she tore him in three/because he had murdered her baby and she." The "B" variant listed in Leach's book is much more of a classic "Pretty Polly" version (although still called "The Gosport Tragedy"), with six stanzas appearing in couplet form with the first line of each verse repeated.[20]

There are many more versions of this song's lyrics to be found in the many collections of ballads available in both printed and online form. (See page 183 below for a list of Internet sites that include ballad texts and page 184 for a list of printed ballad collections.)

One problem with comparing versions and variants of ballads comes to the fore when many ballads contain similar plot elements and even some "floating verses" that become attached to various songs. For many years, ballad scholars have endeavored to decide which folk songs are versions of the "same" song by comparing lyrics, as I have done above, but the first to develop a classification system for ballads was American academic Francis James Child, who numbered English and Scottish ballads from 1 to 305 and in the 1880s published all the versions and variants he had found in existing published and manuscript sources, along with a few field collected songs.[21] He was followed in the middle of the twentieth century by scholar G. Malcolm Laws, who created a system for categorizing American folk songs that grew from British broadsides—Laws assigned letters to topics, giving murder ballads the letter "P," and individual songs numbers within that letter, thus giving the murder ballad "The Cruel Ship's Carpenter" the number P36.[22] This is why succeeding scholars refer to "Pretty Polly," "The Cruel Ship's Carpenter," and "The Gosport Tragedy" as Laws P36. The important work of comparing and grouping versions of ballads continues today with English folk song scholar Steve Roud's folk song and broadside indexes, where "The Gosport Tragedy," "The Cruel Ship's-Carpenter," "Pretty Polly" (and its many other titles) are considered to be versions of the same song, all grouped under Roud Number 15.[23]

Pretty Polly

Now that we have looked at variations in the lyrics of this song, I will do the same for the melodies usually associated with the song. For the sake of comparison, I have grouped together the variant tunes used for "Pretty Polly," as well as synthesizing earlier research done on the tune, which allowed me to construct a timeline for dissemination and variations of the tune (as I outlined in the diagram on page 127 above).

The tune listed on the ca. 1720 broadside—"Peggy's Gone Over the Sea" — probably dates from the late sixteenth century.[24] This tune is in 3/8 meter and major tonality, although ending on the sixth scale degree imparts a minor feel. It contains scalar passages and a repeat of the music for the first and second lines of each verse.

Peggy's Gone Over the Sea
or Peg and the Soldier

A melody often used for the song "The Gosport Tragedy" [25]
(See footnote #1 on page 136 for citation information)

There are some inherent difficulties present in tracing the melodies used for American folk songs before 1900 and "Pretty Polly" is a particularly good example of this. The song was sung throughout America, especially during the latter half of the 19th century, but the tune was often not included in published versions of folk song collections, even if the collector originally noted it; this was most often because of the high cost of printing music. Therefore, the majority of the American "Pretty Polly" tune variants available to us were recorded in the U.S. between 1907 and 1940, the years when collectors began to actively pursue tunes and notate them by hand or record them using early recording equipment, which allowed scholars to track changes in melodies.

The tune most commonly used for "Pretty Polly" during its approximately 150 year history in America, and the tune that is still predominant today, is in a minor key, usually pentatonic, with three distinct four-measure phrases. In the "A" phrase, the tune begins and ends on the minor tonic. In the next phrase ("A prime" or A'), the tune is restated at a perfect fifth above the first phrase. The "B" phrase is basically scalar, descending from the fifth to the first notes of the minor pentatonic scale and ending on the tonic pitch. Ballad scholar Bertrand Bronson termed this the "standard" musical form of the "Pretty Polly" ballad tune with the couplets repeated at the fifth above and makes the stylistically interesting connection to Gregorian chants and the blues.[26] (Although many variants of "Pretty Polly" follow this form, there are some that have the first line repeated three times and some that do not repeat the first line at all.) Below is a musical example of the "standard" form (A A' B) in pentatonic minor and duple meter, collected by Alan Lomax in 1947.[27]

A version of "Pretty Polly" that uses what Bronson calls the "standard" tune
(See footnote #27 on page 138 for citation information)

Of the 21 versions of "Pretty Polly" that appear in Cecil Sharp's Appalachian collections, compiled in the second decade of the 20th century, the majority have tunes that are in the key of G minor, with a flat seventh scale degree (natural minor or Aeolian mode). Six of the remaining variants are in the key of G major, with either a flat seventh or no seventh, while five are in other keys. It is unknown whether the singers actually performed the song in the key of G, or if it was Sharp's convention to use that key in his transcriptions, though the tune does appear in many other collections in and around the key of G. The time signature for the majority of the Sharp variants is 3/4 – fourteen of the variants are given in this meter. Six of the remaining variants are in duple meter (either 2/2 or 4/4) and one (Sharp Q) is in 6/8. It is the form of the tune in which the most variations occur within the versions Sharp collected – five of the variants are in A A' B form (which Bronson calls the "standard" tune, as we've seen) with the first line of text repeated once at the fifth above; five of Sharp's variants are in A A' B C form, a four-phrase form with the first line of the text repeated 3 times; three are in A B form with the first line not repeated; while the other variants are mostly in four-phrase form with the first line repeated 3 times.

I believe B. F. Shelton's 1927 recording of "Pretty Polly," along with other commercial recordings made around the same time, played a key role in codifying the tune into its current "standard" form, i.e. the most commonly recorded lyric and tune combination. Shelton performed twelve verses of the song and sang in G minor in a fast duple meter with banjo accompaniment. The majority of professional recordings made after 1927 are very similar in style and tonality to Shelton's version, indicating that many performers were influenced by his recording of the song. This recording was widely distributed and became very popular with the music-buying public because of the increasing spread of hand-cranked Victrola record players and 78 rpm recordings in the early part of the 20th century. In fact, the majority of transcriptions of "Pretty Polly" collected after the release of Shelton's 78 had tunes that were very similar to the tune he sang.

Those who collected or performed tunes closest to Shelton's include Wyman and Brockway, Niles, Scarborough, Lomax, Ives, and Ball,[28] though Scarborough's "B" variant is in 6/8 and G major, with an occasional raised fifth scale degree, while Combs collected two versions of the tune—one of which is listed as a "fiddling tune" with instrumental interlude and one that he says "is usually plucked on banjo." His "B" variant survives in 3/4 and in A major, which is a departure from the duple meter and minor version which seem to predominate.

Mid-20th-century American versions of "Pretty Polly" from the Ozark region are available on the Max Hunter Folk Song Collection website, which allows interested visitors to listen to field recordings while reading a transcription of each tune, thus making it easy to compare tunes.[29] The Hunter Collection website lists six variants of "Pretty Polly" (under various titles) which Hunter collected between 1958 and 1969 in Arkansas, Missouri, and Kansas. These variants of "Pretty Polly" tend not to follow the standard form of the text or tune, however. For example, Hunter's 1958 recording of Mrs. Ed Newton of Gainesville, Missouri, singing her version of "Pretty Polly," which she titled "Molly Girl" (MH 0109), has eleven verses that are inconsistent in length. The text is A B C D (2 rhyming couplets per verse), but the tune is in A A B C form. The vocal performance has uneven rhythms and many vocal slides throughout, making the melody at times inconsistent. The text is fairly standard, although Willie stabs her with a "pen knife." (There are also a few memory lapses that make the song difficult to follow in the recording.)

Other versions of "Pretty Polly" that appear in Hunter's collection include Harrison Burnett's singing of "Pretty Polly" (listed as MH 0542) which Hunter collected in Fayetteville, Arkansas in 1960; it contains ten verses in the standard A A' B form and ends with "Gentlemen and ladies I bid you adieu,/the song it is ended although it is true." Hunter recorded another version from Fran Majors in 1963 in Witchita, Kansas (MH 1401), which is in A major, 3/4 meter. Although its 7-verse text is in A B A B form, the tune is in A A' A" B. The murderer is "Johnny" and the song is titled "Molly, Pretty Polly," which is an unusual title for American versions (though earlier British versions sometimes use the name Molly, as does the recording from Gainseville, Missouri, mentioned earlier). On Hunter's recording of Sara Joe Bell of Harrison, Arkansas, singing "Pretty Polly," made in 1969 (MH 0832), she sings in D minor with guitar accompaniment in 3/4 meter; this 6-verse version is notable as the only variant that is sung in first person, in Polly's voice. One other variant in Hunter's collection—the 6-verse "Pretty Polly, Come Go Along With Me" (MH 0777), sung by Ollie Gilbert of Mountain View, Arkansas, in 1969, is closer to the "standard" version of the tune than most of Hunter's other Ozark versions. (The recording numbered MH 1329, sung by Sharon Redding of Hot Springs, Arkansas, in 1969, is barely understandable, so there is no musical notation of the melody and no transcription of the lyrics.)

There have been many notable performances of "Pretty Polly" over the past 90 years, showing that traditional songs as vital and striking as "Pretty Polly" are not forgotten, but still speak to performers and audiences. In styles ranging from old-time and bluegrass to rock 'n roll and blues, artists continue to include versions of "Pretty Polly" in their repertoires, a few examples of which will suffice: Pete Seeger recorded the song on his 1957 Folkways album *American Ballads*; Bob Dylan and Erik Darling performed "Pretty Polly" in 1961 (though a recording of that performance was not released until 2011); Judy Collins recorded a fairly traditional version of the tune and lyrics, but at a very slow tempo and with a very modern instrumental accompaniment, on her album *Who Knows Where the Time Goes* in 1968; and finally, also in 1968, the influential rock group The Byrds recorded a version of "Pretty Polly" (though it wasn't added to their *Sweetheart of the Rodeo* album until years after the initial release) which was another fairly traditional version but played at a much faster tempo than the Judy Collins version.[30] Even in the 21st century, there are still many versions of "Pretty Polly" being recorded and sold in various digital formats by many different performers. From B. F. Shelton's 78s produced in 1927 to versions that can currently be downloaded from iTunes, recordings of "Pretty Polly" have been available in one format or another for nearly a century now.

The changes that have taken place in both the lyrics and the tune of "Pretty Polly" since its inception as a broadside ballad, most likely in the first half of the 18th century, and indeed the changes that continue to be made by

Pretty Polly

new artists even today, are consistent with what happens to any song that goes through either oral transmission or simply the artistic process engaged in by individual performers. George Lyman Kittredge expounded upon the importance of such variation in his introduction to a 1904 one-volume edition of Child's opus:

> Old stanzas are dropped and new ones are added; rhymes are altered; the names of the characters are varied; portions of other ballads work their way in...Taken collectively, these processes of oral tradition amount to a second act of composition, of an inextricably complicated character, in which many persons share (some consciously, others without knowing it).[31]

During the period between the first American publication of "The Gosport Tragedy" in the 1790s and the first appearance in print of the "Pretty Polly" text in 1907, and afterwards through the middle of the twentieth century at least, this process of oral transmission and change continued in Appalachia, the Ozarks, and everywhere else folk songs based on the traditional British repertoire were sung in America. There was little variation of the text before 1880, it being standardized to the broadside versions that were distributed in print, but between 1907 and 1930, many variations in both text and tune of versions of "Pretty Polly" were collected. After 1930, however, the ballad appears to have been fairly well "standardized" yet again, perhaps—as we have seen—owing to the popularity of the 1927 B. F. Shelton recording or to the distribution of other recordings or printed folk song collections, many of which were, in their turn, based on the Shelton recording. Later variations, such as those found in the Max Hunter collection, might have resulted from the singers not being exposed to the earlier recordings or sheet music, thus ensuring that the informants had learned the song through oral transmission.

After almost three hundred years, some of the elements from the original printed broadside remain in the versions of "Pretty Polly" being sung today; these are essential text elements that preserve the bare bones of the 34-verse ballad heard in London before the American Revolution—in the voices of singers from the Kentucky hills and elsewhere...the plea to "come go along with me," the fact that Willie "led her over hills and valleys so deep," the way Willie showed Polly a "new dug grave and a spade lying by," and the ending where he kills her, throws her in the grave, and leaves. A simple, repetitive tune, along with these graphic images, have resulted in a song that has both gruesome action and emotional impact, which insured the popularity of "Pretty Polly" as a favorite title in the repertoire of American folk singers for more than 150 years.

Notes

[1] "The Gosport Tragedy; or, the Perjured Ship-Carpenter" [broadside] (London: [1720?]), from the Roxburghe Ballad Collection. British Library Catalog, http://explore.bl.uk—search for title, choose first entry; acc. 6/6/15).

[2] W[illiam] Christie. *Traditional Ballad Airs, Vol. 2* (Edinburgh: David Douglass, 1881): 98.

[3] William K. McNeil. *Southern Folk Ballads, Vol. 1* (Little Rock: August House, 1987): 141.

[4] David C. Fowler. "'The Gosport Tragedy': Story of a Ballad," *Southern Folklore Quarterly,* 43 #3-4 (1979): 157-196.

[5] Fowler, 158.

[6] Two examples:

"The Gosport Tragedy or The Perjured Ship Carpenter. To which is added, Bunny Wully, (a Scotch ballad)" [broadside sheet], (New York: Printed for the hawkers, 1798; microfiche, Early American Imprints, 1st series, no. 33809).

"The Gosport tragedy: shewing how a young damsel was seduced by a ship carpenter, who led her into a lonesome wood, and there destroyed her, and the infant with which she was pregnant; how her ghost haunted him when at sea, and he died distracted. To which is added, Paul Jones, and Mary's dream." [8-page illustrated booklet] (Baltimore: Printed for the purchaser, 1810-19?).

[7] "The Gosport Tragedy" [broadside] (Leonard Deming, Boston, n.d.), Library of Congress. *America Singing: Nineteeth-Century Song Sheets* (http://memory.loc.gov/ammem/amsshtml/amsshome.html; search title, choose #1; acc. 6/15).

[8] Carrie B. Grover. "The Gosport Tragedy" in *A Heritage of Songs* (Norwood, PA: Norwood Editions, 1973): 43-45.

[9] George Lyman Kittredge. "Ballads and Rhymes from Kentucky," *Journal of American Folklore,* 79 (Oct.-Dec. 1907): 251-277; "Pretty Polly" ("Gosport Tragedy" or "Cruel Ship Carpenter"), 261-264.

[10] Cecil J. Sharp and Olive Campbell. *English Folk Songs from the Southern Appalachians* (London: Oxford University Press, 1952, 1932): "The Cruel Ship's Carpenter," 317-327.

Dorothy Scarborough. *A Song Catcher in Southern Mountains: American Folk Songs of British Ancestry* (NY: Columbia University Press, 1937; reprint by AMS Press, 1966): "The Cruel Ship's Carpenter" ("Pretty Polly"), 128-134.

[11] Sharp, 317-327.

[12] Mellinger E. Henry. "Ballads and Songs of the Southern Highlands," *Journal of American Folklore*, 42 (July-Sept. 1929): 254-300; "Come, Pretty Polly," 276-278.

[13] Sharp, 317-327.

Loraine Wyman and Howard Brockway. *Lonesome Tunes: Folk Songs From the Kentucky Mountains* (New York: H. W. Gray Co., 1916): "Pretty Polly," 79-81.

Scarborough, 128-134.

Kittredge, 261-264.

Max Hunter. "The Max Hunter Folk Song Collection," [various titles used for "Pretty Polly"], (http://maxhunter.missouristate.edu; acc. 6/6/15).

[14] Shelton, B. F. "O Molly Dear," *The Bristol Sessions* (Country Music Foundation Records, [LP] CMF-011-L; 1987, 1927).

[15] Célestin Pierre Cambiaire. *East Tennessee and Western Virginia Mountain Ballads (The Last Stand of American Pioneer Civilization)* (London: The Mitre Press, 1934): "The Cruel Ship Carpenter" ("Pretty Polly"), 74-75.

[16] Scarborough, 128-134.

[17] Sharp, 317-327.

Wyman, 79-81.

Henry, 276-278.

MacEdward Leach. *The Ballad Book* (New York: Harper, 1955): "The Gosport Tragedy," 698-700.

[18] Sharp, 317-327.

Scarborough, 128-134.

[19] Josiah Combs. *Folk-Songs from the Kentucky Highlands* (New York: G. Schirmer, Inc.; 1939): "The Gosport Tragedy," 35-37.

20   Leach, 698-700.

21   Francis James Child. *The English and Scottish Popular Ballads*. 5 vols. (NY: Dover, 1965, 1882).

22   G[eorge] Malcolm Laws. *American Balladry from British Broadsides: A Guide for Students and Collectors of Traditional Song* (Philadelphia: American Folklore Society, 1957): "The Cruel Ship's Carpenter," 268-269.

23   Steve Roud. *Folk Song Index* and *Broadside Index* (http://www.vwml.org/search/search-roud-indexes; acc. 6/6/15).

24   "The Gosport Tragedy" – see note #1 above for the full citation.

25   The musical illustration for "Peggy's Gone Over Sea" comes from Claude M. Simpson. *The British Broadside Ballad and Its Music* (New Brunswick, N.J.: Rutgers University Press, 1966): 572.

26   Bertrand H. Bronson. "On the Union of Words and Music in the 'Child' Ballads" in *The Ballad as Song* (Berkeley: University of California Press, 1969): 112-132. [Essay originally published in 1952; on p. 131, Bronson mentions B. F. Shelton's recording of "Pretty Polly" (Victor 35838B).]

27   Alan Lomax. *The Penguin Book of American Folk Songs* (Baltimore: Penguin Books, 1964): 44.

28   Wyman, 79-81.

   John Jacob Niles. *More Songs of the Hill-Folk: Ten Ballads and Tragic Legends from Kentucky, Virginia, Tennessee, North Carolina, and Georgia* (New York: G. Schirmer, Inc., 1936): "Pretty Polly," 2-3.

   Scarborough, 128-134.

   Lomax, 387.

   Burl Ives. "Pretty Polly," *The Wayfaring Stranger* (LP; Columbia, 1955).

   Estil (E. C.) Ball. "Pretty Polly," *Anglo-American Ballads, Vol. 1* (Rounder CD 1511, 1999).

29   The Max Hunter Folk Song Collection (http://maxhunter.missouristate.edu; acc. 6/6/15). An archive of almost 1600 Ozark folk songs recorded by Hunter, a traveling salesman from Springfield, Missouri, who—between 1956 and 1976—took his reel-to-reel tape recorder into the backwoods of the Ozarks, thus preserving the heritage of the region.

30 Pete Seeger. "Pretty Polly," *American Ballads* (LP; Folkways, 1957).

Bob Dylan. "Pretty Polly," *Bob Dylan's Greenwich Village: Sounds from the Scene in 1961* (CD; Chrome Dreams, 2011, 1961).

Judy Collins. "Pretty Polly," *Who Knows Where the Time Goes* (LP; Elektra, 1968).

The Byrds. "Pretty Polly," *Sweetheart of the Rodeo* (CD; Columbia/Legacy, 2011, 1968).

31 George Lyman Kittredge. "Introduction," *English and Scottish Popular Ballads* by Francis James Child, 1-vol. ed. edited by Helen Child Sargent and George Lyman Kittredge (New York: Houghton Mifflin Co., 1904): xvii.

The Gosport Tragedy [broadside], British Library, Roxburghe 3.510-511; found in the English Broadside Ballad Archive, Univ. of California, Santa Barbara (http://ebba.english.ucsb.edu, search "Gosport Tragedy;" acc. 6/6/15)

Materials Consulted to Develop the "Family Tree" on Page 127

Ball, E. C. "Pretty Polly"
1) *Anglo-American Ballads, Vol. 1* (Rounder, CD 1511; 1999).
2) *Through the Years, 1937-1975* (Copper Creek, CCCD-0141; 1997).
3) *Treasury of Library of Congress Field Recordings* (Rounder, CD 1500; 1997).

Brewster, Paul G. "Pretty Polly" in *Ballads and Songs of Indiana*. Indiana University Publications, Folklore Series, No. 1. (Bloomington, IN: Indiana University, 1940): 298-299.

Buchan, Peter. "The Gosport Tragedy" in *Gleanings of Scarce Old Ballads with Explanatory Notes* (Norwood, PA: Norwood Editions, 1974; reprint of the 1891 ed. published by D. Wyllie & Son, Aberdeen, which is a reprint of the original edition, printed in 1825 by Buchan under the title *Gleanings of Scotch, English, and Irish Scarce Old Ballads Chiefly Tragical and Historical*): lyrics on pp. 46-51.

Cambiaire, Célestin Pierre. "The Cruel Ship Carpenter" ("Pretty Polly") in *East Tennessee and Western Virginia Mountain Ballads (The Last Stand of American Pioneer Civilization)* (London: The Mitre Press, 1934): 74-75.

Christie, W[illiam]. "The Gosport Tragedy" in *Traditional Ballad Airs* (Edinburgh: David Douglass, 1881): 98-99.

Collins, Judy. "Pretty Polly," *Who Knows Where the Time Goes* (Elektra [LP] 74033, 1968).

Combs, Josiah. "The Gosport Tragedy" in *Folk-Songs from the Kentucky Highlands* (New York: G. Schirmer, Inc.; 1939): 35-37.

Cox, John Harrington. "Come, Pretty Polly" in *Folk-Songs of the South* (Cambridge: Harvard University Press, 1925): 308-310.

Darling, Erik. "Pretty Polly"
1) *The Best of Traditional American Bluegrass* (Great American Music Company, CD-GA-214; 2010).
2) *Bob Dylan's Greenwich Village: Sounds from the Scene* (Chrome Dreams, CDCD5074; 2011). [Recordings made in 1961.]
3) *Blue Grass Music from the Appalachian Mountains* (Laserlight, CD 12 181; 1993).
4) *Erik Darling Sings and Plays* (Elektra, LP EKL 154; 1959).
5) *Erik Darling* (Collector's Choice Music, CD CCM-623; 2005).

The Forget-Me-Not Songster (Norwood Editions, 1974; reprint of 1835 ed. published by Nafis & Cornish in St. Louis): 232-235.

"**The Gosport Tragedy**; or, the Perjured Ship-Carpenter" [broadside] (London: [1720?]; http://explore.bl.uk—search for title; acc. 6/6/15). [The British Library holds at least 7 copies of this broadside printed between approximately 1720 and 1835.]

Grover, Carrie B. "The Gosport Tragedy" in *A Heritage of Songs* (Norwood, PA: Norwood Eds., 1973): 43-45.

Hunter, Max. "The Max Hunter Folk Song Collection" (http://maxhunter.missouristate.edu; acc. 6/6/15); see "Where to listen to versions of 'Pretty Polly'" (on page 144 below) for a list of titles and catalog numbers.

Ives, Burl. "Pretty Polly," *The Wayfaring Stranger* (LP; Columbia, 1955).

Kittredge, George Lyman. "Pretty Polly" ("Gosport Tragedy" or "Cruel Ship Carpenter") in "Ballads and Rhymes from Kentucky," *Journal of American Folklore,* 20 (Oct.-Dec. 1907): 261-264.

Laws, G[eorge] Malcolm. "The Cruel Ship's Carpenter" in *American Balladry from British Broadsides: A Guide for Students and Collectors of Traditional Song* (Philadelphia: American Folklore Society, 1957): 268-269.

Leach, MacEdward. "The Gosport Tragedy" in *The Ballad Book* (New York: Harper, 1955): 698-700.

Lomax, John and Alan. "Pretty Polly" in *Folk Song USA: The 111 Best American Folk Songs* (New York: Duell Sloan and Pearce, 1947): 387.

McGuinn, Roger. "Pretty Polly," *Cardiff Rose* (sound recording; Columbia 34154, 1976).

McNeil, W. K. "Pretty Polly" in *Southern Folk Ballads, Vol. 1* (Little Rock: August House, 1987): 140-141.

Niles, John Jacob. "Pretty Polly" in *More Songs of the Hill-Folk: Ten Ballads and Tragic Legends from Kentucky, Virginia, Tennessee, North Carolina, and Georgia* (New York: G. Schirmer, Inc., 1936): 2-3.

Randolph, Vance. *Ozark Folksongs, Vol. II – Songs of the South and West* (Columbia and London: University of Missouri Press, 1980; revised ed. with introduction by W. K. McNeil, reprint of 1946-1950 edition published by the State Historical Society of Missouri): 112-114.

Scarborough, Dorothy. "The Cruel Ship's Carpenter" ("Pretty Polly") in *A Song Catcher in Southern Mountains: American Folk Songs of British Ancestry* (New York: Columbia University Press, 1937; reprint by AMS Press, 1966): 128-134.

Sharp, Cecil J. and Olive Dame Campbell. "The Cruel Ship's Carpenter" in *English Folk Songs from the Southern Appalachians: Comprising 274 Songs and Ballads, with Nine Hundred and Sixty-Eight Tunes, Including Thirty-Nine Tunes Contributed by Olive Dame Campbell.* Maud Karpeles, ed. (London: Oxford University Press, 1952, 1932): 317-327.

Shelton, B. F. "O Molly Dear," *The Bristol Sessions* (Country Music Foundation Records, [LP] CMF-011-L; 1987, 1927).

Sing Out! ("Pretty Polly") 11 #1 (Feb./Mar. 1961): 13.

Wyman, Loraine and Howard Brockway. "Pretty Polly" in *Lonesome Tunes: Folk Songs from the Kentucky Mountains* (New York: H. W. Gray Co., 1916): 79-81.

The Gosport Tragedy's *William promises Molly he'll marry her before his ship leaves port.*

Image from Paul Slade's online article about "Pretty Polly"
(See page 143 for URL)

For further information about versions of "Pretty Polly"...

AppLit: Resources for Teachers of Appalachian Literature
Lyrics only (http://www2.ferrum.edu/applit/texts/PrPollyBallad.htm).

Folk Music Index
"Browse," "Title," "Pretty Polly II"; 132+ references to the song; no lyrics or tune notations (http://www.ibiblio.org/keefer/p08.htm).

The Full English
115+ references to the song "Pretty Polly" (Roud #15) in the papers of 19 English folk song collectors; lyrics included, some with tune notations (http://www.vwml.org/search/search-full-english).

Moore, Chauncey and Ethel. *Ballads and Songs of the Southwest* (University of Oklahoma Press, 1964): 158-159; "The Gaspard Tragedy" [lyrics and tune].

Patterson, Daniel W. *A Tree Accurst* (Chapel Hill: University of North Carolina Press, 2000): 106-107; these pages contain a discussion of how broadside songs change through the process of oral transmission using "The Gosport Tragedy/Pretty Polly" as an example.

Rosenberg, Bruce. *The Folksongs of Virginia: A Checklist of the WPA Holdings* (University Press of Virginia, 1969); lists 20 versions of the song; no lyrics or tune notations, just references to the papers.

Roud, Steve. *Broadside Index* and *Folk Song Index*
515+ references to the song "Pretty Polly" (Roud #15); no lyrics or tunes (http://www.vwml.org/search/search-roud-indexes). Some also appear in "The Full English" (above) with lyrics and sometimes tune notations.

Slade, Paul. "Pretty Polly," *PlanetSlade.com*
An nteresting article about the song appears on this British journalist's website (http://www.planetslade. com/pretty-polly.html).

The Traditional Ballad Index
Includes more than 50 citations to books and recordings; no lyrics or tune notations. (http://www.fresnostate.edu/folklore/ballads/LP36.html).

Wikipedia – "Pretty Polly"
Includes a list of 22 performers who have recorded the song. (http://en.wikipedia.org/wiki/Pretty_Polly (ballad)).

[All web pages cited here were accessed on 6/6/15.]

Where to listen to versions of "Pretty Polly" online...

The Digital Library of Appalachia
(http://dla.acaweb.org; search title – 25 recordings by various artists)
Example: Sparky Rucker at Berea College in Kentucky in 1981
(http://dla.acaweb.org/cdm/singleitem/collection/berea/id/2630/rec/15)

English Broadside Ballad Archive
(http://ebba.english.ucsb.edu/search_combined/?ss=gosport+tragedy)
Four "Gosport Tragedy" broadsides incl. lyrics and recordings to listen to

The Internet Archive
Dock Boggs, 1927   (https://archive.org/details/Prettypolly)
B. F. Shelton, 1927   (https://archive.org/details/Shelton)

The John Quincy Wolf Collection of Ozark Folksongs
(http://web.lyon.edu/wolfcollection/ozarks.htm; browse by title)
"Pretty Molly" sung by Mrs. Virgil Lane (Arkansas, ca. 1952-1963)

Traditional Ballads: The Library of Congress Celebrates the Songs of America
Pete Steele, recorded by Alan Lomax in Ohio in 1938
(http://www.loc.gov/item/ihas.200197217)

The Max Hunter Folk Song Collection
(http://maxhunter.missouristate.edu)
Versions from Arkansas, Missouri, and Kansas recorded 1958-1969
    0109 – "Molly Girl"
    0542 – "Pretty Polly"
    0777 – "Pretty Polly, Come Go Along With Me"
    0832 – "Pretty Polly"
    1401 – "Molly, Pretty Polly"

Smithsonian Folkways Online Catalog
    Pete Seeger. "Pretty Polly," *American Ballads* (LP FW02319; 1957)

    Doug and Jack Wallin. "Pretty Polly," *Family Songs and Stories from the North Carolina Mountains* (CD SFW40013; 1995)

YouTube
    The Byrds. "Pretty Polly," *Sweetheart of the Rodeo* (CD C2K 87189; Columbia/Legacy, 2003) (youtube.com/watch?v=fPD9CjiS_P0)

    The Coon Creek Girls. "Pretty Polly," *Early Radio Favorites* (CD 4142; Old Homestead, 2006) (youtube.com/watch?v=V8ZCQmD2m0Q)

[All web pages cited here were accessed on 6/6/15.]

To learn more about broadsides...

Atkinson, David and Steve Roud. *Street Ballads in Nineteenth-Century Britain, Ireland, and North America: The Interface between Print and Oral Traditions* (Burlington, VT: Ashgate, 2014).

Ballads and Broadsides in Britain, 1500-1800, ed. by Patricia Fumerton, Anita Guerrini, and Kris McAbee (Burlington, VT: Ashgate, 2010).

Bennett, Anthony. "Sources of Popular Song in Early Nineteenth-Century Britain," *Popular Music*, 2 (1982), 69-89.

Charosh, Paul. "Studying Nineteenth-Century Popular Song," *American Music*, 15 #4 (Winter 1997): 459-492.

Cohen, Norm. "The Forget-Me-Not Songsters and Their Role in the American Folksong Tradition," *American Music*, 23 #2 (Summer 2005): 137-219.

Henderson, William. *Victorian Street Ballads: A Selection of Popular Ballads Sold in the Street in the Nineteenth Century* (London: Country Life, 1937).

Johnson, C. R. and C. P. Thiedeman. *Street Literature: A Collection of 944 Whiteletter Broadside Ballads* (Cheshire: C. R. Johnson Rare Books, 1980).

Laws, G. Malcolm. *American Balladry from British Broadsides: A Guide for Students and Collectors of Traditional Song*, Publications of the American Folklore Society, Bibliographical and Special Series, Vol. 8 (Philadelphia: American Folklore Society, 1957).

Palmer, Roy. "'Veritable Dunghills': Professor Child and the Broadside," *Folk Music Journal*, 7 #2 (1996): 155-166.

Shepard, Leslie. *The Broadside Ballad: A Study in Origins and Meaning* (London: H. Jenkins, 1962).

Shepard, Leslie. *The History of Street Literature: The Story of Broadside Ballads, Chapbooks, Proclamations, News-Sheets, Election Bills, Tracts, Pamphlets, Cocks, Catchpennies, and Other Ephemera* (Detroit: Singing Tree Press, 1973).

Simpson, Claude. *The British Broadside Ballad and Its Music* (New Brunswick, NJ: Rutgers University Press, 1966).

Würzbach, Natascha. *The Rise of the English Street Ballad, 1550-1650* (New York: Cambridge University Press, 1990).

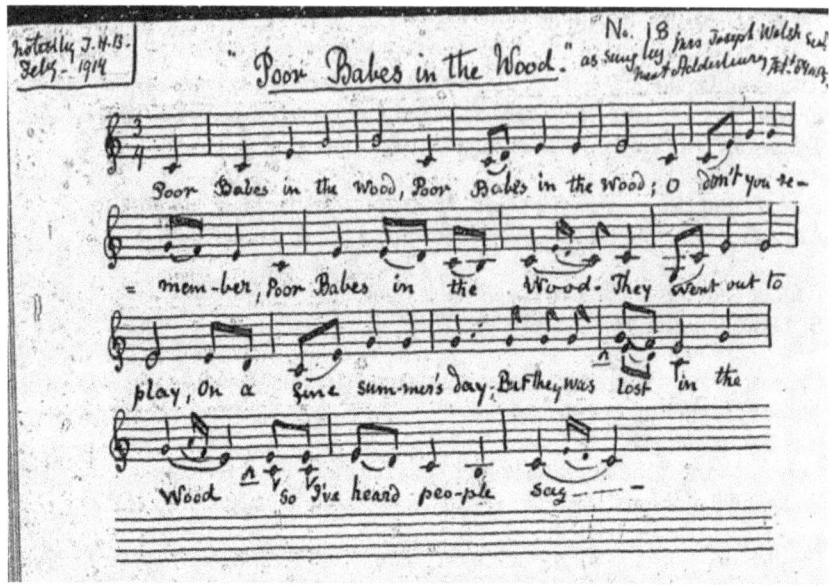

"The Babes in the Wood" – lyrics recorded and tune notated by English folk song collector Janet Heatley Blunt in Oxfordshire in 1914. These two versions are among 15+ available in "The Full English" database at http://www.vwml.org.
(Courtesy of the Vaughan Williams Memorial Library, English Folk Dance and Song Society)

Introduction – "The Babes in the Wood"

An English scholar adds to what we know about a well-loved Ozark song

Steve Roud is an internationally renowned folk song scholar whose name has become synonymous with his most famous creations—the *Folk Song Index* and the *Broadside Index*, often called "The Roud Indexes." A former librarian who currently spends most of his time writing about the folk songs and customs of the British Isles, Steve started his indexes on cards, later shifting to digital databases made available on CDs. Some forty years later, his indexes, now in the form of online databases, are among the largest resources on traditional English-language songs available anywhere. Thanks to the English Folk Dance and Song Society (EFDSS) and the United Kingdom's National Heritage Lottery Fund, Roud's indexes are now freely available at http://www.vwml.org.uk/search/search-roud-indexes, where they have become invaluable access points for anyone researching the traditional songs found in the British Isles and North America during the past 400 years.

Currently containing more than 320,000 records between them, the *Folk Song Index* and the *Broadside Index* allow people to easily find occurrences of traditional songs (and information *about* such songs) that appear in any medium—i.e. books, journals, newspapers, manuscript collections, published and unpublished sound recordings, videos, websites, etc. Some of the indexed materials include only the lyrics of a song, some contain musical notation (with or without lyrics), some include sound recordings, some contain only information about a song, and some have various combinations of these. While the indexes do not contain the songs themselves, they do allow researchers to discover where to find lyrics, tunes, and information about the songs.

In designing these digital indexes, Steve had to figure out a way to designate particular songs as versions or variants of the "same song," despite them having different titles and first lines. The numbering system he developed has become a new set of standard numbers in the vein of those devised by folk song scholars Francis James Child and G. Malcolm Laws. For the past ten years and more, scholars have been using "Roud numbers" to cite songs they write about, in addition to—or instead of—Child or Laws numbers. Steve's work in designing and compiling his indexes was recognized by the American Folklife Center at the Library of Congress in 2011 when he was invited to give a lecture on that work. (You can view a free video of his lecture at http://www.loc.gov/today/cyberlc—search for 5186.)

Lest anyone think that Steve is solely an indexer, a short resume of his other accomplishments soon puts that notion to rest. He served for more than fifteen years as the honorary librarian of England's Folklore Society, he participated in the *Take Six* and *Full English* projects developed and run by the EFDSS's Vaughan Williams Memorial Library (see the EFDSS website for descriptions of these two archival/educational projects), he teaches classes on ballads and broadsides at Cecil Sharp House in London (the headquarters of the EFDSS) and at other venues around England as part of the educational

A poster for Steve's lecture in the Botkin Series at the Library of Congress
(http://www.loc.gov/folklife/events/BotkinArchives/2011flyers/RoudFlyer.html; acc. 6/6/15)

efforts connected with *The Full English* project, and he helps to organize annual meetings, conferences, and special events for the Traditional Song Forum and other groups, of which the Folk Song Conference at Cecil Sharp House in October 2013 was but one example.

Steve has written or co-authored seven authoritative books on the folk songs and customs of England, books that have garnered praise in both the scholarly and popular press. In addition, he has written, co-authored, or compiled several CD collections of folk songs and contributed many short articles, obituaries, and reviews to publications ranging from the scholarly journals published by the Folklore Society and the EFDSS to magazines such as *English Dance & Song* and newspapers such as *The Times* (London) and *The Guardian* (Manchester). One of his most important recent works—*The New Penguin Book of Folk Songs* (co-edited with Julia Bishop)—has been hailed as a major accomplishment and has received many glowing reviews.

Introduction

Among his many honors, Steve can count the Folklore Society's Katharine Briggs Folklore Award for his book *The Penguin Guide to the Superstitions of Britain and Ireland* and the American Folklore Society's Opie Honorable Mention for his *Lore of the Playground*. Steve's extensive and high-quality body of work in the field of traditional songs was also acknowledged by his peers in 2009 when the EFDSS awarded him its Gold Badge, given for outstanding contributions to folk music.

When I mentioned to Steve that we were editing a volume of the *Missouri Folklore Society Journal* on songs and ballads, he said he had been thinking of writing a short reply to an article concerning the song "The Babes in the Wood" that had appeared in our journal years ago. (It's nice to know that our journal reaches people as far afield as England!) We are so glad we can publish even this small portion of Steve's in-depth knowledge of the history of English folk songs, so many of which made the journey from the British Isles to the New World and settled in the Missouri Ozarks, where they have been cherished by generations of singers.

[Note: We left Steve's text as it appeared in his original manuscript—with standard British spellings, word usages, and punctuation. –Eds.]

Broadside sheet of the song "The Babes in the Wood"
(Bodleian Library [Harding B 4(32)]; http://www.bodley.ox.ac.uk/ballads; acc. 6/6/15)

A note from Lyn: I first met Steve at the University of Sheffield in 1998 when we were both giving papers at a conference celebrating the centennial of England's Folk Song Society. We discovered we were fellow librarians who both enjoyed indexing—those of us with that twist of mind find all the minutiae fascinating and are happy to connect with others who have the same obsessions. Steve and I kept in touch, but didn't get together again until 2002 when I invited him to participate in a panel I organized for the Archives and Libraries Section of the American Folklore Society meeting. He graciously agreed to attend and talk about his indexes, probably lured at least in part by the chance to compare notes with the other six folk song index/database producers who attended, among them the Paul Stamler who represented the *Traditional Ballad Index* and whose article appears above. It *is* a small world!

1855 broadside for "The Babes in the Wood"
(Bodleian Library [Harding B 11(123)]; http://www.bodley.ox.ac.uk/ballads; acc. 6/6/15)

A NOTE ON THE SONG "THE BABES IN THE WOOD" (ROUD 288 / LAWS Q34)

Steve Roud

Nearly twenty years may be a rather long time to get around to replying to a point made in an article, but I would like to comment on Karen Sanders' excellent piece "Making the Babes Our Own," which was included in Volume 17 of the *Missouri Folklore Society Journal*, published in 1995.

Sanders quite rightly states that "The Babes in the Wood" song, which was traditional in her family, is a cut-down and rewritten version of a much longer song, originally called *The Norfolk Gentleman's Last Will and Testament*, or *The Children in the Wood*, which goes back to at least 1595, and which in itself retells a story which is even older.

The only quibble I have with Sanders' piece is in her assumption that the new, shorter song was composed in America and is an example of the way many folk songs were remoulded in the New World. Behind this notion lies the idea that, to put it crudely, rugged and practical Americans took the songs of decadent Europeans and refashioned them in their own image. This, like all national stereotypes, whether positive or negative, is largely founded on myth rather than demonstrable fact. Although such a thing might have happened in specific instances, I would argue that it should not be accepted as a general principle without supporting evidence. It is almost certainly wrong in the case of "The Babes in the Wood".

When talking about the history and development of traditional songs, we are always hampered by the highly patchy nature of our knowledge, but in this case there is a fair amount of evidence that the shorter "The Babes in the Wood" was composed in Britain and brought to America – either by immigrants or by way of print – some time later.

Most telling is the information to be found in William Gardiner's book, *Music and Friends, or Pleasant Recollections of a Dilettante* (Vol. III, 1853). Gardiner was born in March 1770, and his book is mainly concerned with his long involvement in amateur and professional music-making in the neighbourhood of Leicester, his home town in the English Midlands. He starts chapter 50 with a piece on 'Mr. Combe':

> While on the subject of ballads, let me speak of some written many years ago, by my friend and fellow-townsman, Thomas Combe Esq., a poet of no ordinary talent. As Lady Ann Lindsay, in her *Auld Robin Gray*, has admirably described the simple manners of the Scotch, so has my friend, in his *Hunting Physician*, hit off the spirit of our Leicestershire Foxhunters. He was equally happy in his bacchanalian and love songs. The taste, however, of Mr. Combe was refined, and of the highest order…

After giving the first ballad they wrote together, Gardiner continues:

> Another early production of mine was the following little song, from a street cry that much interested the children of Leicester. An itinerant vendor of toys, with a musical and plaintive voice, paraded the streets with two little wax figures in a bower, representing "The Babes in the Wood". To this morceau I persuaded Mr. Combe to write some lines, of which I made the song that was published:
>
> The Babes in the Wood!
> The Babes in the Wood!
> Don't you remember the Babes in the Wood?
> When a child on the knee
> How silent I'd be,
> While my mother related the story to me,
> Of the Babes in the Wood, &c.
>
> My dear you must know,
> That a long time ago,
> There were two little children, whose names I don't know,
> Who were stolen away
> On a fine summer's day,
> And left in a wood, as I've heard the folks say.
> Poor Babes, &c.
>
> And when it grew night,
> O, sad was their plight;
> The sun it had set, and the moon gave no light:
> They sobb'd and they sigh'd,
> And bitterly cry'd;
> Then, poor little things, they lay down and died.
> Poor Babes, &c.
>
> A Robin so red,
> When he saw them lie dead,
> Brought strawberry leaves, and over them spread,
> Then all the day long,
> The branches among,
> He'd prettily whistle, and this was his song –
> Poor Babes &c.

When Gardiner refers to the song being 'published', he presumably means in the form of sheet music, and just such an item can be found in an excellent

A Note on the Song "The Babes in the Wood"

private collection owned by John Earl in London. Its title is *The Babes in the Wood, written and composed to introduce an Admired Cry in the Town of Leicester*, and was printed in London by Cabusac & Sons, No. 196, Strand, for Henry Valentine, Leicester. From these details, John Earl dates the sheet to between 1794 and 1798.

The song is mentioned many times in British publications during the 19th century, often with particular affection, and it clearly achieved wide circulation as a piece for the nursery. A correspondent in *Notes & Queries* (4th series 10 (1872) 494), for example, submitted a very similar text which he remembered from sixty years before, and he explicitly states that he never saw the music for it, so he cannot have learnt it from the sheet music. The story of "The Babes in the Wood" was extremely widely known and was immensely popular on the stage, as a play or pantomime, and nearly 50 different productions of that name are known to have been presented during the 19th century. The song, with very similar words to Sanders' family version, was also widespread in the British folk song tradition, having been collected at least a dozen times in the 20th century. The best-known version from England, sung by Bob and Ron Copper of Rottingdean in Sussex, can be heard on the CD entitled *Come Write Me Down* (Topic TSCD 534 (2001)).

However, it was clearly even more popular in North America, where well over 80 traditional versions were documented in 20th century collections, and, as H.M. Belden commented, 'No doubt it is much more widely known than this list would indicate, collectors ignoring it as something universally familiar' (*Ballads and Songs* (1973) 106).

It would be interesting to find out when it first crossed the Atlantic, but we are hampered by the fact that folk song collecting in North America did not get properly underway until the 20th century. For 19th century evidence, we must rely on printed sources like broadsides and songsters, and these have not yet been adequately catalogued and indexed. From our current state of knowledge, however, and considering how popular the song was to become, it seems strangely absent from the major collections of this material, in Britain as well the USA.

We may therefore be looking in the wrong places, and this could be because its appearances were confined to publications aimed at children. George Kitteridge states in a *Journal of American Folklore* issue from 1922 (v. 35, p. 349) that it was included in a tiny volume called *A Song Book for Little Children* printed at Newburyport, Mass., in 1818 (Harvard College Library 25276.43.82), which I have not seen. It is also worth noting that much of the evidence for the song's popularity in Britain comes from brief mentions in memoirs and journalistic pieces, so perhaps it is this type of material which should be consulted to chart its development in America.

Obviously, there is yet much more to be learned about the poor "Babes in the Wood".

To learn more about "The Babes in the Wood"...

Listen to field recordings collected in the Ozarks (browse by title):

    3 collected in Missouri and Arkansas by Max Hunter (http://maxhunter.missouristate.edu/indexsongtitle.aspx?Letter=B)

    3 collected in Arkansas by John Quincy Wolf (http://web.lyon.edu/wolfcollection/songs/songs.html#b)

Listen to two versions of the song in the *Digital Tradition* database on the website at http://mudcat.org (search for the title).

Study five Ozark versions of the song (two with musical notation) in Vance Randolph's *Ozark Folksongs, Vol. 1: British Ballads and Songs* (Columbia: University of Missouri Press, 1980) on pages 365-368.

View copies of the song printed on broadside sheets during the 18th and 19th centuries by going to the *Bodleian Library Broadside Ballads Collection* website—http://www.bodley. ox.ac.uk/ ballads (search for the song title).

[All web pages cited here were accessed on 6/6/15.]

The song "The Babes in the Wood" has been popular for centuries, appearing first on broadsides and later in children's picture books
(http://www.gutenberg.org/files/37690/37690-h/37690-h.htm, click HTML; acc. 6/6/15)

Selected List of Publications By Steve Roud
[Note: Some sources list his name as Stephen Roud.]

"Alice E. Gillington," *Folk Music Journal*, 9 #1 (2006): 72-94; co-authored with Mike Yates; [Gillington was an English folklore / folk song collector].

A Dictionary of English Folklore, co-authored with Jacqueline Simpson (Oxford University Press, 2005); [see a review in *MFSJ*, 26 (2004): 97-102]. [Cover on next page, used by permission of Oxford University Press.]

English Traditional Songs and Singers from the Cecil Sharp Collection, co-authored with Eddie Upton and Malcolm Taylor (EFDSS, 2003).

The English Year: A Guide to the Nation's Customs (Penguin, 2008).

Good People, Take Warning: Ballads by British and Irish Traditional Singers, selected and presented by Steve Roud ([CD] Topic, 2012).

"James Madison Carpenter and the English Mummers' Play," co-authored with Paul Smith, *Folk Music Journal*, 7 #4 (1998): 496-513.

London Lore – The Legends and Traditions (Random House, 2008).

The Lore of the Playground (Cornerstone, 2011). [Cover on next page used by permission of The Random House Group, Ltd.]

Monday's Child Is Fair of Face and Other Traditional Beliefs about Babies and Motherhood (Cornerstone, 2008). [Cover on next page used by permission of The Random House Group, Ltd.]

New Penguin Book of English Folk Songs, with Julia Bishop (Penguin, 2012).

Penguin Guide to the Superstitions of Britain and Ireland (Penguin, 2006); [see a review in *MFSJ*, 26 (2004): 97-102].

Room, Room, Ladies and Gentlemen...The English Mummers' Play, co-authored with Eddie Cass, Malcolm Taylor, and Doc Rowe (EFDSS, 2002).

Roud Indexes (http://vwml.org.uk/search/search-roud-indexes; acc. 6/6/15).

Still Growing: English Traditional Songs and Singers from the Cecil Sharp Collection, co-edited with Eddie Upton and Malcolm Taylor (EFDSS, 2003).

Street Ballads in Nineteenth-Century Britain, Ireland, and North America: The Interface between Print and Oral Traditions, co-authored with David Atkinson (Burlington, VT: Ashgate, 2014).

About: "Steve Roud" (http://en.wikipedia.org/wiki/Steve_Roud; acc. 6/15).

"Roud Folk Song Index" (http://en.wikipedia.org/wiki/Roud_Folk_Song_Index).

  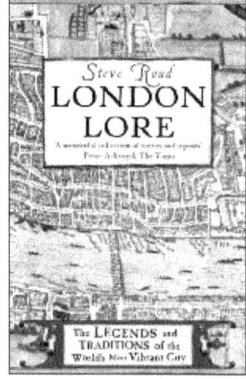

Introduction – "Ozark Ballads as Story and Song"

We hear from a Missouri scholar who's also a ballad singer or, some might say, a ballad singer who's also a scholar!

Julie Henigan's article on ballads found in the Ozarks and Appalachians builds on her personal and scholarly background in American, British, and Irish folk music. Her survey will interest those who have been familiar with ballads for years, as well as those just starting a study of the "story-songs" so common in our culture in past generations. Julie's article will be of interest not only to those studying and performing American and British folk music, but also to those interested in history and storytelling.

Julie, who hails from Springfield, Missouri, holds a master's degree in folklore from the University of North Carolina and a Ph.D. in English from the University of Notre Dame. She has conducted extensive fieldwork, gathering traditional music and song in Ireland, among other projects, and has published a number of articles on Irish and American traditional culture. Her publications vary from the scholarly to the popular, with topics ranging from *sean-nós* singing in Ireland to music parties in a small Missouri town, from oral histories of a Jewish community in the Ozarks to the old-time fiddling of Bob Holt, and from Synge's *Playboy of the Western World* to the dynamics of the Irish song tradition in her book *Literacy and Orality in Eighteenth-Century Irish Song*. (These and others are listed in a selected bibliography of Julie's work on page 181 below.) Her CD, *American Stranger*, which is a mix of traditional American and Irish songs with some of her originals, has received many favorable reviews. (The recording engineer on this project was Paul Stamler, author of the "Freaks and Fiddle Tunes" article in this volume.)

Julie stays very busy, teaching part time and performing all over the country and at international venues. A quick Google search brings up many performances and scholarly events she's been involved with over the years. She even manages to fit in an occasional visit to the MFS annual meeting! So, without further ado, here is Julie's article sharing with us some of the ballads she loves and studies and sings.

Missouri scholar, ballad singer, instrumentalist, author, and poet Julie Henigan
(Courtesy of the author)

>>> Definitions of the Word "Ballad"

OED: The Oxford English Dictionary
(3rd edition, Mar. 2008. http://www.oed.com/view/Entry/14914; acc. 6/6/15)

ballad, n. Pronunciation: Brit. / ˈbaləd/, U.S. / ˈbæləd/

1. b. A popular, usually narrative, song. In the 17th and 18th centuries such songs were often printed as broadsheets, without accompanying music.

    1602   Who makes a ballet for an ale-house doore.

    1704   I know a very wise man who believed if a man were permitted to make all the Ballads, he need not care who should make the Laws of a Nation.

Standard Dictionary of Folklore, Mythology, and Legend
(New York: Funk & Wagnalls, 1972, 1949)

Ballad A form of narrative folk song, developed in the Middle Ages in Europe…This type of folk song varies considerably with time and place, but certain characteristics remain fairly constant and seemingly fundamental:
1) A ballad is a narrative.   3) A ballad is impersonal.
2) A ballad is sung.   4) It focuses on a single incident.

Julie's CD includes traditional American and Irish ballads and songs
(http://juliehenigan.com/cd.html; acc. 6/6/15)

OZARK BALLADS AS STORY AND SONG

Julie Henigan

The performance of narrative songs (called "ballads" by folk song scholars) constitutes a form of storytelling with a long history in the Ozarks. Although the region's ballad tradition is not as well documented as that of the Appalachians, the collections made by Vance Randolph, John Quincy Wolf, Max Hunter, Sidney Robertson Cowell, and others all attest to the once lively and widespread practice of ballad-singing throughout the region. This practice was at once contiguous and continuous with the folktale tradition, occurring, as it did, primarily in intimate performance contexts, and sometimes employing the same narrative in either form: ballads often appear as spoken stories and singers were not infrequently also storytellers. In the following article, I will briefly outline some of the ballad-types most common to the Ozarks and describe their significance and function in the lives of singers and their audiences as both story and song, drawing on the experience of traditional singers from both the Ozarks and the southern Appalachians.

Scholars and collectors have tended to classify American ballads according to format, style, and provenance, designating them, for example, as Old World ballads (of both the "Child" and the printed broadside variety), New World ballads (including murder ballads and other ballads of local and historical interest), parlor ballads, blues ballads, and so on. This method has the virtue—for folk song scholars, at any rate—of conveying the likely structure and style of a song and helping to fix it in time. Thus, while it may not tell you what the ballad is about, it will tell you more or less how the story will be told. For example, if I hear a "Child ballad" (one of those story-songs that nineteenth-century Harvard scholar Francis James Child designated as belonging to an older, oral, often pan-European tradition), I know that it will fall into one of two basic rhyme patterns (including "common meter") and that it will be characterized by compressed montage-like action, dialog, incremental repetition, and a certain range of conventional characters—knights and ladies, servant messengers, cruel mothers, adulterous lovers, and talking birds; as well as by formulaic imagery—"lily-white hands," "milk-white steeds," "dewy dens," and "castles strong." A version of one Child ballad found throughout the southern mountains, "Lord Bateman," was sung by Ollie Gilbert of Timbo, Arkansas:

"Aunt" Ollie Gilbert (Photo by Clay Anderson)

Lord Batesman

There was a man in the state of Georgia,
And he did live to a high degree,
But he could never live contented
Until he taken a voyage on the sea.

He sailed east, and he sailed west,
And he sailed 'til he came to the Turkish shore,
And there he was caught and put in prison,
No hopes of freedom any more.

The jailer had one only daughter,
And she was as fair as fair could be.
She stole the keys of her father's prison,
Saying, "This Lord Batesman I'll set free."

"Have you got a house, have you got land?
Have you got money to a high degree?
And will you give it to a lady
Who will from prison set you free?"

"Yes, I've got a house, and I've got land,
And I've got money to a high degree,
And I will give it to a lady
Who will from prison set me free."

She taken him to her father's cellar,
And there she treated him on wine so strong,
And every glass that she drank with him,
Saying, "Wish Lord Batesman were my own."

She taken him to her father's castle,
And there engaged a ship for him.
"Farewell, farewell, my own true lover;
I'm afraid we'll never meet again."

"Three long years we'll make the bargain,
Three long years, and here's my hand.
If you won't court no other lady,
I'm sure I'll court no other man."

Three long years had passed and over,
Three long years, just one, two, three.
"I'll dress myself in my fine jewels,"
Saying, "This Lord Batesman I'll go see."

> She sailed 'til she came to Lord Batesman's castle.
> She knocked at the door 'til she made it ring.
> "Go out, go out, my poor old servant,
> And see who's there that will come in."
>
> "Here stands a lady at your door,
> And she's as fair as fair can be.
> She wears enough jewelry 'round her neck
> To buy your bride and Comridge Inn."
>
> "Oh, is this here Lord Batesman's castle?
> Or is he here or gone away?"
> "Oh, yes, oh, yes, this is his castle.
> He's just now brought his new bride in."
>
> "Go tell him to send me a slice of his bread,
> And send me a glass of his wine so strong,
> And ask him if he remembers the lady
> Who set him free when he was bound."[1]

Another form of ballad dear to the folk song scholar is the broadside ballad, so-called because it was often printed on the single side of a sheet to be sold on the streets by hawkers and ballad singers. Some dating back to the sixteenth century, this ballad form is typified by an almost journalistic attention to detail, commonplace imagery, the frequent insertion of a moralizing narrator, and a range of typical metrical patterns.

The murder ballad "The Waxwell Girl" is at once a localized example of a British broadside, a classic murder ballad, and a "goodnight" or "gallows" ballad, putatively composed by the criminal on the eve of his execution. This song may date to as early as the 17th century, but it was certainly well-known in the 18th as a printed ballad called "The Berkshire Tragedy, or The Wittam Miller." It subsequently became (variously) "The Oxford Girl," "The Wexford Girl," "The Knoxville Girl," and, in the Ozarks, the "Waxford" or "Waxwell Girl." The ballad tells of a miller who murders a girl whom he has defiled, of his subsequent arrest and repentance, and his final warning to young people to shun his example. Many American-made ballads follow the same pattern. The following version of this ballad was collected by Max Hunter from Mrs. Roxie Phillips of Berryville, Arkansas, in 1958:

Max Hunter (from an article by Doug Johnson, *Kirksville Daily Express*)

"The Berkshire Tragedy, or The Wittam Miller" (London, 1796)
(Bodleian Library, University of Oxford [Harding B 6 (97)])

The Waxwell Girl

It was in the town of Nero,
Where I did live and dwell,
It was in the town of Waxwell
I owned a flour mill.

I fell in love with a Waxwell girl
With dark and rolling eyes;
I asked her to marry me,
And yes, she did reply.

Into her sister's house we went,
The wedding to provide,
I asked her to walk with me
Down by the river side.

We traveled over hill and valley
Till we came to level ground;
I picked up a gambrel stick
And knocked the fair maid down.

She fell upon her bended knees,
"Have mercy," she did cry,
"O, Johnny dear, don't murder me,
I'm not prepared to die."

He gave no heed to the words she said,
But tapped her more and more
Until the ground all around her
Was covered with bloody moor [sic].

He dragged her by the yellow locks,
He dragged her on the ground,
He dragged her by the river side
And plunged her in to drown.

"Lie there, lie there, you Waxwell girl,
Lie there, lie there," he cried,
"Lie there, lie there, you Waxwell girl,
To you I'll never be tied."

It was twelve o'clock or afterwards
When I got home that night,
My mother was sitting there
All in an awful fright.

"O, Johnny dear, where have you been,
There's blood upon your clothes,"
The only answer I could give
Was bleeding at the nose.

She handed me a napkin
To wrap my aching head,
She handed me a candle
That lighted me to bed.

The flames of hell shone 'round me,
The Waxwell girl about.
Her sister swore that it was I
Who took her sister out.

So, early next morning
The Waxwell girl was found
A-floating down the river
That runs through Waxwell town.

They took me on suspicion
They marched me down to jail;
No one to go my security,
No one to go my bail.

Come all you young people,
Take warning here by me,
Don't murder your true lover,
It'll be a cruelty.

It'll bother you, it'll bother you,
Until the day you die,
And then they will hang you
Upon a scaffold high.[2]

Parlor ballads were products of a Victorian and Edwardian sensibility that ran to bathos and contributed hordes of blind orphans, drunken fathers, deserted wives, frozen debutantes, and grieving parents to the cast of narrative song characters. One prime example is "The Fatal Wedding," co-authored by Gussie L. Davis, the composer of such classics as "The Baggage Coach Ahead" and "Why Does Papa Stay So Late?" Vance Randolph recorded the following version in 1941 from Lillian Short. (Note the reference to the song as a narrative tale in the final verse.)

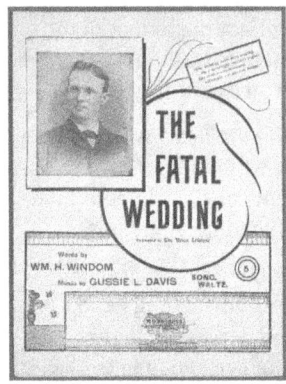

Sheet music for the song "The Fatal Wedding," 1893
(Detroit Public Library, E. Azalia Hackley Collection; http://thehackley.org; acc. 6/6/15; http://digitalcollections.detroitpubliclibrary.org/islandora/object/islandora%3A208850)

The Fatal Wedding Night

The wedding bells were ringing on a moonlight winter night.
The church was decorated, all within was gay and bright.
A mother with her baby came and saw the lights aglow.
She thought of how those same bells chimed for her three years ago.

"I'd like to be admitted, sir," she told the sexton old,
"Just for the sake of baby, to protect him from the cold."
He told her that the wedding there was for the rich and grand,
And that with the eager, watching crowd outside she'd have to stand.

Chorus

While the wedding bells were ringing, while the bride and groom were there,
Marching up the aisle together, as the organ pealed an air,
Telling tales of fond affection, vowing never more to part,
Just another fatal wedding, just another broken heart.

She begged the sexton once again to let her pass inside.
"For baby's sake you may step in," the grey-haired man replied.
"If anyone know reason why this couple should not wed,
Speak now or hold your peace forever," soon the preacher said.

"I must object," the woman cried, with voice so sweet and mild.
"The bridegroom is my husband, sir, and this our little child."
"What proof have you?" the preacher said. "My infant," she replied.
She raised her babe, then knelt to pray; the little one had died.

Chorus

The parents of the groom then took the outcast by the arm,
"We'll care for you through life," they said,
                              "You've saved our child from harm."
The outcast bride and parents quickly drove away;
The husband died by his own hand before the break of day.

No wedding feast was spread that night, two graves were made next day,
One for the little baby, and in one the father lay,
This story has been often told by firesides warm and bright
Of bride and groom, the outcast, and the fatal wedding night.

Chorus[3]

    Another method of classification—according to subject matter—more clearly reflects the kinship between ballads and spoken narrative, and instead of telling us how the story will be told, tells us what it will be about. Common ballad subjects include stories of love, courtship, and marriage; supernatural events; local legends; scatological matters; humorous situations; stories of murders, executions, and other historical events; and so on. This method has the virtue of categorizing ballads by content, a practice more in keeping with the way traditional singers often tend to classify their songs, especially when, for example, one singer specializes in love songs, while another tends to sing mostly comical ditties. According to this system of classification, no hard-and-fast distinction can be made between a parlor ballad, a Child ballad, and a broadside ballad (although it should be noted that many ballad singers have historically recognized the older traditional ballads as a separate genre, usually referred to simply as "love songs").[4]
    Sensitive to such thematic categories, Roger Abrahams noted that Arkansas ballad-singer Almeda Riddle showed a preference for "dying soldier," cowboy, and "parted-lover" ballads.[5] One of her favorites of the cowboy variety was "Texas Rangers."

Ballad singer Almeda Riddle of Heber Springs, Arkansas in 1959
(Photo by Alan Lomax [Cultural Equity]; acc. 9/22/15;
https://www.youtube.com/watch?v=MtbPk5NsEQA)

Texas Rangers

Come all you Texas Rangers, wherever you may be,
I'll tell to you a story that happened unto me.
My name is nothing extra, so it I will not tell,
But here's to all good Rangers, I'm sure I wish you well.

It was at the age of twenty, I joined the Ranger band.
We marched from San Antonio, down to the Rio Grande.
It was here our captain told us, perhaps he thought it right,
"Before you reach the station, boys, I'm sure you'll have to fight."

And when the bugle sounded, our captain gave command.
"To arms, to arms," he shouted, "and by your horses stand."
I saw the smoke ascending, it seemed to reach the sky,
The first thought then that struck me, "My time had come to die."

I saw the Indians coming, I heard them give the yell,
My feelings at that moment, no tongue can ever tell.
I saw the glittering lances, their arrows around me flew,
And all my strength it left me, and all my courage too.

We fought full nine hours before the strife was o'er.
The like of dead and wounded, I never saw before.
And when the sun was rising, the Indians they had fled.
We loaded up our rifles and counted up our dead.

All of us were wounded, our noble captain slain,
And the sun was shining sadly across the flooded plain.
Sixteen as brave Rangers as ever roamed the West
Were buried by their comrades, with arrows in their breast.

'Twas then I thought of Mother, who to me in tears did say,
"To you they are all strangers, son, with me you had better stay."
I thought that she was childish, the best she did not know;
My mind was fixed on ranging and I was bound to go.

Perhaps you have a mother, boy, likewise a sister, too,
And maybe you have a sweetheart to weep and mourn for you.
If that be your situation, although you'd like to roam,
I'd advise you from experience, you had better stay at home.

And now my song is ended, I guess I've sung enough.
The life of a Texas Ranger, boys, is something very tough.
And here's to all you ladies, I am sure I wish you well.
I am bound to go on roaming, so you ladies, fare you well.[6]

Another favorite type of ballad was the bawdy song which, though popular, was seldom sung for collectors. Vance Randolph, however, amassed thousands of this type of song and tale, though he was forced to suppress most of the erotic and scatological pieces in his collection, which were not published until two volumes of these materials came out after his death. These included mid-19th-century music-hall songs like "The Keyhole in the Door," as well as songs like the earthier (and certainly earlier) "Bonny Black Hare," found on several undated British ballad sheets. Vance Randolph collected the following version in 1940 from a man in Walnut Shade, Missouri.

The Bonny Black Hare

On the sixteenth of May, at the dawn of the day,
With my gun on my shoulder to the game field did stray,
In search of some game, if the weather proved fair,
To see if I could get a shot at the bonny black hare.

I met a fair maiden, as fair as a rose,
Her cheeks was as fair as the lilies that grows,
Says I, "My fair maiden, why ramble you so?
Can you tell me where the bonny black hare doth grow?"

The answer she gave me, the answer was "No,
But under my apron they say it doth grow,
An' if you'll not deceive me, I vow an' declare,
We'll go to yon green wood to hunt the black hare."

I walked on beside her an' vowed that I would,
I layed her in the green grass to see if I could,
I pulled out my ramrod, my balls they played fair,
Says I, "My pretty maiden, do you feel the black hare?"

The answer she gave me, the answer was nay,
"How often, young sportsman, do you ramble this way?
If good be your powder, and your balls they play fair,
Why don't you keep firing at the bonny black hare?"

"My powder's all wasted, my balls are all gone,
My ramrod is limber an' I cannot fire on,
But I'll come back in the morning if the weather proves fair,
An' I'll take another shot at the bonny black hare."[7]

Another widespread genre in traditional singing communities, especially since the 19th century, is the ballad of disaster, of which the many variants of "The Titanic," "The Ship That Never Returned," and "The Wreck of the Old 97" are well-known examples. Closer to home, "The West Plains Explosion" (written by Carson J. Robison and made popular by singer Vernon Dalhart) commemorates the explosion of a dance hall in that Missouri town in 1928. The story, which made national news at the time, draws on both the journalistic conventions of the broadside tradition and the sentimental imagery of 19th-century parlor songs. Max Hunter recorded this from Mrs. Iva Haslett:

The West Plains Explosion

In the little town of West Plains
In old Missouri State,
'Twas in the month of April,
They saw the hand of fate.

The springtime flowers were blooming,
The world was bright and gay,
And no one dreamed that danger
Would come to them that day.

Was there the young folks gathered
One fatal Friday night,
And to the dance they wandered
With hearts so gay and light.

And there they spent the evening
Without a thought of fear,
For nothing came to warn them
That death was drawing near.

The dance was nearly over,
The evening nearly past,
When from the floor beneath them
There came an awful blast.

What was left of the West Plains Dance Hall after the explosion in 1928
(From *The West Plains Dance Hall Explosion* by Lin Waterhouse, History Press, 2010;
originally published in the *West Plains Gazette*; courtesy of Russ Cochran)

The building all around them
Came tumbling to the ground;
And there they fought and struggled,
But the hot flames beat them down.

How quick the scene was shifted
From one so gay and light;
How hard the brave men struggled
To save their friends that night.

How sad the fears of loved ones
Who came at break of dawn,
To see the great disaster
Where forty lives had gone.

We can't explain the reason
These awful things must come;
But we should all be ready
To say, "Thy will be done."

And though our hearts are weary,
Our burdens hard to bear,
We have one consolation:
We'll meet them over there.[8]

The emotional impact of such narratives on both singers and their audiences cannot be over-stated. Almeda Riddle, for example, described her childhood reactions to "The House Carpenter"—in which a woman is enticed to elope with her former lover, abandoning her husband and children—in the following terms:

> I loved my father to sing me that. When I was about seven years old, I remember him singing it to me.... I thought that was a terrible thing, this mother leaving that baby. That was the thing that struck me the worst, you know, the mother deserting the child. I wasn't too concerned with the husband at that time. I don't know, maybe I subconsciously felt he got what he deserved—he couldn't hold his wife... And when she drowned, I remembered getting great satisfaction out of the thought that she got her just deserts [sic]. Even a child can have thoughts like that.[9]

Virginia ballad-singer Texas Gladden told Alan Lomax that "most often [she'd] sing something that was jolly if [she] was with a bunch of young people," but would choose sad love songs if singing for those who had been disappointed in love. Remarking that tears would sometimes well up in her listeners' eyes, she commented that they "liked the sad ones."[10]

Texas Gladden, ballad singer from Virginia
(http://www.last.fm/music/Texas+Gladden/+images/73316560; acc. 6/6/15)

In a similar vein, writing in 1945, Randolph remarked that he had seen:

> tears coursing down many a cheek, and have more than once heard sobs and something near to bellowings as the minstrel sang of some more or less pathetic incident, which may have occurred in England three or four hundred years ago. The old song of "Barbara Allen," which Samuel Pepys enjoyed in 1666, is still a moving tragedy in the Ozark hills, and women in Missouri still weep today for young Hugh of Lincoln, murdered across the sea in the thirteenth century, whose story lives in the ballad of "The Jew's Garden."
>
> On one memorable occasion I sat with seven mountain men in a smoky log kitchen, while a very old fellow quavered out the song known as "The Jealous Lover," one verse of which goes something like this:
>
> > Down on her knees before him
> > She humbly begged for life,
> > But into her snow white bosom
> > He pierced the fatal knife!
>
> At this point the old man stopped short with a kind of gasping sob, and then burst out in such a paroxysm of rage that I was startled quite out of my chair. "Oh Gawd!" he shrilled, "the son-of-a-bitch! Dod *rot* such a critter, anyway!" Our host, a hard-faced moonshiner with at least one killing to his credit, muttered some similar sentiment, and there were grunts of sympathetic approval from several other listeners.[11]

Both Almeda Riddle and Kentucky ballad-singer Jean Ritchie have written about the predilection they possessed for "lovely lonesome" songs.[12] Mrs. Riddle, influenced by modern psychological notions, apparently felt it necessary to explain this preference. She told folklorist Roger Abrahams, "I don't want to think that I was a morbid-minded child, but still I loved these sad songs....You know, happy things that tell us good news don't make the papers as often as sad news. And most of the ballads, didn't you ever notice that, are written about sad occurrences."[13] Similarly, Texas Gladden said she liked to hear her mother sing "The Two Brothers" because "it was such a beautiful sad story."[14] In fact, so vivid did she find ballad narratives that she remarked on having "a perfect picture" of every song she sang:

> I can see Mary Hamilton [heroine of a well-known Child ballad], I can see where the old Queen came down to the kitchen, can see them all gathered around, and I can hear her tell Mary Hamilton to get ready. I can see the whole story, I can see them as they pass through the gate, I can see the ladies looking over their casements, I can see her as she goes up the Parliaments steps, and I can see her when she goes to the gallows. I can hear her last words, and I can see all just the most beautiful pictures.[15]

"Last night there were four Mary's, tonight there'll be but three"
(http://en.wikipedia.org/wiki/File: The_Four_Maries,_from_an_Edwardian_ children%27s_
history_book.jpg; Wikimedia Commons; acc. 6/6/15)

Perhaps the compressed, montage-like imagery of many ballads explains much of their impact on singers and their audiences, but ballads also function as an accessory to memory, and much of their meaning can lie in their associations with past events or people. Thus Texas Gladden also spoke of having "a perfect picture of every person" from whom she learned each of her songs: "When I sing a song, a person pops up," she told Alan Lomax.[16] Jean Ritchie recalls her uncle swaying "to the quavery ups and downs" of the family version of that great ballad of adultery and murder "Lyttle Musgrave" while "his eyes clouded over with memories."[17] Madison County, North Carolina ballad-singer Lee Wallin commented, "The old songs has mighty good meanings to them. . . . that makes me think back when I was a young man, away back again when I had such good times, but they passed by and gone, and I like to hear 'em to remember things again by."[18] According to Sheila Kay Adams (inheritor of the Madison County ballad tradition), "The [songs] that are nearest and dearest to me are those that bring back a specific memory from childhood, whether it was handing tobacco, or whenever we would be out in the woods hunting for ginseng; Granny [Dellie Norton] then, of course, would sing one song after another."[19] Almeda Riddle could never remember the songs her older sister Claudia, who died in childhood, sang, although she did recall that "she sang very well and had a beautiful face, long golden hair, and a very sweet voice." Afterwards, "for many months I remember I would only cry and say No when I was asked to sing."[20] Perhaps even more poignantly, she ceased to sing some of her favorite ballads after her husband was killed in a tornado. Of a song about General Custer, she remarked, "I can sing it . . . I know all the words, but I never sing it much, though I love it, for it reminds me of singing with him."[21] Clearly, each singer's memory of, and association with, a ballad influences his or her emotional relationship to it.

The meanings of songs can also vary from singer to singer. We have already seen the way in which Almeda Riddle interpreted "The House Carpenter" in her childhood, through her imaginary identification with children deserted by their mother. It was also in her childhood that Almeda settled on the metaphorical meaning of certain ballad stories. For instance, she was adamant in her belief that the boys in "Lady Gay," in which a woman's dead children return to her from the grave, did not come back as ghosts: "They came back in a dream," she told Abrahams. "She cried so much that the grave became so wet that it wet the winding sheet."[22] On the other hand, Eunice Yeatts MacAlexander, a ballad singer from Meadows of Dan, Virginia, having no quarrel with the concept of returned revenants, focused on what she saw as the moral lesson of the ballad: "the sinfulness of pretty things…too much material pleasure," represented by the fine table and beds the mother has prepared for her children.[23] For North Carolina singer Berzilla Wallin, a ballad in which a man kills his lover because he believes she has betrayed him demonstrated to her "how deep and true love ran in the olden days" and led her to the conclusion that "the trouble with people today was that love was no longer so strong, and so children had less respect for their parents, and husbands for their wives."[24]

Of course, meaning is also partly dependent on the intelligibility of the lyrics, which can sometimes become fragmented and incoherent, though ballad singers vary in the freedom they feel to alter texts that have become garbled or incomplete. Three of the eleven singers interviewed by Ozark ballad scholar John Quincy Wolf on the subject claimed never to have made any alterations in the songs they had learned. Ollie Gilbert, for example, stated that she "never put nothin' in or took nothing' out" of the songs she sang. If she didn't understand a phrase, instead of changing it to make better sense, she attempted to make sense out of the words as she had learned them. For instance, when asked about the phrase "Comridge Inn" in her version of "Lord Bateman," she told Wolf that she "supposed it meant all of Lord Bateman's other possessions."[25] Other singers Wolf interviewed admitted to having "patched many a hole" in songs they had learned. As James Clifton Farrell of Sikeston, Missouri, put it, "If the meter is rough or the tune has a clumsy spot or two, I smooth it out till it sounds better to me."[26] Similarly, W. P. Detherow, from near Batesville, Arkansas, while, as Wolf notes, making "conscientious and intelligent attempts at restoration and not clever improvements," nonetheless "made such changes as common sense demanded."[27] Finally, according to Wolf, "the most inventive and independent" singers he knew—like Almeda Riddle and Jimmy Driftwood (best known for his songs "The Battle of New Orleans" and "Tennessee Stud")—would "adapt the songs to their own artistic judgments and/or permit the songs to evolve into what they feel to be more effective works of art."[28] Although he makes much of Driftwood's ability not only to compose but to "re-create traditional materials," it is Riddle whom Wolf ultimately identifies "more than any other singer" he knew as tending "to create as she [sang]." With her, he remarks, "No songs [were] completely

John Quincy Wolf,
Ozark folk song collector
(Courtesy of Mabee-Simpson Library,
Lyon College; http://web.lyon.edu/
wolfcollection; acc. 6/6/15)

Jimmy Driftwood,
Ozark singer and songwriter
(Courtesy of Caleb Pirtle; photo by J.
Gerald Crawford; venturegalleries.com;
"Prospecting Memories"; acc. 6/6/15)

exempt from change, not even the Child ballads."[29] In what amounted to a manifesto of her approach to traditional singing, she told Wolf, "All my life I've sung for myself, my children, and grandchildren. I sing to please myself and use my judgment on what and how I sing."[30] In all of these varied responses to the concept of re-creation, Wolf presciently recognized, as Eleanor Long was later to put it, "the impact of personality upon tradition."[31]

While this impact sometimes takes the form of expansion of a ballad's narrative elements, it more often leads to a process of condensation—a process that does not, however, necessarily detract from the ballad's overall effectiveness. In fact, many details of a ballad's narrative may be lost while the song retains essential elements, along with its power to move: what Tristram Coffin once famously defined as its "emotional core."[32] Indeed, the very structure of ballads as strophic songs necessitates a compression of action typically less evident in spoken narratives, which, except for some shorter, more formulaic folktales, allow far greater scope to the storyteller for expansion and elaboration of description and action than do ballads. This tendency toward compression—in conjunction with melody—leads, I would argue, to a corresponding intensification of emotional power, for despite the narrative qualities that link them in function, form, and significance to tales, much of the emotional impact of ballads comes from their nature as sung verse as opposed to spoken prose narrative.

Philosophers since the time of Pythagorus, Plato, and Aristotle have contended that music strongly influences the emotions and even the ethics of the listener. In more recent times, the arguments have increasingly involved cognitive studies, although many scholars have challenged the idea of a universal emotional response to music on the grounds that cultural forces play as much or more of a role in determining the reaction of the listener. Since we are dealing with what is virtually a single culture in this case, however, it is less important to establish what gives music its emotional force than to acknowledge it as part of the power of the songs within that culture.

For example, Almeda Riddle recalled being sung to sleep with ballads as a form of lullaby, suggesting that a song's melody could function to soothe as well as to excite.[33] And, speaking of her mother's singing, Texas Gladden remarked that "she could raise the hair on your head with anything she was in a mind to sing."[34] Similarly, Sheila Kay Adams identifies a kind of "weird phrasing that is so common to these love songs, that sets them apart"—a phrasing that "even as a child, just absolutely raised the hair on the back of my neck."[35] She describes Lee Wallin's son Doug as having had "probably the perfect voice for singing the love songs. . . . There was so much feeling and passion in it. I've seen Doug sit on stage when his mother was singing, and the tears'd just run down his face and drop into his shirt."[36] Underscoring the kinship between text and tune in the performance of ballads, Wallin himself once declared that ballad-singing "had to come from the heart." Dan and Beverley Patterson have also noted Wallin's "keen sensitivity to the beauty of words and tunes," observing that "his favorite melodies have a minor cast or are in old five-tone scales. He accentuates the emotional power of this music. While playing and singing 'The House Carpenter,' he paused after the last tone of the third phrase to exclaim: 'Now there's a lonesome note!'"[37]

Berzilla Wallin at home with sons Doug (left) and Jack, Sodom Laurel, NC; 1977
(Smithsonian Folkways LP, *Doug and Jack Wallin*, booklet, p. 1; photo by Rob Amberg, © 2015)

Perhaps because of this combination of emotionally charged lyrical narrative with melody, ballads also lend themselves particularly well to self-entertainment: performing for one's own enjoyment, especially while engaged in chores or while simply walking—both well-known contexts for traditional singing. As Eunice Yeatts MacAlexander told me, her friend Ruby Bowman used to "wander over the hills singing."[38] When asked when she would sing the old "love ballads," Dellie Norton replied: "Anytime when I be by myself, when I get lonesome, way up in the mountains, a-sanging or a-hunting."[39] Almeda Riddle told John Quincy Wolf that "she always sang to her cow as she was milking," thus amusing herself while keeping her repertoire fresh and her cows more productive.[40]

Dellie Norton, ballad singer from North Carolina
(1978 photo reproduced here with permission of photographer David Holt)

As this brief overview has demonstrated, ballads have played an important role in the culture of the Ozarks and throughout the southern mountains, functioning as a form of entertainment, an emotional outlet, a form of socialization, and as a means of self-expression for both the singers and the families and communities that formed their audiences. Whether employed to make work lighter, to while away the time, to incite tears or laughter, to lull infants to sleep, or to make life richer and more full of wonder, they have clearly played a significant role in the lives of the inhabitants of our region—and indeed in the entire ballad-singing world. Ballads convey stories of love, loss, sex, death, lurid crimes, dying soldiers, and solitary cowboys—all told using melody: a seemingly irresistible combination.

Yet relatively few people in the Ozarks—or the United States as a whole—still sing narrative songs. Even on the revival folk scene, the number of ballad singers is miniscule compared to that of storytellers. If both storytelling and ballad singing traditions were equally under threat, it would be easy to ascribe their attenuation to the effects of the mass media, especially television and the Internet—although the latter could, arguably, raise the profile of traditional song by providing clips of ballad singers to a global audience. Perhaps it is a function of our much-diminished attention spans; perhaps modern listeners find many of the melodies too mournful, too repetitive. Whatever the reason, I—as a long-time lover (and performer) of ballads—would be happy to hear of either singers of, or audiences for, this exquisite form of story-telling in the Ozarks: in other words, of evidence that the tradition is still alive. It would be a thousand pities if, after a hundred years of premature lamentations by ballad scholars over the demise of the genre, it should, after all, pass away. I thus venture to hope that more young singers, whatever their backgrounds, will choose to sing ballads and that they will always find people who are eager to listen to the stories they tell.

Notes

[1] "The John Quincy Wolf Collection: Ozark Folksongs" (acc. 10/1/2010; web.lyon.edu/wolfcollection/songs/songs).

The text of the song as given here was slightly edited by the author.

See also *Southern Journey, Vol. 7: Ozark Frontier—Ballads and Old-Time Music from Arkansas* (Rounder CD 1707, 1997), notes; and Vance Randolph, *Ozark Folksongs, Vol. 1*, Rev. ed. W. K. McNeil (Columbia: University of Missouri Press, 1980), 80-88.

Mrs. Gilbert's version of "Lord Bateman" is a truncated one; more complete variants include Bateman's rejection of his new bride and a vow to wed his former liberator. Verses in which Bateman excuses himself to the bride and/or her mother are also typical.

> I own I've made a bride of your daughter,
> But she's none the better nor worse for me,
> She come to me on a horse an' saddle,
> An' she can go back in a carriage an' three. (See Randolph, 83.)

[2] You can listen to the song in "The Max Hunter Folk Song Collection" (Missouri State University; http://maxhunter.missouristate.edu; acc. 6/15).

The text of the song as given here was slightly edited by the author.

[3] These are Short's words from Vance Randolph's recording, which appears on *Ozark Folksongs* (Rounder CD 82161-1108-2, 2001). You can also listen to three other recordings of the song for free online :

> Sung by Fred Smith of Bentonville, Arkansas, in 1969; in "The Max Hunter Folk Song Collection" (maxhunter.missouristate.edu/ songinformation.aspx?ID=689; acc. 12/2012)

"The John Quincy Wolf Collection of Ozark Folksongs" (web.lyon.edu/wolfcollection/Ozarks.htm; acc. 12/19/2012).

> Sung by Mrs. W. N. Osborne of Cord, Arkansas in 1957
>
> Sung by a Mrs. Barnes (no location given) in 1962

[4] Remarks like that of Virginia ballad-singer Texas Gladden are typical: "They weren't called ballads, we just called them love songs." *Texas Gladden: Ballad Legacy* (Rounder CD 11661-1800-2, 2001): notes, 4.

[5] Almeda Riddle and Roger Abrahams. *A Singer and Her Songs: Almeda Riddle's Book of Ballads* (Baton Rouge: Louisiana State University Press, 1970): 158.

[6] Riddle, 14-15.

Recordings of two other versions of "Texas Rangers" appear in "The John Quincy Wolf Collection of Ozark Folksongs" (see note #3 above for URL):

> Sung by Mr. and Mrs. Berry Sutterfield of Big Flat, Arkansas in 1958
>
> Sung by Sarah Fendley and Mary Hensley of Leslie, Arkansas, 1963

[7] Vance Randolph. *Roll Me in Your Arms: Unprintable Folksongs and Folklore, Vol. 1*, ed. by Gershon Legman (Fayetteville: University of Arkansas Press, 1992): 42.

[8] You can listen to Mrs. Haslet sing "The West Plains Explosion" by going to "The Max Hunter Folk Song Collection" (Missouri State University, maxhunter.missouristate.edu; acc. 6/6/13).

See also *The West Plains Dance Hall Explosion* by Lin Waterhouse (Charleston: History Press, 2010).

[9] Riddle, 9-10.

[10] *Texas Gladden*, notes, 7-8.

[11] Randolph, *Ozark Folksongs*, Vol. 1: 34-35.

[12] Jean Ritchie. *Singing Family of the Cumberlands* (Oak, 1955): 123.

[13] Riddle, 33.

[14] *Texas Gladden*, notes, 8.

[15] *Texas Gladden*, notes, 2.

Sheila Kay Adams recalls "acting out" ballads with her cousins, either in play form or using "little sticks and corn-shuck dolls" as puppets. See Paul J. Stamler, "'Just the Thought of Going Home': Sheila Kay Adams and the Singers of Madison County, N.C." *Sing Out!* 46 #2 (Summer 2002): 62.

[16] *Texas Gladden*, notes, 2.

[17] Ritchie, 123.

[18] *Dark Holler: Old Love Songs and Ballads* (Smithsonian Folkways, SF CD 40150, 2005), notes: 7.

[19] Stamler, 67.

[20] Riddle, 5.

[21] Riddle, 69.

[22] Riddle, 116.

[23] Eunice Yeatts MacAlexander, tape recorded interview, Meadows of Dan, Virginia, 1985.

[24] *Dark Holler*, notes, 11.

[25] John Quincy Wolf. "Folksingers and the Re-Creation of Folksong," *Western Folklore*, 26 #2 (April 1967): 104.

[26] Wolf, 106.

[27] Wolf, 107.

[28] Wolf, 111.

[29] Wolf, 108.

[30] Wolf, 108.

[31] Eleanor R. Long. "Ballad Singers, Ballad Makers, and Ballad Etiology" in *The Anglo-American Ballad: A Folklore Casebook* (New York: Garland, 1995): 237; originally published in *Western Folklore*, 32 (1973): 225-236. Long delineates four distinct types of singers (on pages 240-242):

> "Perseverating" – conservative singers who tend to retain even the most garbled phrases in their attempt to faithfully reproduce a song
>
> "Confabulating" – stylistic improvisers who feel free to revise a song
>
> "Rationalizing" – who also feel free to manipulate materials, but are possessed of more abstract motivations
>
> "Integrative" – those who, with "the value-system of a poet," not only remake received material, but also create new songs

Wolf's singers exemplify all of these types.

[32] Tristram Potter Coffin. "'Mary Hamilton' and the Anglo-American Ballad as an Art-Form," *Journal of American Folklore*, 20, #77 (1907): 209.

[33] Riddle, 6.

[34] *Texas Gladden*, notes, 6.

[35] Stamler, 67.

[36] Stamler, 64.

[37] *Doug and Jack Wallin: Family Songs and Stories* (Smithsonian Folkways, SF CD 40013, 1995); notes by Dan and Beverly Patterson, 7.

[38] MacAlexander. After this remark, Eunice, who felt she was a ballad-singer by default—not because she chose to learn the songs, but because they simply stuck in her mind—commented matter-of-factly, "I didn't do that."

[39] *Dark Holler*, notes, 21.

[40] Wolf, 108.

This National Geographic LP, released in 1972, includes four Ozark ballads
(http://www.discogs.com/Various-Music-Of-The-Ozarks/release/2754062; acc. 6/6/15)

Selected Writings by Julie Henigan

"Art Galbraith, Ozark Fiddler," *Come For to Sing*, 9 #4 (Fall 1983): 26-28.

"'Circumstances Alter Things': Oral History and the Life of a Jewish Community," *OzarksWatch*, 12 #1-2 (May 1999): 3-8.

DADGAD and DGDGCD Tunings (Pacific, MO: Mel Bay, 2013).

"'Folk' vs. 'Literary' in Eighteenth-Century Irish Song" in *Anáil an Bhéil Bheo: Orality and Modern Irish Culture* (Cambridge Scholars Press, 2009): 41-50.

"'For Want of Education': The Origins of the Hedge Schoolmaster Songs," *Ulster Folklife*, 40 (1994): 27-38.

"*I'm Old But I'm Awfully Tough*: The Making of a Great Record," *Come For to Sing*, 6 #3 (Summer 1980): 5-9.

Literacy and Orality in Eighteenth-Century Irish Song (London: Pickering & Chatto, 2012).

"Max Hunter: The Traveling Salesman Who Rescued a Folk Heritage," *Springfield Magazine*, 2 #5 (October 1980): 40-42.

"The McClurg Music Parties: A Living Tradition," *Old-Time Herald*, 4 #5 (Fall 1994): 20-22.

"'Play Me Something Quick and Devilish': The Old-Time Square-Dance Fiddling of Bob Holt," *Old-Time Herald*, 4 #6 (Winter 1994-95): 26-30.

"Print and Oral Culture in the Eighteenth-Century Irish Ballad" in *Studies in Eighteenth-Century Culture*, 41, ed. by Lisa Cody and Mark Ledbury (Baltimore: Johns Hopkins University Press, 2012): 161-183.

"*Sean-Nós* in Donegal," *Ulster Folklife*, 37 (1991): 97-105.

"Social Structure and the Irish and American Jack Tales," *North Carolina Folklore Journal*, 34 #2 (Fall-Winter 1987): 87-105.

To learn more about ballads and their music...

Atkinson	*The English Traditional Ballad*
Cheesman	*Ballads Into Books: The Legacies of Francis James Child*
Coffin	*The British Traditional Ballad in North America*
Conroy	*Ballads and Ballad Research*
Dugaw	*The Anglo-American Ballad: A Folklore Casebook*
Dugaw	*Warrior Women and Popular Balladry, 1650-1850*
Edwards	*Narrative Folksong, New Directions*
Fumerton	*Ballads and Broadsides in Britain, 1500-1800*
	Folk Music Journal (English Folk Dance & Song Society)
	International Folk Ballad Conference. *Proceedings*
Leach	*The Critics and the Ballad*
Lyle	*Ballad Studies*
McCarthy	*The Ballad Matrix*
McKean	*The Flowering Thorn: International Ballad Studies*
Porter	*The Traditional Music of Britain and Ireland: Research Guide*
Riddle	*A Singer and Her Songs: Almeda Riddle's Book of Ballads*
Ritchie	*Singing Family of the Cumberlands*
Russell	*Folk Song: Tradition, Revival, and Re-Creation*
Shepard	*The Broadside Ballad*
Shields	*Narrative Singing in Ireland*
Simpson	*The British Broadside Ballad and Its Music*
Spencer	*The Ballad Collectors of North America*
Wells	*The Ballad Tree: A Study of British and American Ballads*
Wilgus	*Anglo-American Folksong Scholarship Since 1898*
Wilgus	*The Ballad and the Scholars*

Finding ballads on the Internet...

Some of the following websites contain lyrics only, some add musical notation and/or recordings, and some also include information about the songs.

The Bodleian Library Broadside Ballads Project [England]
(http://www.bodley.ox.ac.uk/ballads; includes broadside images)

The Broadside Ballad Index [primarily British Isles]
(http://www.fresnostate.edu/folklore/Olson; tunes in ABC)

The James Madison Carpenter Collection [primarily British Isles]
(http://www.hrionline.ac.uk/carpenter)

* **The Digital Tradition** [English language]
(http://www.mudcat.org; includes discussion forum)

* **The English Broadside Ballad Archive** [England]
(http://ebba.english.ucsb.edu; includes broadside images)

Folk Music: An Index to Recorded Sources [English language]
(http://www.ibiblio.org/folkindex)

The Full English Project (includes the Take Six Project) [England]
(http://www.vwml.org.uk/vwml-projects/vwml-the-full-english)

* **The Max Hunter Folk Song Collection** [Ozarks]
(http://maxhunter.missouristate.edu; includes field recordings)

Roud Folk Song Index / Roud Broadside Index [English language]
(http://www.vwml.org.uk/search/search-roud-indexes)

The Traditional Ballad Index [English language]
(http://fresnostate.edu/folklore/BalladIndexTOC.html)

* **The John Quincy Wolf Collection of Ozark Folksongs** [Ozarks]
(http://web.lyon.edu/wolfcollection/ozarks.htm; includes field recordings)

[All web pages cited here were accessed on 6/6/15.]

* = You can listen to recordings of songs on these free websites.

Note: The words in brackets indicate the geographic location of the singers/songs. English language = songs in English from any location, though usually from the United Kingdom, the United States, Ireland, Canada, and/or Australia

Published folk song collections that include ballads...

Belden	*Ballads and Songs Collected by the Missouri Folklore Society*
Bronson	*The Traditional Tunes of the Child Ballads* (4 vols.)
Brown	*Folk Ballads from North Carolina*
Child	*The English and Scottish Popular Ballads* (5 vols.)
Cox	*Folk-Songs of the South*
Davis	*Traditional Ballads of Virginia* and *More Traditional Ballads*
Friedman	*Viking Book of Folk Ballads of the English-Speaking World*
Greig, et al.	*The Greig-Duncan Folk Song Collection* (8 vols.)
Henry	*Sam Henry's Songs of the People*
Kennedy	*Folksongs of Britain and Ireland*
Kidson	*Traditional Tunes: A Collection of Ballad Airs*
Laws	*American Balladry from British Broadsides*
Laws	*Native American Balladry*
Leach	*The Ballad Book*
Lomax	*American Ballads and Folk Songs* and *Our Singing Country*
McNeil	*Southern Mountain Folksongs: Folk Songs from the Appalachians and the Ozarks*
Moore	*Ballads and Folk Songs of the Southwest*
Quiller-Couch	*The Oxford Book of Ballads*
Rainey	*Songs of the Ozark Folk*
Randolph	*Ozark Folksongs* (4 vols.)
Roud/Bishop	*The New Penguin Book of English Folk Songs*
Scarborough	*A Song Catcher in Southern Mountains*
Sharp	*English Folk Songs from the Southern Appalachians*
Warner	*Traditional American Folk Songs*

A Short History of Ballad-Collecting

Ballads were first collected by amateur historians (often called "antiquarians") in the British Isles, beginning as early as the 17th century. In the late 1800s, American scholar Francis James Child spent many years gathering English and Scottish narrative songs from thousands of books and manuscripts for his monumental collection *The English and Scottish Popular Ballads*. The numbers he used to identify the 305 ballads he included in his collection became *de facto* standard numbers used to identify ballads in most collections published subsequently and are still used by scholars today.

Ballads also appeared on penny-sheet broadsides that circulated in the British Isles for centuries. Many of those songs traveled with immigrants to the United States, where they were later collected by ballad-lovers and scholars. These songs, along with the so-called "Child ballads," became the basis of the repertoire of singers all over America. Some of these people also kept hand-written "ballet" books, which were cherished by individuals and families up through the 20th century. Some of the same people or their descendants also sang for collectors who roamed the country to capture songs.

Those of us who love ballads are the lucky inheritors of songs from previous generations of singers and from the many devoted collectors who worked all over the English-speaking world to preserve these songs for future generations, including those in our own region such as Vance Randolph, Max Hunter, Mary Celestia Parler, John Quincy Wolf, Loman Cansler, and Joan O'Bryant, for whose labors we are profoundly grateful.   [The Editors]

Vance Randolph's 4-volume collection of Ozark folk songs and ballads is one of the standard sources of American folk songs for both scholars and singers (University of Missouri Press, 1980; composite of the covers of Vols. I and III)

Introduction – "A Shivaree in Thornfield, Missouri

Coincidences, curses, and choruses……a shivaree gone wrong

Pauline Greenhill, professor of Women's and Gender Studies at the University of Winnipeg in Canada, has graced us with a fascinating article on an unfortunate experience that happened during an event called a shivaree in Thornfield, Missouri, in 1962…..an occasion that was supposed to be light-hearted fun, but resulted in court cases and bad feelings instead.

Dr. Greenhill has been researching and writing for several years now about the custom usually known in scholarly circles today as charivari, an old European tradition that was transplanted to the New World by immigrants. Known variously as shivaree, chivaree, and rough music (among other names), it is a custom that has functioned in many different ways over the centuries. Pauline's book on shivarees—*Make the Night Hideous: Four English Canadian Charivaris, 1881-1940*—was published in 2010 by the University of Toronto Press. She found a surprising number of law cases in North America dealing with examples of charivaris gone wrong, several of which resulted in deaths. Her research also uncovered this more recent case from Missouri in which only hurt feelings and court costs were at stake, not someone's life.

Thornfield is located in an unincorporated area of Ozark County, which today consists of a few buildings and a cemetery located near the intersection of Ozark County Road 916 and Missouri State Highway 95 at the Little North Fork of the White River which feeds into Bull Shoals Lake. This area, near the edge of what is today the Mark Twain National Forest, is about 22 miles from the Arkansas state line.

The location of Thornfield in Ozark County, Missouri
(http://en.wikipedia.org/wiki/Thornfield,_Missouri; acc. 6/6/15)

In 1962, Thornfield had a larger population than it does now and was also the site of a retreat center called Cedar Heart of the Ozarks. This center was either owned or rented by a Merle E. Parker, a free thinker who would today probably be called a Libertarian. He was – among many other things – the leading light of the Foundation for Divine Meditation in California and the founder of the Citizens' Legal Protection League. In some of his publications he is listed as "Rev. Dr. Parker." One reference says he had a PhD in religious philosophy, though we have not been able to independently verify that. He seems to have split his time between the rural retreat in the Ozarks and several different towns in California, among them Valley View and San Ysabel. Parker is perhaps best known for his hobby of bringing lawsuits, many of which today might be called "nuisance suits," though one of his suits did result in an important decision regarding religious publishing and IRS rules.

Many Missourians, including some members of the Missouri Folklore Society, are familiar with shivarees from reading about them in history books and fiction, from seeing them in movies and television, or from personal experience. There are even members who, in planning their own honeymoon, had to keep the location a secret lest their friends find out and "serenade" them with loud fiddles, drums, and fireworks….and this has even happened at least as recently as 1979! We think you will enjoy reading this account of a small community dealing with the unexpected outcome of an episode of "rough music" that occurred a mere fifty years ago in the Missouri Ozarks.

Note: Throughout this article (unless otherwise specified) numbers in parentheses after quotations represent the location of that statement within the transcript of case #1147, Circuit Court, Ozark County (5/21/1963). Appeal Case File #8256, Missouri State Archives.

>>> Definitions of the Word "Shivaree"

OED: Oxford English Dictionary
(2nd ed., 1989; online. http://www.oed.com; acc. 6/6/15)

> **Shivaree**, n. *U.S.* and *Cornwall* Corrupt form of <u>CHARIVARI</u>
>
> **Etymology:** < French *charivari* (14th cent.); *caribari*, Medieval Latin
>
> A serenade of 'rough music', with kettles, pans, tea-trays, and the like, used in France, in mockery and derision of incongruous or unpopular marriages…hence a confused, discordant medley of sounds...

The Free Dictionary
(http://www.thefreedictionary.com/shivaree; acc. 6/6/15)

> **Shiv-a-ree** (shĭv'ə-rē', shĭv'ə-rē') [Alteration of CHARIVARI.]
> *n. Midwestern & Western U.S.*
>
> A noisy mock serenade for newlyweds. Also called regionally *charivari, belling, horning,* and *serenade.*

A SHIVAREE IN THORNFIELD, MISSOURI: COINCIDENCES, CURSES, AND CHORUSES

Pauline Greenhill

"Charivari"
(With the permission of the artist, Dan Junot; http://danjunot.com; acc. 6/6/15)

A community celebration for a newlywed couple in a southern Missouri county in 1962 offers a window into a tradition usually called "shivaree" in the Ozarks but more often called in the folklore literature "charivari." This custom dates to colonial times in North America, and much earlier in Europe, and continues today in parts of Canada and the United States. This relatively well-documented range of practices in its older forms in Europe condemned specific types of marriages—usually between older, previously married, age-disparate, or interracial couples.[1] But more recently, as in the case of the Thornfield shivaree in Missouri in 1962, the custom of charivari is used rather to mark appropriate marriages—ones the community approves of and wants to celebrate together.[2]

In the style of Mark Twain's famous witticism—that rumors of the death of the charivari have been greatly exaggerated—the traditional custom of charivari was pronounced dead as early as the mid-nineteenth century. Many people, particularly historians, thought charivari had ceased by that time. English historian E. P. Thompson commented:

> ...the forms of rough music and of charivari are part of the expressive symbolic vocabulary of a certain kind of society—a vocabulary available to all and in which many different sentences may be pronounced. It is a discourse which (while often coincident with literacy) derives its resources

from oral transmission, within a society which regulates many of its occasions—of authority and moral conduct—through such theatrical forms as the solemn procession, the pageant, the public exhibition of justice or of charity, public punishment, the display of emblems and favours, etc.[3]

Modern society on the whole does not give moral weight to public theatrical forms with the possible exception of protest demonstrations. As John T. Flanagan noted about the difficulty of getting "shiveree" into Webster's American lexicon (quoting an 1872 complaint): "Perhaps by the time the custom which it denotes has become obsolete even in the backwoods, the word will become part of standard English."[4] However, charivari—both the word and the custom—endures today in parts of New Brunswick, Ontario, and Alberta in Canada and among communities and interested families elsewhere in southern Canada[5] and the United States.

The study of charivari has been part of folkloristics and ethnology since the beginnings of those disciplines in the nineteenth century. Cognate forms of the tradition can be found in various European locations, with an especially broad range in England that includes "skimmington,"[6] "riding the stang," and "rough music," some of which were known in early colonial America.[7] "Shivaree" is also well known in the United States, its etymology "satisfactorily established" as being from the French, since "although raucous celebrations are common in rural England following unpopular or atypical weddings or as a form of social censure, the French term does not seem to be part of the British folk vocabulary."[8]

Charivari has been extensively misunderstood as a destructive practice— especially by historians—because the vast majority of written works about it that survive document cases where something went seriously wrong. For example, an online legal database search for "charivari" conducted in 2003 uncovered 49 pre-1944 and seventeen post-1944 cases in the U.S. Most of the charivaris in these appeal cases did not appear to denounce the nature of the marriages, and yet eight resulted in homicide,[9] eight in assault and battery, weapons, and injury-related cases short of homicide,[10] six in riot or disorderly conduct,[11] four in property crimes,[12] and one in an employer's liability case (for a charivari during a late night theatre performance).[13] Certainly, the combination of shotguns and rifles as noisemakers and alcohol for social lubrication can in part explain these results. However, to base one's understanding of charivari upon those cases which reached the legal records and newspapers would be akin to explaining the tradition of office parties using only those which led to court cases or were reported by journalists; not everyone enjoys and appreciates either office parties or shivarees, though most are relatively benign events, and even when there are problems with either type of event, the majority of participants deal with the results within their own groups and communities. However, in the case of the Billingsley shivaree in Thornfield, a set of three coincidences led to a notoriety more widespread than the usual appearances in the local newspaper and in local gossip.

But for this series of coincidences, the charivari (shivaree) of newlyweds Judy (Farnsworth) and Gene Billingsley in the town of Thornfield in Ozark County, Missouri, on June 23, 1962, would never have received any attention beyond the community. Like the vast majority of such events across North America, it was a friendly, good-natured affair, enjoyed by all participants. The first coincidence was that Thornfielder Marcus Murray, who had a heart condition, had had an attack that afternoon. His family, concerned that despite their requests some of the revelers would "shoot off dynamite" (17-18)[14] and cause another attack, called Ozark County law enforcement officer Sheriff Kelley Sallee. The second was that on this occasion, Sheriff Sallee apparently lost some of the *sang-froid* expected of law enforcement officers. He had difficulty serving a traffic ticket, misplaced his notebook, and, after one of his tires was apparently slashed, threatened to "take care of the dirty son-of-a-bitch that stuck that knife in my tire" (23). The third coincidence was that one of those charged with an offense as a result of that night was the Reverend Dr. Merle E. Parker, D.D., the founder, director, prime functionary, and Supreme Grand Counselor of the International Fraternal Order of the Foundation for Divine Meditation, located in Santa Ysabel, California, which also held summer conclaves at Cedar Heart of the Ozarks in Thornfield. These three coincidences synergistically built into a case that eventually resulted in a reported appeal, which brought it to this author's attention.

The First Coincidence – A Shivaree, a Sick Man, and Some Dynamite

Judge Justin Ruark's description of the charivari tradition is a good one:

> In the hill country of Missouri [shivarees] became...a combination of celebration and surprise party by the neighbors for the newlyweds. The surprise was usually announced by the banging on pans or plowshares and the blowing of horns, if available. Sometimes shotguns were fired. When the horse was still essential to our way of life, the surprise was often announced by the "blowing of anvils" [author's note: that is, setting off a charge of black powder between two anvils]. Usually the bride and groom were (and sometimes still are) subjected to some good natured hazing, after which refreshments are served.[15]

The trial accounts of the Billingsley charivari also mention the use of gunpowder and dynamite respectively as explosive announcements heralding the beginning of the event. Though shooting shotguns and even rifles seems to be a more common opening salvo (replaced in current Canadian charivaris by the honking of car horns and the running of chainsaws[16]), the idea is the same. Sudden loud noise should startle the newlyweds, interrupt whatever they may be doing, and signal the start of sociability—but also usually the start of traditional pranks directed at the newlyweds themselves, their house, their car, and their property and outbuildings.

Ruark continues:

> In this particular instance, the shivaree was held at the house of...a sister of the bridegroom, where the young couple were staying....A large crowd of neighbors and friends were present, a goodly number of them mature men with their families. The crowd included relatives of the couple and also a group of younger people near the age of the newlyweds. Some mention is made of cake and coffee; on the whole we gather than the shivaree was a combination surprise party and celebration, roughly corresponding to a reception, which concluded with "dunking" the newlyweds in a nearby creek.[17]

This description pretty well approximates the majority of charivaris I've heard about. A house visit—albeit a very distinctive one—from friends, relatives, and neighbors "welcomes" the newlyweds.[18] The scene was set, however, for the kind of event that might be disturbing to a sick person, particularly one with a heart condition; estimates of the numbers in attendance range from about 50 to over 200 people. Sheriff Sallee testified that "the majority of 'em were minors," and that "there was quite a lot of...girls from fifteen or sixteen to twenty-one" (27).[19] Defense witness Judy Jones said they were "just average families, some old and some young....probably more women and children" (51). Several defense witnesses testified that they attended the charivari with their families.

The culmination of this shivaree seems to have been the dunking of the bride and groom. Witness Bill Hartgraves said "we...took him down and threw him in the creek" (72); Fremon Farnsworth (Judy Billingsley's father) said "they took those kids to the creek and give 'em a duckin'" (104). Herbert Howerton's testimony suggests that after "they took Gene [Billingsley] to the creek and threw him in...people was leavin'" (88). Although the bride may not have actually been dunked, her clothes were wet enough that she needed to change. Gene Billingsley testified "I got thrown in the creek, and then I got on the fender of a car and rode back up to the house and Judy and I went up the house and we changed into dry clothes, and then somebody said that there was trouble goin' on down there, that Kelley Sallee had come down there and was making an arrest or had made an arrest—arrested Judy Jones" (114-115). Howerton said, "There was just a bunch of young people there having a good time until this all came up" (93).

The Second Coincidence – Sheriff Kelley Sallee Is Not Amused

"A Good Old Fashioned Chivaree"
(With the permission of the artist, Taral Wayne, deviantart.com; acc. 6/6/15)

Arriving in Thornfield, Sheriff Sallee observed some charivariers "drinking, and especially one had a can of beer in his hand" (17). By all accounts, including his own, the problems began when Sallee tried to serve a parking ticket on Judy Jones and her husband Lynn. Though this incident was immaterial to the actual assault charge eventually leveled against the Rev. Dr. Merle Parker, it takes up the majority of the original trial transcript. These questions were significant to a jury trial because in the view of folk justice, if not in that of the formal legal system, the person who instigates a problem is extensively responsible for whatever follows. Therefore, if Kelley Sallee started the altercation, he must accept substantial culpability in the result.

In sum, Sallee testified that the Jones vehicle was "slaunchways the road" (19), that he asked Judy who was at the wheel to move it, and that she refused. Jones herself testified that she could not move her car because the sheriff's car was blocking it, and that she did not go home immediately afterwards because she was waiting for her husband. Several defense witnesses concur. Herbert Howerton said "she was settin' across this road, she backed out across the road there kindly, had her lights on and her motor runnin' and waitin' for her man to get in the car to go home" (88).

Some others in attendance objected to Sallee's actions, and he says "they just kept vilifying me, telling me I didn't have the authority....There was quite a lot of vilifying from the crowd....at me—about what a sheriff I was, and wasn't worthy to wear the badge and should take it off...[and] job it up the hind end" (19). Sallee served the ticket and left, followed, he said, by "a good portion of the crowd [who]....kept on with their vilifying and, I call it black guarding [sic], indecent language" (24), but returned when he realized he had lost his notebook. At this point, someone unidentified by Sallee or the defense witnesses apparently stuck a knife in Sallee's tire. "I could hear the air whizzing out of the tire, and so I got out and it made me mad....I said, 'Well, I can take care of the dirty son-of-a-bitch that stuck the knife in my tire'" (22-23). Shortly afterward, Sallee testified "Parker grabbed me by the left arm and said, 'I'm making a citizen's arrest for you swearing in a crowd—or in public'" (23). Judy Jones testified, "I believe his exact words were he wasn't supposed to use foul language in front of all them women and children out there, he was going to make a citizen's arrest" (55). Along with all the other defense witnesses, she claimed that Parker never touched Sallee, but "he was just out in front of him, pointing his finger at him" (55).

The issue of who was swearing is also the subject of much testimony. Sallee and his deputy J.B. Taylor claimed it was the crowd. He testified, "They was all a-hurrahing and going on 'til you couldn't hear nothing hardly....calling [Kelley's] name all the time, calling him all kind of names....Some of 'em was vile and vulgar both" (34). But the defense witnesses all testified that the "vile and vulgar language" came only from the sheriff. Bill Hartgraves heard from the crowd "quite a few catcalls, stuff like that around there, but as far as swearing, I couldn't say I heard too much of that....And they got to singin' songs....I heard a bunch of 'em singing 'Kelley was a jolly good fellow,' and I heard 'em singing 'When the roll is called up yonder he'll be there'" (68-69). (I concur with Judge Ruark's comment "We suspect the words were changed somewhat" [278]!). Herbert Howerton also testified, "Oh, some of them, girls or something sung 'Happy Birthday' and he thanked 'em for that" (91). Fremon Farnsworth said "They was singing some little jingles—songs, something like that....The crowd was just—seemed like in an utterance after things got started" (110). Gene Billingsley claimed that "They were singing to him, going on, it was pretty noisy around" but asserts that from the crowd there was "no real serious cussing like 'God-damn' or anything" (123).

Cleo Welch testified that the sheriff said "'I'll whip the low-down, God-damn, dirty son-of-a-bitch that done that'" (77). Fremon Farnsworth quoted him as saying "'The low-down, God-damn son-of-a-bitch that stuck that knife in there, I can take care of him'" (107). Gene Billingsley says his words were "'I'll whip the God-damn dirty son-of-a-bitch that done that'" (115). In recalled rebuttal evidence, asked if he had said the latter, Sallee answered "I did not" (136). On cross examination, he reiterated that he had said "I could take care of the dirty son-of-a-bitch that stuck that knife in my tire" (137).

Finally, another subject of intense scrutiny was the question of whether or not Sallee hit the groom, Gene Billingsley, with a flashlight. The sheriff's own testimony suggested that he and the groom approached one another in a fighting stance. He claimed that he had not hit Billingsley, but that four men, including Merle Parker, had physically restrained him from behind.

I think one may be excused for wondering if this minor incident becoming a fairly seriously altercation might have to do with community opinion about the sheriff—and his of them. There are only two clues in the available material. Perhaps the Billingsley's were upset with Sallee because, as he testified "We...got a call and arrested a younger Billingsley boy up here in town prior to this....at least eight months or more" (29). Another hint comes in Cleo Welch's comment that "I had seen him go berserk one time and pull a gun and empty it in a crowd" (80). However, the reason it actually became a legal case can be directly credited to one individual—the Rev. Dr. Merle Parker.

The Third Coincidence — Enter Merle Parker

According to Fremon Farnsworth, Merle Parker "was there all the time of the charivari, amongst everybody else, was visiting and having a good time there—everybody." During the ticketing of Judy Jones, "he was standing up there and it didn't seem like he was going to—I just wondered if he was going to have anything to say about it. Well, I never seen much out of him 'til after Kelley cursed" (109).

Though in addition to the ticket he wrote that night, Sallee summoned "three boys to appear here...in Magistrate Court" (30)—the transcript is unclear about which three boys he refers to—he did not then arrest Parker, who instead was served on August 9th, some six weeks after the event. There is no testimony on what might have caused the delay, but it may be that Sallee was irked by Parker's advocacy for those charged, including Judy Jones. In a letter written to the Honorable Robert Kennedy, then Attorney General of the U.S., on May 26, 1964, Parker commented "The others who were accused of various 'crimes' were also innocent—at least three of the four were, to my knowledge, and the fourth I have no personal knowledge of, either way. However, they lacked the money to fight."[20] Most individuals served with a summons for a misdemeanor would (as for a traffic ticket) simply pay the fine—whatever they might feel about the merits of the case. In the same letter, Parker asserts "I obtained a trial ONLY after my church sent letters to the citizens of the county demanding that I be tried" [emphasis in original].

But Merle Parker was not a conventional person. In 1955, he and his organization published a pamphlet entitled *Instant Healing Now!*, in which he identifies himself as "The Rev. Dr. Merle E. Parker, Ps.D., D.D., Founder and Director of the International Fraternal Order of The Foundation for Divine Meditation [(F.D.M.], Santa Ysabel, California...founded in 1948."[21] He also wrote several other books during the sixties and seventies including *Miracle Methods of the Masters*, *Taxpayers' Power*, *How to Be Your Own Lawyer and Sue to Win*, and *How to Be Your Own Lawyer: Facts Lawyers Won't Tell You*, in addition to publishing at least two periodicals during the 1960s—the *American Liberty Crusader* and *Taxpayers' Power*.[22] The combination of topics covered by Parker and his organization may seem unorthodox. However, as Laird Wilcox, an expert on extremist groups, has commented, "The populist arm of the American right-wing is infested with miniscule groups like [Parker's]."[23]

Parker was no stranger to litigation. According to *Parker v. Summerfield* (105 U.S. App. D.C. 167; 265 F.2d 359 [1959]), "On April 24, 1953, the then-Solicitor of the Post Office Department instituted a proceeding...against Merle E. Parker, alleging that he was obtaining money through the mails for a course of instruction called 'The Sacred Laws Behind Miracles' and one called 'Secrets of Wealth, Power and Success,' by fraudulent pretenses, representations and promises" (361). The appeals court reversed the original court's decision on the former title, but held that the latter title showed "such a reckless disregard for truth that [a fraudulent] intent may be inferred from all of the testimony and the circumstances involved."[24] Parker sought review of the decision, and then appealed that result. In this appeal, he noted the court's finding of fact that the course "discloses no method of acquiring material wealth, and such a course of instruction is of no value, and all of the evidence adduced demonstrates an intent to deceive" (363). However, calling the latter finding "supported by sufficient evidence" and seeing "no substance" in Parker's argument that his constitutional rights were violated and other errors, the appeal found against him. His petition for rehearing (105 U.S. App. D.C. 243; 265 F.2d 960 [1959]) was denied.

Parker v. Commissioner of Internal Revenue (365 F.2d. 792 [1966]) explains that "in 1954 F.D.M. filed an application for exemption from taxation" (795) under an Internal Revenue Service code exempting "corporations...organized and operated exclusively for religious...purposes...no part of the earnings of which inures to the benefit of any private shareholder and individual" (Ibid.). The exemption was denied by the Commissioner in 1955, and upheld by the Tax Court, finding that the activities of F.D.M. were not "exclusively to the pursuit of religious purposes" (796). Parker's request to appeal this case to the Supreme Court was denied (385 U.S. 1026; 87 S. Ct. 752). It is now a leading case on the topic of religious publishing.[25]

In the meantime, "In 1956 a criminal action was instituted against Dr. Parker for contributing to the delinquency of a minor" (*Parker v. Commissioner*: 801). Found not guilty, "Dr. Parker instituted a civil slander action against a medical doctor and the mother of the minor to whose delinquency Parker was alleged to have contributed" (ibid.). The result of the tort case was not reported. Parker was also the subject of a successful action by the Director of Public Health of the County of San Diego against himself and F.D.M., "enjoining the defendants from preventing plaintiffs from inspecting the swimming pool on defendants' premises" (in *Askew v. Parker* [1957] 151 CA2d 759, n.p.).

Clearly, Merle Parker was extensively engaged in confrontations with the authorities, and wanted to confront Kelley Sallee as well. So, almost eleven months to the day after the Billingsley charivari, on May 21 and 22, 1963, Judge Joe C. Crain and a jury heard the case in the Circuit Court of Ozark County. Charged that he did "in a rude and insolent manner, unlawfully touch and assault one Kelley Sallee," Parker pleaded not guilty, but the jury found him guilty of common assault. They were unable to agree upon a punishment so Judge Crain assessed a $25 fine and court costs.

Parker's appellant's brief states that his Constitutional rights were violated, that the conviction "was had upon perjured testimony and against the overwhelming weight of credible evidence...that [he] was denied a fair and impartial trial and was deprived of his rights under due process of law." An affidavit accuses Kelley Sallee of perjury and notes that he and a number of witnesses "have indicated their willingness to be examined with the assistance of a 'Lie Detector' device." On January 3, 1964, he fired his attorney, Charles A. Moon, whom he accused in the letter to Robert Kennedy (quoted above) of conspiring against him. He appeared on his own behalf for the appeal.

Judge Ruark commented that the appellant's brief "is of little value to us. It is principally concerned with 'constitutional questions,' none of which were raised in the first instance" (276). Such remarks usually do not augur well for those who receive them! Since appeals deal with legal issues, not with matters of fact, they are overwhelmingly difficult for lay people to argue. Yet Judge Ruark held that there had been a technical error in the summoning of the jury. And as judges sometimes do, he also found a roundabout route to deal with his fundamental agreement with Parker's concern that there had been a miscarriage of justice.

He identified the problem, more or less in passing, as follows: "All these [defense] witnesses say that no one grabbed Sallee from behind and all say that *Parker never touched Sallee*; but, if we follow the usually accepted rule, we must assume that they all lied and Sallee, and only Sallee, told the truth, although it is quite distasteful to have to assume that all of these neighbors are perjurers" (emphasis in original, 279). He explained that "the general rule is that evidence favorable to the verdict is taken as true; that all favorable inferences which may reasonably be drawn from the evidence are indulged; that credibility of witnesses is first for the jury and second for the trial court; and that the appellate courts will not pass on the weight of substantial evidence unless it appears that the trial court has abused its discretion." This means that the Judge would be obliged to accept Kelley Sallee's testimony as accurate and factual, to take the jury's implied assessment of the defense witnesses as not credible at face value, and not to weigh the evidence since the jury had a right to do so.

Yet, citing a Criminal Rule which "provides that plain errors affecting substantial rights, although not raised or preserved, or defectively raised or preserved, may be considered when the court deems that manifest injustice or miscarriage of justice has resulted therefrom" (281), he nevertheless was willing to "consider whether there is sufficient evidence to establish that an offense [*sic*] was committed" (281). In short, though the appellant had not actually made this argument in any form, Ruark held that in his altercation with Gene Billingsley, "Kelley Sallee was acting only in the position of a private citizen then engaged, or about to engage, in an affray" (283), not as a sheriff making an arrest, and therefore Parker's intervention was not illegal:

> According to [Sallee's] testimony, he had used the words "son-of-a-bitch" in an angry manner. We are not an authority on whether "swearing" is considered by the general public to consist only in taking the Lord's name in vain. Certainly in Southern Missouri the words "son-of-a-bitch" when used in an angry manner are considered "fighting words" and a breach of the peace likely to produce a more violent breach. The touching of the arm, or the taking hold of the arm, was not accompanied by any other force or threat. It was but a temporary, almost momentary, restraint which we believe the defendant had a right as a citizen to impose under the circumstances. This being true, no assault was committed. Accordingly, the judgement of conviction is reversed and the defendant is ordered discharged (283).

Parker was very fortunate that one of the Missouri Court of Appeals judges involved in the Thornfield case (in fact, the judge who wrote the unanimous decision) was Ruark, whose ethnographic understanding of the Ozarks is also well reflected in his 1960 definition of "hillbilly" from *Moore v. Moore* (337 S.W. 2d. 781):

> We suggest that to refer to a person as a "hillbilly"...might or might not be an insult, depending upon the meaning intended to be conveyed, the manner of utterance, and the place where the words are spoken. *Webster's New International Dictionary* says that a hillbilly is "a backwoods man or mountaineer of the southern United States; often used contemptuously." But without the added implication or inflection which indicates an intention to belittle, we would say that, here in Southern Missouri, the term is often given and accepted as a complimentary expression. An Ozark hillbilly is an individual who has learned the real luxury of doing without the entangling complications of things which the dependent and over-pressured city dweller is required to consider as necessities. The hillbilly foregoes the hard grandeur of high buildings and canyon streets in exchange for wooded hills and verdant valleys. In place of creeping traffic he accepts the rippling flow of the wandering stream. He does not hear the snarl of exhaust, the raucous braying of horns, and the sharp, strident babble of many tense voices. For him instead is the measured beat of the katydid, the lonesome, far-off complaining of the whippoorwill, perhaps even the sound of a falling acorn in the infinite peace of the quiet woods. The hillbilly is often not familiar with new models, soirees, and office politics. But he does have the time and surroundings conducive to sober reflection and honest thought, the opportunity to get closer to his God. No, in Southern Missouri the appellation "hillbilly" is not generally an insult or an indignity; it is an expression of envy.[26]

Back to the Charivari

Ruark's decision is valuable not only as an indication of the ways in which judges may sometimes work very diligently to produce an outcome that furthers substantial justice as they see it, but also as a document on the tradition of charivari. First, it shows that charivari was still part of active tradition, enthusiastically practiced in southern Missouri in the early 1960s. Second, it contains many insightful details on how the practice was pursued, both generally and specifically. But finally, it also shows something of a change of attitudes toward charivari. In the Canadian charivari legal cases I have located so far, from the mid-nineteenth to the early twentieth century, both newspapers and the legal system tended to excoriate the tradition unequivocally. For example, in an 1881 charivari homicide case from Ottawa, Ontario, the judge's charge to the jury was described thus:

> ....the annoyance given by the charivari parties to the people in Mrs. Cooper's house was great, and that custom was no excuse for the rowdy conduct which then took place. He condemned the whole practice in strong terms and said there could be no doubt of the household being in considerable fear. Had Wetherill fired on the crowd and killed someone, he no doubt would have been acquitted. Parties who took part in such proceedings as charivaris, if life was lost in them, they were responsible for that loss of life.[27] His lordship pointed out that the conduct of the whole of the parties about the house of Mrs. Cooper on the night in question was most unwarrantable and held that Wetherill did not exceed his rights in going out and giving chase to any...he thought he could apprehend.[28]

The newspapers were even more scathing. The Hamilton *Spectator* noted that: "A charivari is in itself an outrage and a breach of the peace. It is the outcome of that lowest form of vulgarity which takes pleasure in giving annoyance to others....This brutal custom ought to be punished with the greatest severity, and frowned out of existence."[29] The Toronto *Evening Telegram* said: "The charivari has had its day and has lived five hundred years, and the sooner it is abolished the better."[30] The Toronto *Evening News* noted that "The occurrence is a disgrace to our civilization."[31] The Brantford *Telegram* commented, "Many good people look upon charivaria as harmless pieces of fun which need not be condemned if they cannot be encouraged. To our mind they are incentives to rowdyism and should not be tolerated in any community."[32] The London (Ontario) *Advertiser* said: "Whatever might be said of the charivari—or 'shiveree,' as there is some authority for calling it—in the early days of the country, when means of entertainment were low, and a wedding was the occasion of social jollification, it is now only a display of rowdyism of the worst kind. Like the public address, or the annual presentation of a photograph album to the district school teacher, it has been tolerated, although regarded as a social nuisance. No charivari ever occurred that was not an invasion of private rights."[33] And the Toronto *Globe* stated:

"In many cases, it is to be feared, the perpetrators of this form of social outrage are simply ignorant and thoughtless youths spoiling for some sport. The fun, the sole element of which consists of the annoyance caused to others, is unworthy of a civilized being....We do not know what remedy the law provides for the punishment of the horn blowing, the tin pan beating, gun firing, &c., and similar form of annoyance, but they should certainly be made indictable offences liable to severe penalties."[34]

On another charivari, which resulted in personal injury but not death to the charivariers, a newspaper in Manitoba, Canada, editorialized: "If young men will persist in disgracing the age in which they live, by such obsolete and barbaric practices, they may, if disaster overtakes them, expect but little sympathy from peaceable law-abiding citizens. The charivari is as much a thing of the dark ages as the thumb screw and the rack or trial by ordeal."[35]

Yet by the middle of the twentieth century, charivaris appeared more often in the newspapers as examples of quaint customs still practiced in the backwaters. Ruark's decision, then, stands out as neither a condemnation nor a dismissal of the practice. His comments clearly reflected his understanding of charivari as part of contemporary life in parts of southern Missouri. Yet his position as an arbiter of the law and representative of the power of government and law did not lead him to condemn it. Perhaps, indeed, Justin Ruark can be counted as the final coincidence of this case—a judge who understood not only the formal legal system of his time, but also the community's sense of self-regulation and celebration.

Notes

[1] Jacques Le Goff and Jean-Claude Schmitt, eds. *Le Charivari* (New York: Mouton, 1981). The practice of charivari has also been used to condemn actions/practices that range from the political (denouncing unpopular individuals and actions) to the personal (marking sexual indiscretions and variations from standard gender roles).

[2] Pauline Greenhill. "Welcome and Unwelcome Visitors: Shivarees and the Political Economy of Rural-Urban Interactions in Southern Ontario," *Journal of Ritual Studies,* 3 #1 (1989): 45-67.

[3] E. P. Thompson. *Customs In Common* (NY: New Press, 1993): 479.

[4] John T. Flanagan. "A Note on 'Shivaree'," *American Speech,* 15 #1 (Feb. 1940): 109-110.

[5] This conclusion is based on my research, funded by a Standard Research Grant from the Social Sciences and Humanities Research Council of Canada, 2004-2007, which involved interviews with and questionnaire responses from over 800 people across southern Canada from Prince Edward Island to British Columbia.

[6] John Hamilton Baker. *An Introduction to English Legal History*, 4th ed. (London: Reed Elsevier, 2002).

[7] Paul A. Gilje. *Rioting in America* (Indiana University Press, 1996): 47.

[8] Alva L. Davis and Raven I. McDavid, Jr. "'Shivaree': An Example of Cultural Diffusion," *American Speech*, 24 #4 (Dec. 1949): 249-250. Charivari is also now spelled in ways that more closely approximate its English pronunciation; "shivaree" or "chivaree" can often be found in Canadian and American dictionaries. Less standard spellings can be attributed to the fact that their users rarely, if ever, encounter the term in written form.

In the US, besides "shivaree," other terms used for charivaries include:

(Ohio) "Belling." Florence Halpert. "Belling: An Ohio Custom," *Journal of American Folklore*, 61 (1948): 211-212.

(Nebraska) "Belling." Mamie Meredith. "Belling the Bridal Couple in Pioneer Days," *American Speech*, 8 (1933): 22-24.

(New England) "Serenade." Miles Hanley. "'Serenade' in New England," *American Speech*, 8 (1933): 24-26.

(Mennonites) *"Polterabend."* Pamela Klassen. "Practicing Conflict," *Mennonite Quarterly Review*, 72 #2 (April 1998): 225-241.

[9] Patten v. People, 18 Mich. 314 1869: Choate v. State, 37 Okla.Crim. 314 (1927); State v. Countryman, 57 Kan. 815 (1897); State v. Adams, 78 Iowa 292 (1889); Havens v. Commonwealth, 26 Ky.L.Rptr. 706 (1904); Walker v. Commonwealth, 235 Ky. 471 (1930); State v. Voss, 34 Idaho 164 (1921); Tharp v. State, 65 Okla.Crim. 405 (1939).

[10] Bruno v. State, 165 Wis. 377 (1917); Palmer v. Smith, 147 Wis. 70 (1911); Higgins v. Minagham, 76 Wis. 298 (1890); Gilmore v. Fuller, 99 Ill.App. 272 (1901) and 198 Ill. 130 (1902); White v. State, 93 Ill. 473 (1879); People v. Warner, 201 Mich. 547 (1918); Ryan v. Becker, 136 Iowa 273 (1907); State v. Parker, 378 S.W.2d. 274 (1964).

[11] Kiphart v. State, 42 Ind. 273 (1873); State v. Voshall, 4 Ind. 589 (1853); Cherryvale v. Hawman, 80 Kan. 170 (1909); State v. Brown et al., 69 Ind. 95 (1879); Bankus v. State, 4 Ind. 114 (1853); St. Charles v. Meyer, 58 Mo. 86 (1874).

[12] Bruno v. State, 171 Wis. 490 (1920); Lebanon Light, Heat & Power Co. et al. v. Leap, 139 Ind. 443 (1894); Cline v. LeRoy, 204 Ill.App. 558 (1917); Combs v. Ezell et al., 232 Ky. 602 (1930).

[13] Novelty Theater Co. v. Whitcomb, 47 Colo. 110 (1909).

[14] Throughout this article, unless otherwise specified, numbers in parentheses after quotations represent the location of that statement within the transcript of case no. 1147, Circuit Court, Ozark County, MO; 5/21/63. Appeal Case File #8256, Missouri State Archives. I thank the Archives staff for their friendly and expert assistance.

[15] State v. Parker (378 S.W. 2d. 274): 276-277.

[16] At a charivari I attended in rural Ontario, for example, the couple was serenaded with car horns and chainsaws for some fifteen minutes, beginning around midnight. Their farmhouse, car, trees, and farm buildings were covered in toilet paper. The bride's female friends and relatives turned her house topsy-turvy, moving furniture and other contents from room to room. They put cereal in the bed, displayed her underwear on the kitchen cupboards, and tied all the socks in the house together in one long rope.

[17] *State v. Parker (*78 S.W. 2d. 274): 277.

[18] By far the most common explanation for charivari from those who answered my questionnaire and participated in interviews is that it is "a welcome."

[19] A reminder seems appropriate here: Numbers in parentheses, unless otherwise specified, represent the location of the quotation before the parentheses in the trial transcript of the Thornfield case. (See note #14 for the full case citation.)

[20] This letter from Parker to Attorney General Bobby Kennedy also appears in the Missouri State Archives appeal case file. (See note #14.)

[21] Merle E. Parker. *Instant Healing Now!* (Santa Ysabel, CA: Foundation for Divine Meditation, 1955): 4.

[22] Complete publishing information for books by Merle E. Parker:

Miracle Methods of the Masters (Santa Ysabel, CA: Foundation for Divine Meditation, 1964).

Taxpayers' Power (Thornfield, MO: American Liberty Crusader, 1968).

How To Be Your Own Lawyer and Sue to Win! (Sanford, FL: Citizens' Protective League, 1976).

How To Be Your Own Lawyer: Facts Lawyers Won't Tell You (Sanford, FL: Citizens' Protective League, 1979).

[23] Laird Wilcox, letter to the author, 2006. The Wilcox Collection of Contemporary Political Movements is held by the Spencer Research Library at the University of Kansas. It consists of an estimated 5000 monographs, 4500 serials, 800 audiotapes, and 80,000 pieces of ephemera, in addition to the personal correspondence of Laird M. Wilcox and others involved in the study of Left- and Right-wing politics. It includes materials from politically based left and right wing groups, as well as items from other types of "fringe" groups in America.

[24] *State v. Parker* (378 S.W. 2d. 274): 277.

[25] I.R.S. *Internal Revenue Manual*, "Religious Publishing," (02-23-1999), 7.25.3.6.8 (http://www.irs.ustreas.gov/irm/part7/irm_07-025-003-cont01.html). "2. In a Tax Court case, an organization sold a large volume of literature to the general public by mail. Some of the literature had little or no connection to the beliefs held by the organization...The court held that this was not a religious organization, but rather a trade or business. Foundation for Divine Meditation, Inc., 24 T.C.M. 411 (1965), affirmed sub. nom. M.E. Parker v. Commissioner, 365 F.2d 92 (8th Cir. 1966), cert. denied, 385 U.S. 1026 (1967)."

[26] Quoted in *Tom Beveridge's Ozarks* (Boxwood Press, 1979).

[27] This was the outcome nearly thirty years later in Manitoba, Canada, when a Grand Jury found "No Bill" in a manslaughter case against a bridegroom who shot and killed a charivarier, so his case never actually went to trial. See Pauline Greenhill, "Make the Night Hideous: Death at a Manitoba Charivari, 1909," *Manitoba History* 52 (2006): 3-17.

[28] Quoted in the *Ottawa Daily Citizen*, October 15, 1881.

[29] Ibid.

[30] Ibid.

[31] Ibid.

[32] *Ottawa Free Press*, August 16, 1881.

[33] *Ottawa Daily Citizen*, August 17, 1881.

[34] *Ottawa Free Press*, August 17, 1881.

[35] *Western Canadian*, September 13, 1906.

Author's Note

This paper constitutes a preliminary examination of the 1962 Thornfield shivaree case. I would be very interested in locating individuals who might be able to help me understand shivarees in Missouri, the community of Thornfield, and/or the specific parties involved in this case. If you would like to contribute any information on these topics, please contact me at:

> Pauline Greenhill, WGS
> University of Winnipeg
> 515 Portage Ave.
> Winnipeg, Manitoba R3B 2E9, Canada
> p.greenhill@uwinnipeg.ca
> (204)786-9439

Dr. Greenhill and friends
(http://www.usu.edu/usupress/books/index.cfm?isbn=7810; acc. 6/6/15)

The American School of Mentalvivology
Founded in the 1960s by Dr. Merle E. Parker, it grew out of his Foundation for Divine Meditation which he established in 1948 in Santa Isabel, California. Mentalvivology was a science of mind. Its goal was to produce whole people. The basic course involved teaching the student to produce any sensation at will, to use the mind to affect "faith healing," and to use the inner mind to set goals and accomplish them. Advanced courses—dealing with mysticism, ritual magic, and ancient wisdom—were originally published by the Aquarius School of the Masters, now defunct. All courses were by correspondence.

[This information was culled from *The Encyclopedia of American Religions*, 2003; "New Thought," #1493. (http://www.encyclopedia.com/article-1G2-3402400131/new-thought.html; scroll down to entry 1493); acc. 6/6/15).]

To learn more about...

Shivarees

Alford, Violet. "Rough Music," *Folklore*, 70 #4 (Dec. 1959): 505-518.

Blair, Nina. "The Ozark County Shivaree," *OzarksWatch*, 13#1 (2000): 29-32.

Boehrer, Bruce T. "*Epicoene*, Charivari, Skimmington," *English Studies*, 75 #1 (Jan. 1994): 17-33.

Conway, Michele. "The Shivaree," *Kansas Heritage*, 6 #3 (1998): 3.

Davis, Natalie Zemon. "The Reasons of Misrule: Youth Groups and Charivaris in Sixteenth-Century France," *Past & Present*, 50 (1971): 41-75.

De Caro, Frank. "Charivari in Nineteenth-Century New Orleans," *Louisiana Folklore Miscellany*, 6 #3 (1990): 78-83.

Finch, L. Boyd. "A Shivaree in Prescott, 1864," *Journal of Arizona History*, 31 #4 (Winter 1990): 425-428.

Greenhill, Pauline. "Make the Night Hideous: Death at a Manitoba Charivari, 1909," *Manitoba History*, #52 (June 2006): 3-17.

Gunn, Rex. "An Oregon Charivari," *Western Folklore*, 13#2/3 (1954): 206-07.

Hamner, Earl Jr. and Max Hodge. "The Shivaree," *The Waltons*. Season 3, episode 20; aired January 30, 1975.

> Olivia Walton's namesake Young Olivia brings her city-bred husband Bob to Walton's Mountain for their wedding. Realizing that Bob would neither understand nor appreciate the old mountain custom of the "shivaree," John-Boy calls off this traditional event, but forgets to tell Ike and Yancy.

Hancock, Norma. "Shivarees," *Western Folklore*, 14 #2 (1955): 136-137.

Johnson, Loretta. "Charivari/Shivaree: European Folk Ritual on the American Plains," *Journal of Interdisciplinary History*, 20 #3 (Winter 1990): 371-387.

Marks, Patricia. "Charivari: American Style," *Arnoldian*, 7 #2 (1980): 31-52.

Marshall, Gordon. "Shivaree: A Midwestern Welcome to Marriage," *Iowa Heritage Illustrated*, 77 #2 (1996): 66-69.

McKnight, Mark. "Charivaris, Cowbellions and Sheet Iron Bands: Rough Music in New Orleans," *American Music*, 23 #4 (Winter 2005): 407- 425.

Milburn, George. *Julie* (New York: Lion Library Editions, 1956).

> A novel set in Pineville, Missouri. The first 88 pages describe a wedding and shivaree. Vance Randolph says in his Ozark folklore bibliography that the author's dialect is exaggerated, but that the material seems to be fairly authentic.

Morris, Mark. "The Tradition of the Shivaree," *Midwestern Folklore*, 22 #1 (Spring 1996): 5-15.

Morrison, Monica. "Wedding Night Pranks in Western New Brunswick," *Southern Folklore Quarterly*, 38 #4 (1974): 285-297.

Meyers, Vest C. "An Ozark Charivari," *Southern Literary Messenger*, 6 (1944): 281-286.

Patrick, Michael D. "Traditional Ozark Entertainment," *Missouri Folklore Society Journal*, 3 (1981): 47-57.

Savory, Gerold. "Charivari: British Style," *Arnoldian*, 7 #2 (1980): 7-28.

Seal, Graham. "A 'Hussitting'," *Folklore*, 98 #1 (1987): 91-94.

Shields, Kenneth. "Rattleband(ing) 'Shivaree': Another Pennsylvania Variant," *American Speech*, 68 #2 (Summer 1993): 220-22.

Tharp, Mel. "Shivaree," *Kentucky Folklore Record*, 22 (1976): 102-103.

Thompson, E. P. "Rough Music," *Folklore*, 103 #1 (1992): 3-26.

West, Jessamyn. *Friendly Persuasion* (NY: Harcourt, Brace, and Co., 1945).
> About the Birdwell family, Quakers living in Indiana following the Civil War. The second chapter is titled "A Shivaree Before Breakfast."

Thornfield, Missouri

Evans, Mrs. Al. "Thornfield, Missouri," *White River Valley Historical Quarterly*, 5#1 (Fall 1973): 14-19. (Also available online at http://thelibrary.org/lochist/periodicals/wrv/V5/N1/f73e.html; acc. 6/6/15.)

§§§§§§§§§§§§§§§§§§§§§§§§§§§§§§§§§§§§§§

Selected Writings by Merle E. Parker

American Liberty Crusader [serial] (Thornfield, MO; No. 1, April 1967- ?).

How to Be Your Own Lawyer and Sue to Win! (Sanford, FL: Citizens' Legal Protective League, 1976).

Instant Healing Now! (CA: Foundation for Divine Meditation, 1955).

The Mentalvivology Story (Thornfield, MO: 1969).

Taxpayers' Power (Thornfield, MO: American Liberty Crusader, 1968).

Voice of Aquarius [serial] (CA: Foundation for Divine Meditation, 1964- ?).

Selected Writings by Pauline Greenhill

Ethnicity in the Mainstream: Three Studies of English Canadian Culture in Ontario (McGill-Queen's University Press, 1994); [cover courtesy of press].

Make the Night Hideous: Four English Canadian Charivaris, 1881-1940 (University of Toronto Press, 2010); [cover image courtesy of the press].

"Neither a Man Nor a Maid: Sexualities and Gendered Meanings in Cross-Dressing Ballads," *Journal of American Folklore*, 108 (1995): 156-177.

"'Places She Knew Very Well': The Symbolic Economy of Women's Travels in Traditional Newfoundland Ballads" in *The Flowering Thorn: International Ballad Studies*, ed. Thomas McKean (Utah State Univ. Press, 2003).

"Traditional Ambivalence and Heterosexual Marriage in Canada," co-authored with Angela Armstrong; *Ethnologies*, 28 #2 (2006): 157-184.

"'Who's Gonna Kiss Your Ruby Red Lips': Sexual Scripts in Floating Verses" in *Ballads into Books: Legacies of Francis James Child* (Peter Lang Publ. USA, 2001).

"'Your Presence at Our Wedding Is Present Enough': Lies, Coding, Maintaining Personal Face, and the Cash Gift," co-authored with Kendra Magnusson; *Journal of Folklore Research*, 47 #3 (2010): 307-333.

Co-Editor

Encyclopedia of Women's Folklore and Folklife (Greenwood Press, 2009).

Fairy Tale Films: Visions of Ambiguity (Utah State University Press, 2010); [book cover image above courtesy of the press; http://www.upcolorado.com/utah-state-university-press/item/2305-fairy-tale-films; acc. 6/6/15].

Transgressive Tales (Wayne State University Press, 2012).

"Your Folk Connection"
KRCU 90.9 FM / Cape Girardeau, Missouri
Saturdays at 7 p.m.

In 1996, Terry Wright, Barney Hartline, and Jim Hickam started a radio show. Jim died in 2008, but the show is still going strong and honors his memory. (http://krcu.org/programs/your-folk-connection)

Terry Wright
(http://krcu.org/people/terry-wright; acc. 6/6/15)

Barney Hartline
(http://krcu.org/people/barney-hartline; acc. 6/6/15)

In Memoriam

THE LASTING LEGACY OF JIM HICKAM – A REMEMBRANCE

Lyn Wolz

Though I was one of the founding members of the reorganized Missouri Folklore Society (MFS) in 1977, I was not able to attend most of the annual meetings between 1978 and the late 1990s because I had gone east to attend the graduate folklore program at the University of North Carolina, Chapel Hill, after which I went off to work at a small college in Virginia. I don't know when Jim Hickam started attending the MFS meetings, but I do know that when I started going regularly again (when I moved to Kansas City in 1995 to start working at the University of Kansas), there was a marvelous presence making himself felt, especially during the late evening jam sessions—a big man with a shy smile and a lovely speaking voice with just a hint of soft southern Missouri drawl. At first you thought he would stay in the background, but then he'd let loose with a rendition of "Butter Beans" or some other absurdly funny song none of us had ever heard, just grinning at the song and at himself. He had an enormous repertoire of songs serious and comic and a fascinating way of playing guitar that I had never seen anyone else use before (or since), but I loved the sound. He could tell a tall tale or a joke with the best of them and spent many a long evening exchanging whoppers with Irvin Rice and other MFS raconteurs. The MFS meetings were, and continue to be, a joy, but the ones since 2008 have left us all feeling like something's missing because Big Jim is no longer there. However, as his good friend Judy Domeny Bowen said at that 2008 meeting, "Let's not mourn for Jim; let's celebrate his life!"….so that's what we did and that's what we do.

Jim Hickam doing his radio show on KRCU in Cape Girardeau, Missouri
(http://missourifolkloresociety.truman.edu/emails.html [scroll down to "H"]; acc. 6/6/15)

For those of you who weren't lucky enough to know Jim, I put together this information about him so you could get some inkling of his background and his accomplishments. Though these things weren't the reasons he meant so much to all his friends, this will hopefully help you to get a sense of the person he was. Here are the dry facts of his life as published in the obituary that appeared in the *Missouri Folklore Society Newsletter* (Fall 2008):

> James Lester Hickam, 71, of Jackson, MO, died Friday, September 5th, 2008, at Jackson Manor. He was born October 10th, 1936, in Cape Girardeau, son of Milford Lester and Elsa May Dow Hickam. Hickam was a 1955 graduate of Central High School and received a bachelor of science in elementary education from Southeast Missouri State University in 1963. He taught sixth grade at Jefferson School for 32 years, retiring in 1996.
> Hickam served in the U. S. Army from 1957 to 1959, of which 19 months were spent in Germany. He was a KFVS 12 weather watcher and co-host of *Your Folk Connection* on KRCU radio. He was a much-loved member of the Missouri Folklore Society, serving on its Board of Directors for several years and sharing his musical talent and great sense of humor at numerous Society functions. He was also a member of the SEMO Astronomy Club and active in youth league baseball. Survivors include a brother, Jon Hickam, and a sister, Dorothy Hickam, both of Jackson. He was preceded in death by his parents and a sister. He will be greatly missed.

This bare bones description doesn't do much to bring Jim alive for readers, so now I'll let Jim tell you in his own words how he became interested in folk music. He wrote this piece for the website for *Your Folk Connection*, the radio show he started on station KRCU in Cape Girardeau in 1996 with fellow Shade Tree Folk Company singers (and MFS members) Terry Wright and Barney Hartline.

> Among my earliest memories is sprawling on the floor in front of the big radio listening to the "Grand Ole Opry" and hearing the music of old-time string bands with all the colorful characters who made up the Opry cast. In my early high school days, I discovered Burl Ives, Josh White, Harry Belafonte, and Lonnie Donegan. The rhythm and blues being played by Gene Nobles and John R., disc jockeys of the time, broadened my musical horizons. The sudden prominence of the Kingston Trio; Ian and Sylvia; Peter, Paul and Mary; Joan Baez; Bob Dylan, and so many more of the folk performers of that era fueled my growing appreciation of music. The fiddle playing of my grandfather and uncle made a big impression on me as well. These varied sources served to expand my musical tastes beyond the early rock and country being played on the radio.
> Somewhere in my late high school years, I bought an old banjo and later a guitar. I was shown how to tune the banjo to an open G and a few chords by my uncle. And when the guitar came along, I lowered the pitch of the little E string and could play what little I knew on the first four strings of the guitar, too. I never figured out how Uncle Dave Macon of Opry fame played his

banjo, but I developed a style of playing that some people, not wishing to hurt my feelings, have called "unusual."

In 1965, I met a most uncommon man named Ralph "Bones" Gentry. His hospitality to me and many others brought a whole host of pickers and singers together. Among the many, Terry Wright and Barney Hartline came to play and sing. We three formed a trio called "The Shade Tree Folk Company" and played harvest festivals and state parks. We decided to approach the local public radio station, KRCU, about starting a folk music program. To our surprise and consternation, they said, "Sure, why not?" and "Why don't you guys do it?"

And so *Your Folk Connection* was born. We play a wide variety of music loosely described as folk. The regular listener will quickly discover that each of us brings a selection of music to the program based on our own unique tastes. We feature live interviews with artists and sponsor concerts with some of the leading folkies as they pass through our area.

We owe much to a number of people – David and Suzie Walls of Steele, Mo., for introducing us to many of the singer/song writers; Judy Domeny Bowen for introducing us to Cathy Barton and David Para and their friend, Bob Dyer; the aforementioned Para's for introducing us to the many performers who have played at their Big Muddy Folk Festival; and to the station manager, Greg Petrowich, for allowing three complete novices to conduct our program in our own blundering manner.

To complete Jim's story of how he and Barney and Terry started their folk music show, here's a piece he sent to Cathy Barton and Dave Para—they passed it on to me when I told them I'd like to include something about Jim in this issue of the journal. It's a fun and unassuming little reminiscence that sounds like Jim's voice telling a story. I hope you'll enjoy his recollections and his self-effacing humor as much as we did.

"Somebody ought to start a folk music show!" These words were repeated often in a circle of friends who met for an occasional picking session. In particular, Barney Hartline, Terry Wright and I could be heard chanting this mantra with some frequency. Then one day it occurred to us, "Hey! We <u>are</u> somebody!" And so I was designated to visit the public radio station located on the campus of Southeast Missouri State University to inquire about how to get such a program on the air. We really did not intend for this to be a do-it-yourself project. We just wanted to make known to the station that there was interest out there for such a program. I met with the station manager, Jay Landers, and was pleased that he seemed to be quite favorably disposed to the idea. However, he was thinking in terms of a locally produced show with us as the hosts. I was introduced to the assistant manager, Greg Petrowich, and we three discussed the idea in general terms. I then returned to my friends with the assurance that such a program could, indeed, be started.

Being potential members of "Procrastinators Anonymous" (although we just haven't gotten around to joining yet), the three of us continued to talk about the idea for several weeks — all talk, no action! Eventually, Barney decided it was time to do something, and so we three met at the station with Greg Petrowich, who was now station manager. We were taken on the grand tour of the facility as well as encouraged to commit to doing the program for a minimum of three months.

The first challenge we faced was the lack of recorded folk material in the station's archives. Fortunately, each of us had our own collection of LPs, tapes, and CDs at home. We decided to record a couple of shows and see how it went. We then developed a simple format. Our thought was to record in advance so as not to tie ourselves up every Saturday evening by having to do a live show. Also, we were totally new to this and the fear of making on-air mistakes was on our minds. We each brought, without consultation, enough material to fill a twenty-minute segment, and we began recording with the help of one of the station engineers. On June 18th, 1996, and with Cathy Barton and David Para's "Marmaduke's Hornpipe" ringing out as our theme, we were broadcast for the first time.

We quickly discovered that we each had different tastes in folk music. The groups who came just at the end of the 1960's folk boom heavily influence Terry's tastes—the Beatles, James Taylor, the Eagles, Pure Prairie League, and others of that ilk were favorites of his. The three of us share an affection for the folkies of the '60's, such as Dylan, Baez, Ian and Sylvia, The Kingston Trio, and Pete Seeger. Barney and Terry both feature bluegrass in their sets. Barney tends to favor singer/songwriter types. He prefers music that tells a story and has a story behind it. My own tastes run more to the string band and older-time music. Dave Macon, the Skillet Lickers, the Blue Sky Boys, and Mac Wiseman are more my preference than the bluegrass they evolved into. I have a bent for odd sounds like Lonnie Donegan, Australia's John Williamson, England's the Wurzels, and the Yetties, et al. None of our tastes are exclusionary; we are each apt to play things that come from the others' "territory."

We really have not established any set method of selecting our material. We tend to be three little programs within the context of the hour. We bridge this disjointedness with comments and jibes we inflict on each other's choice of songs. We add information about songs; we tease and criticize and compare renditions of songs with good-natured banter. All said and done, we have a good time enjoying each other's musical choices.

In the course of our show, we have been privileged to have guests stop by. We've done shows with the Grace family and their friend, Sally Rogers. Bill Staines, Bob Dyer, Judy Domeny, Michael Jonathan, Suzanne Vega, and a number of others have also graced our program.

One of the things we hoped to accomplish was to promote folk music at the local level. To this end, we have been able to sponsor several concerts at the university. Our station manager has been very cooperative in helping us in this regard. We've had concerts by Bill Staines; Tom May; Bryan Bowers; Bok, Muir, and Trickett; Barton and Para; Chuck Brodski; the Graces; Small Potatoes; and others. We have used local talent on our fund drive shows, and we've discovered that there is a lot of talent in the area. In addition, we've lent our support to the concert series organized by Jack Smoot, site supervisor for Bollinger Mill State Historical Site.

> Our show has been picked up for broadcast by the public radio station in Carbondale, Illinois, and its two repeater stations. We are now heard in western Indiana, the southern third of Illinois, a little of northern Kentucky, and our own little section of southeast Missouri. Our station is in the process of expanding its power and coverage area and has hopes of establishing repeater stations of its own. We three look forward to being heard by an increasingly large number of listeners. Judging by comments we receive and fund drive responses, our audience appears to be steadily growing. Our web page can be accessed at http://krcu.org/programs/your-folk-connection....

Your Folk Connection is still running on radio station KRCU in Cape Girardeau with Barney and Terry serving as its hosts, though Jim's contributions are not forgotten – here are some of the comments posted by Jim's friends on the Mudcat forum when they learned of his death:

> I was blessed to have played in several "house" hootenannies with Jim and always enjoyed his music and loved his stories. He [had] a wealth of knowledge. I kind of figured that the angel Gabriel, being the consummate musician that he is, needed some lessons in playing the guitar in open G tuning, and as many of you know, Jim is just the man for that job.
> – Jerry Swan

> I am very sorry to learn of....Jim's death. He and I had become friends a few years ago when we met at a festival in Memphis. [He] was very knowledgeable about folk music of all kinds, and we hit it off. One of my fondest memories of Jim is when he came on my tour to N. Ireland. He loved the Giant's Causeway, and just sat on the stones soaking it all in. I have a photo of him with a big smile on his face, the picture of contentment, sitting there absorbing everything - the ocean air, the breeze, the smells, the view. I believe he'd be sitting there yet if we didn't have to go for dinner and a session! When [Jim] asked to borrow my guitar to do his party-piece, I was only too happy to let him tune it to open G and sing away. He was a big man with a big heart, a magnanimous spirit, a gentle soul, and I for one am honored to have known him. – Seamus Kennedy

> Jim had a beautiful spirit. He was an easy man to be with, a gentleman and what a joy to be in his company, a man you don't meet every day.
> – Declan Ford

> I only knew Jim from the Mudcat [Café Forum], but he was so generous spirited and decent that it came across in all his dealings and conversations. I wish I'd known he'd been over in Ireland. I would have made the trip over just to meet him. A terrific chap. – Al Whittle

Jim's passing was a hard thing for all of us, but we're greatly comforted by his lasting legacy—the joy of sharing "home-grown" music with our friends.

In Memoriam

Dr. Adolf E. Schroeder
Co-founder of the reorganized Missouri Folklore Society
(Photo courtesy of Shannon Robb and the *Columbia Missourian*)

DOLF SCHROEDER

The Missouri Folklore Society (MFS) lost one of its pillars with the death of Dr. Adolph Schroeder, professor emeritus of the University of Missouri (MU) and co-founder of the reorganized MFS. "Dolf," as he was known to scores of Society members and other friends, passed away in March of 2013 at the age of 97 after an active and productive life. He is survived by his wife Rebecca (Becky) Boies Schroeder, his son Richard Schroeder, and his grandsons Michael Schroeder and Luke Schroeder. (His son Christopher Schroeder predeceased him.)

Dolf was born in 1916 in Covington, Virginia, to German immigrants Richard Ernst Schroeder and Rosa Kordula Schroeder. At age five, he was sent to Germany where he lived with foster parents until 1938, when he returned to the U.S. He graduated from the University of Illinois with the class of 1941, then took his master's degree at Louisiana State University and his doctorate at Ohio State University, receiving his PhD in 1950. He worked at a number of universities before moving to Missouri in 1969 to teach at MU in Columbia, where he was a mainstay of the German department until his retirement in 1985. The faculty of the university later acknowledged his accomplishments at MU and his contributions to scholarship by awarding him emeritus status.

In the late 1970s, Dolf and Becky had the idea of reforming the Missouri Folklore Society, which had been established in 1906 by MU English professor H. M. Belden, but had been moribund since the 1920s. The Schroeders called a meeting to be held in Ellis Library at the university on March 30, 1977. At that meeting, the Society was officially reactivated. Among the attendees were Don Lance, Don Holliday, Jim Vandergriff, Cathy Barton, Ruth Barton, Dave Para, Lyn Wolz, and many others who have since been active members, helping to guide the Society. Cathy Barton, who knew Dr. Schroeder and his wife through the society, said Dolf was a "cultural gem." "Those are the people you're glad to know in your life," said Dave Para, Barton's husband and Missouri Folklore Society treasurer.

Dr. Schroeder's son Richard said that the time his father spent living in Germany had fueled a desire to teach others about Germany's rich heritage. Dolf especially enjoyed teaching Americans who had little knowledge of German history and culture, mainly as a result of anti-German sentiment in the U.S. during and after World Wars I and II. Richard continued: "A lot of the Germans here in the state deliberately wouldn't talk about their history… they wouldn't even speak their language." Dr. Schroeder tried to overcome the loss of pride felt by many of the people with German ancestry living in Missouri— he researched, wrote, edited, and produced books, journal articles, videos, exhibits, and events that explored, documented, and celebrated Missouri towns and individuals who had backgrounds rich with German culture. After his retirement from MU, Dr. Schroeder also led groups to Germany so the participants could reconnect with the homeland of their ancestors. "People are interested in their own backgrounds," Richard Schroder pointed out, "They're interested in their histories and their families and he helped them."

Dolf spent a considerable amount of time during his years in Columbia visiting, photographing, and conducting interviews in areas of both German and French settlement in Missouri. He and Becky also collected folk songs and stories from many other locations around the state. With his vast knowledge of Missouri and its history, Dolf eagerly assisted students, researchers, and writers with their projects and served as a mentor to younger scholars. In addition, he and Becky frequently opened their home to visitors from all over the world, extending their gracious hospitality by warmly welcoming both friends and fellow scholars.

In recent years, despite his age, Dolf remained active in the Society, rarely missing the annual meeting, where he and Becky presided over the book display room and networked with everyone interested in any aspect of the history and folklore of Missouri, be they academics or tradition-bearers (a newfangled term for "just folks"). He and Becky attended their last meeting in 2011 in Ste. Genevieve, after which traveling became too difficult for them.

Dolf's absence will be strongly felt by his family, his friends, and his fellow historians and folklorists. The members of the Missouri Folklore Society will also keenly feel the loss of his leadership, his seemingly endless well of knowledge, his wonderful sense of humor, and his friendship, which we were lucky enough to enjoy and benefit from for so many years.   – LW / JV

A remembrance of Dolf from Jim Vandergriff

I first met Dolf in 1977, when, at the urging of Don Lance, I attended a meeting called to revive the Missouri Folklore Society. I interacted with Dolf two or three times a year after that, mostly involving MFS issues, though he and Becky visited my mother and stepfather in Richland on one occasion, and I went to their home a few times, as well.

A few years after that initial meeting, I learned that Dolf had been at Ft. Leonard Wood during World War II, working as a liaison with the German prisoners who were confined there. I began to pester him fairly regularly about his experiences during the War, my interest motivated by the fact that I, too, had lived on the Fort during the war where some of the German prisoners did yard work and household chores for us. I was very young at the time – three when the war ended – so my memories are generally not detailed, but are nonetheless pleasant. I remember the prisoners being quite nice guys. (One memory that is still with me is that one of the young prisoners cried when he learned he had to go back to Germany.)

Aside from that, I regularly rubbed shoulders with Dolf at MFS meetings, as we both spent a lot of time in the book display room and/or attending to other kinds of necessary Society chores. He was someone I truly liked and respected throughout the 30+ years I knew him – a gentleman and a scholar, and most of all, a dear friend I will greatly miss.

Mim Carlson tells us about a way to remember Dolf <u>and</u> help students

As I walked past the book room at the MFS meeting in Ste. Genevieve in 2011, Dolf was singing out in a big booming voice that startled and impressed me. I had not heard him sing before and wondered if someone from MFS had ever recorded him. It turns out that no one ever had! I thought that it was a shame to pass up the opportunity to make a lasting document on this facet of Dolf's life which most of us had never known about.

I asked Sam Griffin if he would be willing to provide his expertise to record Dolf (with Dolf's permission, of course!) and within two weeks, Sam had made beautiful recordings of Dolf singing acapella in German, returning later to record him singing German Christmas songs. We were then fortunate enough to get transcription and proof-reading help from one of Dolf's friends, which made completing the CD possible. We designed a cover using some photos from Becky and had 100 copies made.

The cost of the CD is $17.00. All proceeds will go to the Dolf and Becky Schroeder Foundation to fund scholarships for graduate and undergraduate college students taking folklore courses. Email donjcarlson@donjcarlson.com for the snail mail address where you can order your copy.

§§

A Selected List of Publications by Adolf E. Schroeder

The Arts and Architecture of German Settlements in Missouri: A Survey of a Vanishing Culture by Charles Van Ravenswaay; edited by Adolf Schroeder (University of Missouri Press, 2006, 1977).

Bethel German Colony, 1844-1879: Religious Beliefs and Practices, co-authored with David N. Duke (Historic Bethel German Colony, 1990).

Bethel German Colony: 1844-1879: "Viele Hande Madchen Bald Ein Ende [Many Hands Make Light Work]" (Historic Bethel German Colony, 1989).

"Bruns, Henriette" in *American National Biography Online*, 2000.

Concordia, Missouri: A Heritage Preserved: Essays on Cultural Survival (University of Missouri Press, 1996).

Hold Dear, As Always: Jette, a German Immigrant Life in Letters, written by Jette Bruns, edited by Adolf Schroeder and Carla Schulz-Geisberg (University of Missouri Press, 1988).

Image and Word: A Missouri Mosaic; A Tricentennial Exhibit on the German Experience in Missouri, with Jerry Berneche (University of Missouri, 1983).

The Immigrant Experience: Oral History and Folklore Among Missourians from German and German-Speaking Groups: Suggested Guidelines for Collectors (University of Missouri, 1976).

"The Karl Becker Manuscripts: A German Folk Song Collection in the Library of Congress," *Jahrbuch für Volksliedforschung*, 21 (1976): 178-182.

Little Germany on the Missouri: The Photographs of Edward J. Kemper, 1895-1920, co-edited with A. K. Hesse (University of Missouri Press, 1998).

Longer Than a Man's Lifetime in Missouri by Gerhard Goebel; translated, edited, and introduction written by Adolf Schroeder, Elsa Nagel, and Walter Kamphoefner (State Historical Society of Missouri, 2013).

Missouri Origins: The Landscape of Home (University of Missouri Extension Division, 1981); [a three-part series of programs on Euro-American traditions in Missouri in a slide/tape presentation format].

The Musical Life of Bethel German Colony, 1844-1879, by David N. Duke; co-edited with Julie Youmans (Historic Bethel German Colony, 1990).

My Life Story by Jette Bruns; co-edited with Claudia Powell (University of Missouri, 2008).

"Nineteenth-Century Folksong Collectors in the Rhineland," *Semasia*, 2 (1975): 295-324.

Remembering Eliza Missouri Bushyhead, co-written with Rebecca Schroeder and Donald M. Lance (Missouri Chapter, Trail of Tears Association, 2001).

Report on a Journey to the Western States of North America and a Stay of Several Years Along the Missouri During the Years 1824, '25, '26, and '27 by Gottfried Duden; co-edited with James W. Goodrich and Elsa Nagel (State Historical Society of Missouri and the University of Missouri Press, 1980).

"Robert L. Ramsay and the Study of Missouri Place Names," *Interesting Missouri Place Names*, 1 (1982): 1-21.

Selections from "My Journey to America, 1836-1843" by Jakob Naumann; edited by Adolf Schroeder (Brush and Palette Club of Hermann, Mo., 2000).

"The Survival of German Traditions in Missouri" in *The German Contribution to the Building of America*; co-edited with G. Friesen and W. Schatzberg (University Press of New England, 1977): 289-313.

In Memoriam

SUSAN PENTLIN

(Photo courtesy of Matt Bird-Meyer, digitalBURG.com; 3/18/14)

Long-time Missouri Folklore Society member Dr. Susan Lee Pentlin died on Christmas day of 2013 at her home in Warrensburg, Missouri. She earned her doctorate from the University of Kansas and was a professor of modern languages at Central Missouri State University from 1970 through 2005. Among other awards, she was named a Fulbright Exchange Teacher (she taught in West Germany), attended a Fulbright Summer Seminar, and received a Fulbright Scholar-in-Residence Grant.

Susan's abiding academic research interest was the Jewish Holocaust, an area in which she worked for more than 40 years. She was particularly interested in the story of Holocaust survivor Bronia Roslawowski and also wrote extensively about Holocaust denial. She presented papers nationally and internationally—twice at Oxford, as well as in Berlin, Jerusalem, Tel Aviv, and Prague. She was a prolific writer, producing articles and reviews for numerous journals, in addition to editing a book, and she was working on another book at the time of her death. Related to her interest in the Holocaust, Susan had a passion for human rights, as shown in her service as a member of the Missouri Commission on Human Rights from 1996 until 2012; she was the longest serving member on this important commission.

Through Susan's long association with the Missouri Folklore Society and her service as the editor of the Johnson County Historical Society newsletter, she demonstrated her dedication to Missouri history, folklore, and culture. MFS members are greatly saddened by the loss of this stalwart scholar, colleague, and friend. – LW / JV

JOHN SCHLEPPENBACH

(Photo courtesy of Jeff Spear, Hansen-Spear Funeral Home, Quincy, IL; 5/21/14)

Missouri Folklore Society member Dr. John M. Schleppenbach passed away peacefully in his home on February 24th, 2014. John and his lovely wife Barbara were the proud parents of three children. In addition to his many other varied interests, he was an avid Cubs and Packers fan and the devoted owner of two beagles.

John was a well-loved and dedicated professor of communication at Quincy University in Illinois, where he worked tirelessly to improve the lives of students from 1972 until his death. Among his many contributions to the college, he developed an internship program with local businesses and founded the Learning Skills Center and the Ameritech Center for Communication.

John received his bachelor's degree in comparative literature from the University of Wisconsin-Eau Claire, his master's degree in medieval literature from the University of Washington, and his Ph.D. in linguistics and folklore from Florida State University. One of his main contributions to the field of folklore was his many years of working with famed folklorist Harry M. Hyatt, whose monumental collection of beliefs from African-American communities in the southern United States is housed in the Department of Special Collections at Quincy University's Brenner Library.

Most MFS members will remember John as a frequent contributor to our annual conferences. He was the president of MFS in 2008 and organized the annual meeting which was held in Hannibal in November of that year. Everyone who knew John will greatly miss his gentle smile, his low-key enthusiasm, and his knowledgeable and gentlemanly presence.   – LW / JV

In Memoriam

MILDRED LETTON WITTICK
Our Mysterious Benefactor

Lyn Wolz

(Photo courtesy of Linda Schmidt, Lyons Memorial Library, College of the Ozarks)

In 2008, MFS treasurer Dave Para received a letter from a lawyer and was pleasantly surprised to learn that the society had just received a gift of $5,000 from the estate of one Mildred Wittick. While we were all thrilled about such an unexpected donation, no one on the Society's board of directors or other long-time members of the Society could remember ever knowing or hearing about this person. Wittick had never been a member of MFS, as far as we could tell, and no one could remember her ever having attended one of the annual meetings. Finally, long-time MFS board member Jim Vandergriff dredged up a memory of sitting in an airport waiting for a flight to a professional meeting and talking to the woman sitting next to him. It turned out they were both professors of education and Jim remembers he told the woman about his work with the Missouri Folklore Society. It must have been a memorable conversation, because that's the only connection we can find between Dr. Wittick and any of our members, though our research into her past eventually revealed that she had long-ago ties to Missouri.

She was born Mildred Celia Letton, most likely sometime between 1905 and 1910,[1] though I've been unable to verify an exact birth date. Her parents Riley and Celia (Warmoth) Letton lived in Kansas City, Missouri, at the time. I haven't found much information about Mildred's childhood, but was able to pick up the trail in 1925, when she became a student at the Teacher's College of Kansas City, where she took classes through 1927. She began teaching in the public schools in Kansas City, Missouri, during that period, staying with the district until 1939. She received her BS in Education from the University of Missouri in 1932 and her MA in 1935.[2] Letton next served as an instructor at the University of Missouri for a short time before leaving the state in 1939 to teach middle school at the University of Chicago Lab School. She taught there until her marriage to colleague Eugene Charles Wittick in 1945, returning in 1947 and remaining until 1954. She probably went back to graduate school full-time in 1954 or 1955, because she received her PhD from the University of Chicago in 1958. In 1959, she became an assistant professor of education there, but left later that year to teach English at Paterson State College in New Jersey, where she remained until her retirement.[3] Wittick died on February 22nd, 2007.[4]

I feel that this bare bones recitation of facts doesn't do justice to Wittick's full and interesting life, of which I found hints in unexpected sources. For example, while I was reading articles that cited her dissertation, I serendipitously found an article *about* Letton, which listed her hobbies as "collecting antiques, photography, writing, and attending the ballet."[5] Another interesting bit of information, provided by Wittick to the publisher of *Who's Who of American Women*, gave three addresses for her as of 1961: South Shore Drive in Chicago, Windy Hill Farm in Indiana, and Paterson College in New Jersey.[6]

The earliest printed evidence I found relating to Wittick was several mentions of her in the University of Missouri's *Missouri Alumnus* newsletter, most under her maiden name of Letton. Her name first appears in a list of MU students who participated in a month-long tour sponsored by the MU Geography Department—they visited twelve western states and Mexico during August 1930, traveling a total of 6,250 miles by "luxurious motor coach" and visiting four national parks and many cities along the way.[7]

From the extensive research I did in education journals, Wittick seems to have had a well-established and creditable career in that field. Her dissertation, titled *Individual Differences in Interpretive Responses in Reading Poetry at the Ninth-Grade Level*, was especially influential, having been cited in many journal articles during the 1960s and '70s.[8] She was also an active book reviewer in her field, writing for the *Elementary School Journal* and other education journals in the late 1950s and early 1960s. Along with colleagues from the University of Chicago, she also compiled bibliographies on elementary, middle, and high school teaching for education journals over a period of many years.[9]

Dr. Wittick was also active in various professional education organizations during most of her long career. According to her listing in *Who's Who of American Women* (1961), she was a member of the New Jersey Education Association, the National Conference on Research in English, the National Society for the Study of Education, the American Education Research Association, and the National Council of Teachers of English. In addition, she served as president of the Chicago section of the Association for Childhood Education from 1944 to 1946 and was a member of their advisory board from 1946 to 1956.[10] She also served as an educational consultant to several organizations and companies during the 1940s and '50s, including the Kellogg Foundation; the National Dairy Council; textbook publisher Scott, Foresman & Co.; the Illinois Secondary School Curriculum Program; and *Food News* magazine.[11] She also dedicated herself to mentoring and training teachers, presenting at many University of Chicago annual education and reading conferences over the years, among many other continuing education events designed for teachers.

Wittick continued to express her dedication to education even in her retirement by contributing money to colleges offering excellent teacher education programs for qualified, but less affluent, students—among them Alice Lloyd College in Kentucky and the College of the Ozarks in Point Lookout, Missouri, where she established two teaching awards and a scholarship.[13] Curious as to why she chose that particular college in Missouri, I called the Lyons Memorial Library at the College of the Ozarks to ask if they had any information about Dr. Wittick and the connection she had to their school. Librarian Linda Schmidt kindly looked into that question and within a couple of days had found some very useful materials, including the photo that appears at the beginning of this article. It turns out that Dr. Wittick had been involved with Alice Lloyd College in Kentucky when Dr. Jerry C. Davis was president there, though I was unable to find out what initiated the original contact. When Davis later became president of the College of the Ozarks, she "followed" him, so to speak. Evidently, she felt some kind of resonance between the philosophy underpinning those two colleges and the work of the Missouri Folklore Society, which led to her support of our organization's mission through her financial gift. I hope someone will be inspired by this brief description of her long and distinguished academic career to do further research and write a more substantial biography of Dr. Wittick, a Missouri born and bred educator who generously and unexpectedly gave money to support the work of our Society.

Acknowledgements and a Request

The research I did for this biography began with the help of Gary Cox of the University of Missouri Archives, Columbia librarian/researcher Janice Dysart, and our own Dave Para. I discovered more about Wittick's career through the University of Kansas Libraries' online resources and through general Internet searches. If you have any further information about Dr. Wittick, especially her well-hidden birth date, please contact me at: lwolz@ku.edu.

Notes

[1] Most of the biographical information in this article comes from:

"Wittick, Mildred Celia," *Who's Who of American Women, 1961-62* (Wilmette, IL: Marquis Who's Who, 1961): 1075.

Additional information: *World Who's Who of Women* (4th ed. 1978): 1273.

Since Wittick herself provided the information included in her entries in *Who's Who* publications (as do all people included there), I did not try to independently corroborate the information those sources provided.

Despite searching all the online resources I have access to through KU Libraries, as well as free online sources, I have so far been unable to find Wittick's birth date. I calculated the approximate date given in this article by counting backwards from her enrollment in college in 1925 at what I assume to have been the age of 18, although I am aware that, especially in earlier times, college students sometimes started their studies at an earlier age than most students do now.

[2] I have assumed that Wittick must have attended university classes while she was working or during her summers off in order for her graduation dates and employment dates to mesh.

[3] According to Wikipedia, the school was founded in Paterson, New Jersey in 1855. In 1950, it moved to its current location in Wayne, New Jersey and in 1997, it was renamed William Paterson University of New Jersey. (http://en.wikipedia.org/wiki/William_Paterson_University; acc. 6/6/15).

Based on the fact that Dr. Wittick appears listed as "professor emerita" in the William Paterson University catalogs, I assume she must have taught there until her retirement, if that school follows the usual academic traditions.

Paterson University. *Retired Faculty Association Bulletins and Meetings Archive* (http://www.wpunj.edu/faculty-and-staff/rfa/rfa_arch_bulletins andmeetings.dot; acc. 6/6/15).

Paterson University. *Undergraduate Catalog, 2003-2005*, page 356 (http://cdm15701.contentdm.oclc.org/cdm/compoundobject/collection/ p15701coll4/id/1107; in right-hand box, scroll down and click on WPU_UGC_2003-05small 358; acc. 6/6/15).

[4] "Mildred (Letton) Wittick" ["In Memoriam" column], *EdLife '08*, College of Education, University of Missouri (http://education.missouri.edu/edlife/ 2008/people/alumni_updates.php; acc. 4/2/10).

5   "Miss Letton Succeeds Mr. Mosier," *The Propagandist* (University of Chicago Lab School), 1 #4 (1945): 3.

   I found this article reproduced in an article by one of Dr. Letton's fellow University of Chicago Lab School teachers:

   Merrick, Nellie L. "The Class Newspaper as a Learning Experience," *School Review*, 53 #4 (April 1945): 218-226 [found in *JSTOR*].

   One of the other teachers mentioned in that issue of *The Propagandist*, the student newspaper of the University of Chicago Lab School, was one Mr. Wittick, the future husband of the then Miss Letton.

6   *Who's Who of American Women*.

7   "Geography Department Inaugurates Annual Field Trip," *Missouri Alumnus*, University of Missouri—Columbia, October 1930, p. 38 (http://digital.library.umsystem.edu/cgi/t/text/textidx?page=home;c=alum; acc. 6/6/15).

8   Letton, Mildred Celia. *Individual Differences in Interpretive Responses in Reading Poetry at the Ninth-Grade Level* [PhD dissertation] (University of Chicago, 1958): 308 pages.

9   *Who's Who of American Women*.

   A selected list of Dr. Wittick's writings appears at the end of this article.

10 *Who's Who of American Women*.

11 *Who's Who of American Women*; WorldCat (OCLC).

12 *Elementary School Journal*, "News and Comment," [column] (May 1964): 416; *Reading Teacher* (April 1955): 248; (Feb. 1956): 182-183; (April 1958): 278.

13 Dr. Mildred Letton Wittick Professional Achievement Award, College of the Ozarks (www.cofo.edu/images/OzVisitor/sum04vis.pdf; acc. 4/26/10).

   Dr. Mildred Letton Wittick Professional Teaching Award, College of the Ozarks (www.cofo.edu/images/OzVisitor/sum03vis.pdf; acc. 4/26/10).

   Dr. Mildred Letton Wittick Book Scholarship, College of the Ozarks (www.cofo.edu/Catalog20052006/costfinaid.asp?page=2; acc. 4/26/10).

Geography Department Inaugurates Annual Field Trip

Mildred Letton's student trip was sponsored by the University of Missouri
(*Missouri Alumnus*, Oct. 1930, p. 38; courtesy of University of Missouri Archives; acc. 6/6/15; http://digital.library.umsystem.edu/cgi/t/text/text-idx?page=home;c=alum; search "October 1930")

The University of Missouri Geography Department's first annual field trip through the West was held during the month of August, 1930. During the 30 days of the tour, the party traveled in a big, luxurious motor coach, visiting twelve Western states and Old Mexico in the course of a 6,250 mile journey. Although the primary purpose of the field trip was to better acquaint the students with geographic conditions in the United States through personal observation and lectures by the conductors, time was found for viewing many natural wonders and for visiting some of the principal towns of the West. Four national parks—Yellowstone, Grand Teton, Yosemite, and the Grand Canyon—were included in the itinerary. The month-long tour proved so attractive to the members of the party that many wanted to make a similar tour to some other part of North America the next summer.

Selected Publications by Mildred Letton Wittick

Here is a sample of the wide variety of materials Dr. Wittick produced during her long career. I have interfiled articles/books for which she was the sole author and those she co-wrote with others (alphabetical by title). Though she wrote under both her maiden name and her married name, I have interfiled all works regardless of which name she used for any particular item.

Civics for Youth, co-authored with James Edmonson and Arthur Dondineau (NY: Macmillan, 1946).

Clubs Are Fun, co-authored with Adele M. Ries (Chicago: SRA, 1952).

"Correctness and Freshness: Can Children's Writing Have Both?" *Elementary School Journal* (March 1960): 295-300.

Hello, U.S.A.! (Chicago: National Dairy Council, 1948).

It's Always Breakfast Time Somewhere (Chicago: Nat'l. Dairy Council, 1947).

"Language Arts [column]," *Elementary School Journal*, (Nov. 1956-1964).

"Language Arts for the Disadvantaged" in *Teaching Culturally Disadvantaged Pupils* (Springfield: Thomas, 1969): 109-149.

"Language – Improving Thought Articulation," *Instructor* (Dec. 1966): 106+.

"Let's Teach Children to Proofread," *Midway* (July 1960): 47-57.

The Lore and Language of Schoolchildren by the Opies [review], *Elementary School Journal* (Oct. 1960): 46-47.

Man's Ways and Times by Lewis Todd and Kenneth Cooper, teaching guides by Helen Flynn and Mildred Letton (NY: Silver Burdett, 1954).

Pasture Trails, co-authored with Charles and Sara Whittier (National Dairy Council; 1941).

"Progress Report on Johnny's Reading," *Elementary School Journal* (Dec. 1955): 143-149.

"Status of the Teaching of Listening," *Elementary School Journal* (Jan. 1957): 181-192.

Ways of Our Land by Clarence W. Sorensen, teaching aids and guides by Mildred Letton (NY: Silver Burdett; 1954).

"White House Conference on Education," *Elementary School Journal* (Dec. 1954): 187-199.

Your Child's Leisure Time (NY: Teachers College, Columbia Univ., 1949).

[*Note:* Please contact me at lwolz@ku.edu if you'd like me to send you an expanded bibliography of Wittick's work.]

Selected Publications by Lyn Wolz [Available at: kuscholarworks.ku.edu]

"Anglo-American Folk Music in Missouri: An Annotated Bibliography," *Missouri Folklore Society Journal*, 4 (1982): 51-104.

"Annabel Morris Buchanan and Her Folk Song Collection" in *Folk Song: Tradition, Revival, and Re-Creation*, ed. by Ian Russell and David Atkinson. Elphinstone Institute Occasional Publications 3 (Aberdeen: Elphinstone Institute, University of Aberdeen, 2004): 299-312.

"Annabel Morris Buchanan: Folk Song Collector," *Ferrum Review* [Ferrum College, Ferrum, VA], (1982): 27-34.

"Ballads" in *Storytelling: An Encyclopedia of Mythology and Folklore, Vol. 1*, ed. by Josepha Sherman (Armonk, NY: M. E. Sharpe, 2008): 51-53.

"British Folklore and Superstitions: A Review of Two New Classics," *Missouri Folklore Society Journal*, 26 (2004): 97-102.

"Buchanan, Annabel Morris" in *Dictionary of Virginia Biography, Vol. 2, Bland-Cannon*, ed. by Sara Bearss, John Kneebone, Jefferson Looney, Brent Tarter, Sandra Treadway (Richmond: Library of Virginia, 2001): 363-365.

"*The Dictionary of Missouri Biography*" [review], *Arkansas Review*, 31 (Aug. 2000): 159-161.

"Folk Music in Missouri: An Annotated Bibliography," *Missouri Folklore Society Journal*, 8-9 (1986-87): 193-213; [supplement to my earlier article].

[Index to] *Happy in the Service of the Lord* by Kip Lornell (Urbana: University of Illinois Press, 1988): 165-171; [first edition only].

"Index to the *Missouri Folklore Society Journal*, Vols. 1-10," *Missouri Folklore Society Journal*, 11-12 (1989-90): 225-249.

"Index to the *Missouri Folklore Society Journal*, Vols. 11-16," *Missouri Folklore Society Journal*, 17 (1995): 163-195; [Dr. Donald Lance > 15-16].

"Resources in the Vaughan Williams Memorial Library: The Anne Geddes Gilchrist Manuscript Collection," *Folk Music Journal*, 8 #5 (2005): 619-639.

"A Sampling of Folk Song Databases," *Missouri Folklore Society Newsletter*, 29 (Mar. 2005): 5-8.

"Two Gardeners of Song: Exploiters or Preservers?" co-authored with Linda Plaut, *Journal of the Appalachian Studies Association*, 7 (1995): 41-49.

REVIEWS

Literary Legacies, Folklore Foundations: Selfhood and Cultural Tradition in Nineteenth and Twentieth Century American Literature by Karen E. Beardslee (Knoxville: University of Tennessee Press, 2001. 202 pp., notes, bibliography, index. ISBN 1572331526. $27.00).

Reviewed by: Adam Brooke Davis, Professor of English
Truman State University, Kirksville, Missouri

Beardslee's book is neither as comprehensive in its subject matter nor as theoretical in its approach as one might think from the title. Nonetheless, it leads the reader through a series of valuable appreciations of a number of worthwhile works, some more familiar than others. Without going into excessive detail, the author sets the work within some sort of life-crisis of her own, having to do with a search for self. Observing that this quest is a dominant theme of twentieth-century literature, Beardslee finds that the problem is unlikely to be adequately addressed by a literature of alienation, and proposes that folklore and literature rooted firmly in folklore hold more promise. In each of four chapters, she pairs a nineteenth-century text with one from the twentieth century – Harriet Beecher Stowe's *The Minister's Wooing* with Whitney Otto's *How to Make an American Quilt*; Charles Chestnutt's *The Conjure Woman* with David Bradley's *The Chaneysville Incident*; Zitkala Sã's *American Indian Stories* with Leslie Marmon Silko's *Ceremony* and María Cristina Mena's "The Birth of the God of War" with Roberta Fernández's *Intaglio: A Novel in Six Stories*.

The first pairing illustrates well enough the strengths and weaknesses of an idiosyncratic and personalized approach to a profound and wide-reaching (if largely self-inflicted and even assiduously cultivated) modern ill. Beardslee's interests, be it noted, are in significant measure pedagogical. A teacher in the trenches, she is looking for ways to engage students who may not be immediately disposed to seeing these works as relevant to their own concerns, or even intelligible, and of getting them to perceive thematic continuities between authors and eras widely separated from one another.

This is the work of an expositor; it is an appreciative walk through a series of texts related by theme and imagery – though the relation has less to do with literary history, about which the volume has little to say, than with the author's selection. What is genuinely common to all the texts Beardslee selects is a protagonist's problem of identity. And here, perhaps, the reader can answer a single question in order to determine whether the book will appeal: how does the phrase "the search for self" strike you? For some it is an urgent problem, both personal and universal, the key challenge of the modern world, and Beardslee proposes, not unreasonably, that a person embedded in a traditional community is less likely to suffer from it. However, there are those for whom uttering that phrase would be like chewing tinfoil; for them, it reeks of self-absorption, and disappears miraculously when one is presented with some less philosophical challenge, for example a subpoena or an enlarged spleen. For my own part, I've found digging ten yards of two-foot trench does the trick. In either case, there's a romanticism and a piety about the folk, their life and ways that mars the volume: there is a reason why people attempt to escape the sometime claustrophobic culture of origin, and even if they find themselves counting the cost later, serious re-immersion is both difficult and disillusioning.

This book is recommended for teachers of American literature and for those who cherish the particular texts studied; Beardslee is a genial, insightful, and articulate companion.

Legend and Belief by Linda Dégh (Bloomington: Indiana University Press, 2001. 498 pp., notes, bibliography, index, illus. ISBN 0253339294. $49.95).

Reviewed by: Adam Brooke Davis, Professor of English
Truman State University, Kirksville, Missouri

This is clearly intended to be a career-capping work by one of the most senior of scholars. It's a monograph on legend as a genre, but it never reaches a useful definition. Indeed, most of its energy goes into sometimes picayune fault finding with the definitions of others – circumstances under which one could imagine a definition proving problematic, leaving her with nothing more informative than legend being things which people may or may not believe. "The legend is a legend once it entertains debate about belief." This is a not uninteresting observation, but little comes from it, and it comes at the end of a long effort to disallow anything else to be said on the subject. In fact, the whole book is a kind of rear-guard action against other students of the genre, with Jan Brunvand casting a particularly long shadow, and the consistency with which his work is mentioned as "popular" and in contrast to "serious" scholarship is a rhetorical misfire, undermining the seriousness of this study.

Typical is the extremely long section where she rehearses her efforts with her husband, the late Andrew Vázsonyi (d. 1975) to invalidate the "*volkskundliches* Experiment" of Walter Anderson (whom she refers to as a "tireless polemicist"), work which amounted to a serious methodological critique and forced a ratcheting-down of claims, but whose presence and prominence here, a quarter of a century later, is hard to account for. It's just catty. Contempt is the dominant note sounded throughout the book...for scholars, for legend-tellers, and for what she deems irrationality, which as near as I can tell seems to be an element in her understood definition. It is, in short, puzzling that she could bear to have devoted so much attention to things and people she plainly doesn't much enjoy or admire.

Dégh's most sustained theme in this work is the need for rich information on the context of a particular performance, a view to which most folklorists would subscribe. But the point is hardly novel, and loses strength when the descriptions advanced for particular legend-telling events yield no interesting analysis – indeed, there is hardly the effort. The insistence on the importance of going back to the archives comes to seem like a justification for maintaining the archives, and leads Dégh to ignore the serious comparative work that has been done on the structure of what have come to be called "urban legends" (concerning which term she scores some valid, if belated points). What's lacking here is a mature recognition that there is something to be gained—and something to be lost—should either the "lumpers" (who look for broad patterns and risk losing crucial details) or the "splitters" (those who preserve detail, but miss the proverbial forest) should prevail altogether. If ever there were a demonstration of the value of multiple and conflicting perspectives, this is it.

The legend is indeed notoriously hard to define, difficult to separate from rumor and panic, and problematic even in attempts to define in terms of narrative. There are, for example, allusive references which imply narrative without themselves taking the form of narrative. The sections of the book are loosely connected, the few sustained discussions serving, in an unfortunately nannyish sort of way, to criticize popular taste for the gory and gruesome and popular indifference to solid science. Presumably the rational approach would make all those legends go away. (Dégh seems to include religious belief in this category, though her disdain does not extend to a spiritualist with whom she spent a great deal of time).

Most dishearteningly, Dégh neglects numerous occasions to engage the scholarship of orality and literacy, established for decades at the writing, precisely at those points where they might serve her purposes; that is, when she wishes to distinguish her own work—collecting face-to-face in the field—from that of "other" researchers whom she assumes collect their samples entirely from the media (as indeed some do, though their conclusions regularly acknowledge the dynamics of this form of communication and indeed make that a study in itself).

Perhaps the most interesting section is that where Dégh proposes "I lived in a haunted house" as an autobiographical sub-genre of the legend. Unfortunately, the interest lies mainly in the stories related, not in the analysis, of which there is little. One wants very much to praise a master's final performance, and had the rest of the book been of a piece with this section, it would have been easy to do so. As it is, there is no getting around the recognition that there's something fundamentally small in this very large book.

Medieval Folklore: A Guide to Myths, Legends, Tales, Beliefs & Customs,
Carl Lindahl, John McNamara, and John Lindow, eds. (New York: Oxford
University Press, 2002. 470 pp., illus, index, index of tale types. ISBN 01951-
47723. $24.95).

Reviewed by: Adam Brooke Davis, Professor of English
               Truman State University, Kirksville, Missouri

This brief volume of encyclopedic entries is accurately described by its title and belongs on the bookshelf of every medievalist and every folklorist, academic or amateur. It is by no means comprehensive, but both a handy reference and – for those who cannot simply look up one thing and get back to business – a serious temptation to fact-snacking.

Let's begin by acknowledging the fairness of the easiest charge to lay on any such work: there are things missing that one thinks ought to be here – the bear totem is here; why not then the boar so beloved of Beowulf and his friends? Conversely, we find some hyper-specific items (flyting) whose presence is puzzling in the absence of those other things one sought in vain (the wifely curtain-lecture, for example – though I'd have made the call in exactly the same way). The authors shrug, and reasonably point out that they could easily have made the volume many times larger. As it is, it attempts to cover Celtic, English, French, German, Italian, Islamic, Jewish, Scots, Eastern Slavic, Irish, Scandinavian, Welsh, Baltic, Finno-Ugric and Hungarian, in 261 articles written by 115 scholars under the supervision of 16 editors.

Rather than comprehensiveness, the book seeks representativeness and this is the key to its value. It is intended for those at least minimally knowledgeable in either medieval studies or in folklore, and the articles do a solid job of demonstrating how the one discipline informs the other. Those already well-grounded in either or both areas will, of course, have much larger and more specific references on which they rely. The value of the present volume is as a demonstration of integration.

The articles are written by scholars of standing in both medieval and folklore studies, including Samuel Armistead (Hispanic tradition), Joseph J. Duggan (*El Cid, Chanson de Roland*), Stephen O. Glosecki (shamanism), Constance B. Hieatt (foodways), Carl Lindahl (motifs and tale-types, Chaucer), Wolfgang Mieder (proverbs), Stephen A. Mitchell (Scandinavian), Joseph Falaky Nagy (Irish), W.F.H. Nicolaisen (onomastics), John D. Niles (*Beowulf*), and Lea Olsan (medicine).

The editors have an explicit agenda to remove certain common stereotypes and preconceptions about both folklore and the Middle Ages – that folklore can be easily separated from official culture, that the folk and their lore are static and unresponsive to historical processes, and (with due deference to what we recognize as features of wide or even nearly universal distribution) that folklore can be understood outside of its particular context.

The editors distance themselves equally from elitist and popularizing stances with regard to a particular segment of their intended readership: young people who find themselves fascinated by these two subjects, and especially by their conjunction. The editors are aware of a tendency to romanticize both the Middle Ages (princesses and ponies) and the folk (pretty little pagans). Keeping this volume by one's bedside as fall-asleep reading for a couple of months will take a young person a long way in the direction of serious scholarship without loss of the fascination on which true scholarship will always depend.

For this rather tricky purpose, writers were given instructions to begin articles with the most thoroughly established and consensus-ratified observations and only then to move into more speculative areas (clearly identified as such). Mauss' famous reference to "the primitive" as "that about which any nonsense may be believed" is equally true of folklore and medieval studies, and so, for example, in the entry on Arthur, the "Sarmatian connection" which is offered in the recent film as the "historical" basis for the legend of the great king is given fair treatment, but very far along in the article. Under "Witchcraft," the view that certain practices were survivals of pre-Christian fertility cults is given due and brief notice as an example of a now-discredited theory, while we are spared altogether any mention of the White Goddess or claims of continuity between these putative cults and sundry modern belief-systems. And in a further example, the tortured topics of the mythic underpinnings of *Beowulf*, in particular the relation of Christian and pre-Christian elements, are skillfully handled and provide an admirably efficient history of the criticism of the poem.

The volume under discussion here would prove useful to the serious undergraduate, while more advanced students would do better to purchase the two-volume *Medieval Folklore: An Encyclopedia of Myths, Legends, Tales, Beliefs and Customs* (put together by the same editors and published in 2000) for a more thorough bibliographical treatment of the subject.

The Meaning of Folklore: The Analytical Essays of Alan Dundes, Simon Bronner, ed. (Logan: Utah State University Press, 2007. 580 pages + index, ISBN 978-0874216837. $39.85).

Reviewed by: Adam Brooke Davis, Professor of English
               Truman State University, Kirksville, Missouri

Alan Dundes' epigoni are known to have appeared at conferences wearing buttons that carried the letters *WWDS*. And apparently there were few attendees who could not instantly expand the abbreviation (but, in case you're among them, it was "What would Dundes say?"– it would take pages to unpack the many levels of irony in the gesture). Dundes was also among the few who could provoke a mass walkout from an invited lecture (I was there; he did what appeared to be an impromptu riff on the sick-joke cycle emerging from the then-very-recent *Challenger* disaster). [Editor's Note (LW) – I attended Dundes' presidential address at the American Folklore Society meeting in 1981 where he spent two hours dissing all German people because they have a fixation with bodily functions (!?!). I didn't walk out like many others did, because I was just a lowly graduate student, but as Adam says, you couldn't be neutral about Alan Dundes!] Yes, he inspired strong feelings, strong reactions. His theatrics and polemics, his entrepreneurship and chutzpah rubbed many the wrong way, and his exit – literally dropping dead in front of his class – was of a piece with the rest of his lifework – and he himself, his very persona, was in some significant measure his lifework. Is the observation on my part tasteless? I have full confidence that Dundes would have thought so – and approved. He would have explained, and at some length, exactly how it was tasteless, and why the tastelessness was significant. Dundes was, beyond doubt or denial, a performer, but he was also an explainer, and that is what comes through Simon J. Bronner's collection.

When Dundes burst upon the scene (everything was a scene for Dundes, and he had no way of entering upon anything that did not involve explosions), the field was empirical and object-oriented; the folklorist's duty was to acquire (accumulate, hoard) materials, texts. That was the first part of the classic tripartite program: *collect-classify-analyze*. In Dundes' view, that first phase came to overshadow the others. In typical fashion, that very fact itself would be subject to analysis (he tended towards the view that it documented the anal-retentive character of that generation of scholars).

It did not matter whether you agreed with Dundes' analyses. I certainly didn't. Though less dogmatic in his later years, he was a fairly orthodox Freudian. Freud, like Lacan, tended to attract disciples for whom his metaphors were meaningful (and to alienate those who didn't "get it" by explaining their obtuseness to them in ways that were meant to pre-empt and disenfranchise their own self-understandings. This was characteristic of all the hermeneutics of suspicion, and was part of what made them both attractive and infuriating). Such analyses, it seemed to me, were validated by aesthetic rather than empirical warrants. I was always put off as well by the difference between the meaning of Freud in the United States, where he was taken primarily as a philosopher of mind and language, and his native Europe, where he emerged first and foremost as a physician, developing methods for the relief of pain and disease. Perhaps they were less in need of a sexual revolution than we were. But this, as Bronner argues forcefully in the introduction, was Dundes' contribution – not particular analyses, but the impulse to analyze, and the conviction that meaningful analysis was possible, even a duty. As Freud thought that the dreams of an individual encoded things he or she would find it intolerable to address directly, consciously, explicitly,

Dundes could imagine folklore as a kind of "public dreaming" (to borrow a useful phrase from Jungian mythography).

But that required a reconsideration of both *folk-* and *-lore*. Dundes arrived at a definition of the former as any group of people with at least one thing in common, and the latter as whatever symbolic materials they might exchange. His formulations across the years would include the canons of repetition and variation. Many would rightly ask what could possibly be excluded under such a definition, but the power of Dundes' view to bring interesting things under inspection is not to be underestimated. He more than anyone else caused us to recognize that the folk are not exclusively or even primarily rural, and that lore is not vanishing. He brought us xerographic lore ("tales from the paperwork empire") and taught us to understand it as a corpus, a cumulative discourse that reflected our ambivalence about the dehumanizing cubicle-culture in which so many of us began to find ourselves during those years. His insights, in tandem with the work of his somewhat elder contemporaries, Vance Randolph and Gershon Legman, licensed exploration of the significance of the taboo in even the more-traditionally recognized folk materials (i.e., the rural and soon-to-vanish) as expressions of anxieties and hostilities not otherwise given voice or vent.

No reader of Dundes should balk in the face of an assertion that a well represents a womb, or the phallic implications of naming a rocket "Apollo;" those particular assignments can seem arbitrary and silly (or, I suppose, to those in possession of the same decoder-ring, insightful and inevitable). That's not the point. Dundes' key insight was that folk-groups are polymorphous entities with fluid boundaries who repeat and vary lore as part of the very process of self-constitution in discourse. One need not share his readiness to see scatological meaning (something I believe begs for analysis itself) in order to recognize the aptness of a more general formulation for the meaning of a discourse of ambivalence – *something here stinks*.

Dundes was prolific, and even he did not bother keeping track of all his publications, in a wide variety of venues (including popular magazines all over the world, and ephemeral forms like dittography or even transcribed talks and lectures). Bronner has gathered shorter pieces, some really quite inaccessible until this collection, and organized them into two sections, one representing Dundes' methodological contributions ("Structure and Analysis") and another providing examples of the method at work ("Worldview and Identity"). Purely as an individual reader and scholar, I find the analyses sometimes "on," and other times quite otherwise. Like the man himself, the collection is both provoking and provocative, exasperating and exhilarating. One admires the sheer energy. As Dundes famously observed, the content of lore is strictly cultural, the form transcultural – maybe we all dream about dogs, but my dog may mean something very different from yours. It really doesn't matter whether Dundes read "Snow White" *right* – he taught us to read it. Strongly recommended for all folklorists, from advanced undergraduate to professional.

Living Sideways: Tricksters in American Indian Oral Traditions by Franchot Ballinger (Norman: University of Oklahoma Press, 2006. xii + 212 pages; preface, intro., notes. ISBN: 9780806137964. $19.95).

Reviewed by: Jim Vandergriff, Professor of Education (Ret.)
              Tucson, Arizona

Living Sideways is a very interesting work, one with value for every scholar of Native American culture and literature. It does an admirable job of arguing its central point that, while the Trickster is still a living part of American Indian oral tradition, it is not so easily defined as earlier scholars would lead us to believe. Ballinger also makes a very strong case that while the Trickster figure is quite pervasive among native cultures, it is far from the same in all cultures.

As a result, we readers learn much about Indian philosophies from this book. Ballinger makes it quite clear that the lines between sacred and secular, truth and fiction, reality and non-reality are not so clearly drawn in Native American world-views as they are in Euro-American philosophies. Thus, as we read these stories and discussions, we must struggle with comprehending the underlying belief systems.

The book, then, is not exactly an easy read. I, at least, went into it seeking a once-and-for-all definition of Trickster, but I didn't get it. As I read, I thought of a story some Inuit women once told me about their own encounters with an Inyukon. The Inyukon hid in the head-high willow shrubs that clustered near the water's edge. As the women pushed through the willows, the Inyukon hit them on the backs of their legs with willow switches.

Under my probing, the women told me that the Inyukons are Indians who had been killed in an Inuit/Indian battle about 300 years before. But, they insisted, they aren't ghosts and they aren't spirits. And they don't seriously hurt you, but you should be afraid of them.

I still don't really know what Inyukons are, but then neither do I know exactly what Tricksters are. I do, though, feel considerably better about not knowing. Of his study, Ballinger says, "Much in this book will illustrate the fact that when it comes to tricksters, experience, indeed, has many sides and is a mosaic of values, not all of which fit the others quite neatly enough to satisfy the Euro-American way of looking at the world." (p. 18)

The book, from my perspective, has a couple of non-critical flaws that I would hope might be fixed in later editions. First and foremost is an annoying dearth of translations of words from Indian languages. Am I really expected to know what a "manidog" is, or is the book only aimed at scholars who do know? And what is a "marplot" – an English word I think, but I also think it is not a word most will know. Likewise, Ballinger writes the name of the Arapahoe trickster in phonemic characters but doesn't give a pronunciation guide to go with them. So, who is the intended audience?

A second flaw is that Ballinger, far too often for my comfort, alludes to exemplifying instances rather than recounting the actual narrative for us. I believe the book would be much more instructive, for both lay readers and those like myself who are more than lay readers, but who are, nevertheless, not Trickster scholars, if he would just spell out the examples.

My third objection is the large quantity of material in the notes. In many cases, perhaps most, that material would be of more use in the main text.

All three of these flaws, I think, are the by-product of trying to save space, but I think they would be better done otherwise.

Despite these few problems, the book is well worth reading. Ballinger has devoted virtually a lifetime of study to the subject, has an excellent grip on the other research and writing in this field, and most assuredly gives us our money's worth. We come away with a much clearer understanding of a very complex topic. He analyzes previous Trickster scholarship, finding serious fault with most of it, while insisting that it is nonetheless insightful. He names Jarold Ramsay's *Reading the Fire* as "the most responsive to the facts of American Indian oral traditions." (p. 25) Too much of the accumulated scholarship, he argues, views Trickster more as a Euro-American picaroon: Trickster "in much contemporary writing may be largely the creation of dominant culture scholars and writers...."' (p. 27).

Overall, I found this to be an excellent book and I recommend it to everyone interested in Native American oral traditions.

Family Fun and Games: A Hundred-Year Tradition by Carolyn Gray Thornton and Ellen Gray Massey (Dallas: Skyward Publishing, Inc., 2002. xxii +213 pages; foreword, bibliog., index. ISBN: i881554- 09-0. $16.95).

Reviewed by: Jim Vandergriff, Professor of Education (Ret.)
Tucson, Arizona

This is an interesting book that everyone will probably find some use for. While the authors don't spend a lot of time discussing the folk roots of these games, they do a fine job of providing readers with the circumstances under which they might be played and under which the authors encountered them and/or played them. In fact, they answered for me, as Garrison Keeler might say, "one of life's persistent questions" – that is, exactly how does one play "Fox and Geese"? I've wondered about that for decades. It's a game mentioned in numerous stories about or set in American colonial days, as well as in the early days of the Republic, not to mention in Shakespeare and other Renaissance writers. But, until now, I didn't know how it was played, so, thank you, Carolyn and Ellen!

The organization of the book is very helpful, in that it categorizes the games by type—specifically, those that require no special equipment or elaborate pre-planning, those best for larger groups, those for big occasions, and so on. Some require careful attention, some require word skills, spelling skills, etc. Some require less physical activity than do others, and can be played anywhere – including long car trips. I remember vying with my three brothers for who could count the most windmills as we drove old Route 66 across Oklahoma and Texas in the early 1950s. We also spent some of our time trying to be first to spot a Burma Shave sign. Those games, I'm sure, helped preserve my parents' sanity as they travelled with four boys (ages 12, 10, 9, and 7). This book would have been a great resource for that trip from Laclede County, Missouri, to Phoenix, Arizona, and back!

So, it's a very useful book – one of the blurbs on the back cover calls it a "stupendous book" and encourages family service programs to use it. I recommend it to anyone who wants, in the authors' words, "family fun."

Older Than America, an independent film directed by Georgina Lightning and produced by Adam Beach (IFC Films, 2008. DVD, 101 min., $16.00).

Reviewed by: Jim Vandergriff, Professor of Education (Ret.)
               Tucson, Arizona

The film "Older Than America," which premiered in 2008, was written by Georgina Lightning and Christine Kunewa Walker and directed by Georgina Lightning. It stars Adam Beach as local lawman Johnny Goodfeather, Wes Studi as Richard Two Rivers, and Dennis Banks as Pete Goodfeather. Quite a line-up for an Indie movie. Writer/director Georgina Lightning plays Aunt Rain, but the actor most closely connected to the Missouri Folklore Society is Tony Flores, who danced for the MFS meeting in Columbia in 1978 and again in Kirksville in 2008. (Tony is the tall young man on the right in the photo on the next page.) His role in this movie is not a big one at all – a bit part, really. He plays a hospital nurse who comes in to give an injection to one of the main characters, says a few words, and walks off…but he's *our* Tony.

The film's story is an interesting probing of the efforts to take Native lands and cover up boarding school abuses in rural Minnesota. Though reviews of the movie are all over the place, it was the winner of the 2008 Flyway Film Festival Award for Best Dramatic Feature. It's an interesting movie in its own right and is readily available on Amazon.com. I recommend it to anyone interested in Native American issues, especially when such issues are explored in films conceived of and produced by Native Americans.

Tony Flores, one of the actors in the film *Older Than America* (reviewed on the facing page), danced with his family at the Missouri Folklore Society meeting in Columbia, Missouri, in 1978 and again in Kirksville in 2008. (Tony is the young man standing on the right in this photo.)

(Courtesy of the Missouri Folklore Society and Jim Vandergriff)

ABOUT THE AUTHORS

[Note: These bios were updated in 2013/14. – Eds.]

Susan C. Attalla
Sue is retired from Tulsa Community College (TCC) where she taught English and academic skills. During her last nine full-time years at TCC, she coordinated the Developmental English program at TCC's West Campus and was also president of the Oklahoma Association for Developmental Education. Since retirement, she has continued teaching online as adjunct faculty, as well as completing the Community Scholars workshop offered by the Missouri Folk Arts Program of the Missouri Arts Council. Her interest in folk music has led to six Missouri Folklore Society and two Ozarks Studies Symposium presentations, and she is currently scheduled to give two presentations in Aurora, MO—appropriately, the home of the Houn' Dawgs! Years of reading newspaper microfilms and scouring special collections have kept Sue busy while she completes the research for her book about the Ozark houn' dawg song (best known under its published title of *They Gotta Quit Kickin' My Dawg Aroun'*). Great-granddaughter of a ragtime composer, Sue has also given ragtime-related presentations at the Society for American Music and Sedalia's Scott Joplin International Ragtime Festival and has served on the Board of Directors of the Ragtime for Tulsa Foundation. In addition to her part-time teaching and music research, she is an avid genealogist. Sue and her husband live in Broken Arrow, Oklahoma; are the proud parents of two daughters; and dote on their exceptional grandchildren!

Beth Brooks
Beth Brooks holds a Master of Science in Music Technology degree from Indiana University – Purdue University, Indianapolis (IUPUI) and a Bachelor of Music Education degree from Indiana University in Bloomington. She has completed all three levels of certification for the Organization of American Kodaly Educators and is actively involved in the Indiana Kodaly Educators and the International Kodaly Society. She taught band and strings in the Indianapolis Public Schools until moving to a vocal/general position in 1991; she has been at the same school since that time. Beth is a recipient of the Metropolitan Opera Guild's grant for Creating Original Opera, for which she collaboratively produced an opera with her students and another teacher for four years in a row. She is also a recipient of the Lilly Teacher Creativity Fellowship for study at the Edinburgh Arts Festival in Scotland and the Indiana Department of Education Chinese Cultural Fellowship for study in China and Hong Kong. She has also been a presenter at the Midwest Society for Ethnomusicology conference at Western Kentucky University and has twice served as a clinician for the "Start the Music" early childhood education conference at IUPUI.

John Garst

John is a native of Jackson, Mississippi, who now lives in Athens, Georgia. His interest in American traditional music began seriously when, at age 12, he started playing cornet with the junior high school band. "Cornet" meant "jazz" (Louis Armstrong, Bix Beiderbecke), "jazz" meant "blues," "blues" meant "spirituals," "spirituals" meant "folk songs" ... somehow it all grew. In 1997, he retired from the University of Georgia where he was a chemistry professor, which allowed him to spend time pursuing the historical backgrounds of traditional American songs such as "Wayfaring Stranger," "Man of Constant Sorrow," "Ella Speed," "Delia," and "John Henry." He is currently working on a book on John Henry.

Pauline Greenhill

Professor of Women's and Gender Studies at the University of Winnipeg in Manitoba, Canada, Pauline's recent books include *Transgressive Tales: Queering the Grimms* (co-edited with Kay Turner, 2012); *Fairy Tale Films: Visions of Ambiguity* (co-edited with Sidney Eve Matrix, 2010); and *Make the Night Hideous: Four English Canadian Charivaris, 1881-1940* (2010). She has had articles published in *Atlantis*, *The Canadian Journal of Cardiology*, *The Canadian Journal of Women and the Law*, *Canadian Woman Studies*, *Ethnic and Racial Studies*, *Ethnologies*, *Fabula*, *The Folklore Historian*, *The Journal of American Folklore*, *The Journal of Canadian Studies*, *The Journal of Folklore Research*, *Manitoba History*, *parallax*, *Signs*, *Western Folklore*, and *The Journal of Ritual Studies*, *Marvels & Tales*, among others. In addition to her recent research on queer and transgender fairy tales and fairy-tale films, she is currently exploring ethnic drag and masquerade in western Canada.

Betty Craker Henderson

Betty draws on a lifetime of personal Ozark experience to write her short stories, fiction, and non-fiction, almost all centered on her home region. Prior to a successful freelance career in newspaper and magazine work, she was a librarian and a news editor. Today she still finds time to write, in addition to caring for her husband and watching over numerous children, grandchildren, and greats. Occasionally, she manages to get to the computer for a short time, to an occasional writers' event, and once in a great while manages a trip to see something of this great world. She is the author of several books, the latest being a young adult mystery novel titled *Junkyard Bones* (2011) and a personal memoir called *The Evolution of an Ozark Junkyard* (2010). Her novel *Child Support* won the Missouri Writers' Guild Romance Novel of the Year award in 2001. Betty's short fiction has also been featured in a number of anthologies. She is currently working as an Acquisitions Editor for Sky High Tales, the juvenile division of High Hills Press.

Julie Henigan
Originally from Springfield, Missouri, Julie holds a Master's in Folklore from the University of North Carolina in Chapel Hill and a Ph.D. in English from the University of Notre Dame. She has conducted extensive fieldwork on traditional music and song and has published a number of articles on both Irish and American traditional culture, including two pertaining specifically to the Ozarks, "'Play Me Something Quick and Devilish': The Old-Time Square-Dance Fiddling of Bob Holt" and "The McClurg Music Parties: A Living Tradition" (both for *The Old-Time Herald*). Julie is also a musician and singer specializing in the traditional songs, ballads, and dance music of Ireland and the American Upland South and performs all over the United States and in various locations around Ireland and the U.K. Her concert performances, her CD (*American Stranger*), and her books and articles have garnered many enthusiastic and positive reviews.

Steve Roud
Steve's more than thirty years of research into English folklore have resulted in his status as an internationally recognized expert on the folk songs, superstitions, customs, and traditional drama of the British Isles. He served for more than fifteen years as Honorary Librarian of England's Folklore Society and recently retired from his position as Local Studies Librarian for the London Borough of Croydon (basically equivalent to a local history/genealogy librarian in the United States). Steve works closely with the English Folk Dance and Song Society's Vaughan Williams Memorial Library staff to provide access to the major manuscript and sound collections of the past. He is also the designer and compiler of two major folk song resources (*The Folk Song Index* and *The Broadside Index*) which are used online by folk song scholars and enthusiasts from around the world. In addition, his output as a freelance writer is formidable—he has written or co-authored seven authoritative books on the folklore, customs, and superstitions of England, books that have garnered praise in both the scholarly and popular press. Among his many honors, Steve can count the Folklore Society's Katharine Briggs Folklore Award for his book *The Penguin Guide to the Superstitions of Britain and Ireland* and the American Folklore Society's Opie Honorable Mention for his book *The Lore of the Playground*. His extensive work in the field of traditional song was also acknowledged by his peers in 2009 when the English Folk Dance and Song Society awarded him its Gold Badge, given for outstanding contributions to folk music. Steve currently lives in the village of Maresfield in East Sussex, England.

About the Authors

Paul J. Stamler
Born into a family active in the folk revival of the 1940s and '50s, it is not surprising that Paul Stamler has had lifelong involvement with traditional music. In the late Sixties, he discovered the wonder and power of source performers when he encountered field recordings in the Washington University and St. Louis Public libraries. Inspired by these recordings, he has long performed traditional vocal and instrumental music himself, currently performing for the St. Louis English Country Dancers as the leader of the Original Speckled Band. Over the years, Paul's folk-related activities have included managing several coffeehouses (including St. Louis' Focal Point in its earliest years), producing a concert series, recording performers in the Midwest and beyond, and running concert sound for many different acts. Since 1987, Paul has become well known nationally for hosting the weekly radio program "No Time to Tarry Here" on KDHX-St. Louis, a show which focuses on traditional music performed in many styles—from Dock Boggs' 1927 Bristol sessions to Boiled in Lead's 2005+ efforts; the show was awarded "Best Folk Show" by St. Louis' *Riverfront Times* newspaper in 2012. Among Paul's other notable scholarly endeavors is his work as one of the founding contributors to the *Traditional Ballad Index*, an online annotated collaborative reference work—he edited the original keyword index and has contributed most of the listings for 78 rpm recordings. Most recently he contributed two articles on early collectors of folk music (Robert Winslow Gordon, Loraine Wyman, and Carl Sandburg) to the book *Ballad Collectors of North America*. In 2013, Paul received his M.A. from Webster University in St. Louis, having written his master's thesis on the origins of country music recording in the early twentieth century. He is currently a highly regarded adjunct faculty member in the Department of Audio Aesthetics and Technology at Webster.

Alex Usher
Raised in a refined and artistic family in St. Louis, Alex somehow became enamored of folk music as a teenager during the folk boom of the 1950s. Performing on local TV stations and at a national folk festival before she could even play complex guitar chords, she relied on her singing to entertain people. She has been collecting and performing folk songs for over fifty years now, along the way becoming a nationally known autoharpist, recording artist, and author of books on singing and playing folk music. In addition to teaching private music lessons at the Music Folk store in Webster Groves for many years, she has taught workshops at countless festivals, as well as performing for many Elderhostel (now Road Scholars) classes, hospitals, church groups, libraries, schools, and other civic and cultural organizations. In recent years, she has also presented a program of folk songs called "Hand-Me-Down Music" for the Missouri Humanities Council, as well as sharing her love of music with her four grandsons.

Jim Vandergriff

As noted in the introduction to Jim's article, he is a born and bred native Missourian, with roots in the state that go five generations deep. His Vandergriff ancestors arrived in North America when the Dutch still held "New Amsterdam," his Armstrong and Dodson ancestors came in the early 1700s (from Scotland and Ireland), and his Gibson and Perkins forebears came from Wales in the late 1700s. In fact, his first Missouri ancestor, John Gibson, bought land from the Spanish government. Despite Jim's origins, though, during his lifetime he has lived outside Missouri more than *in* it – including stints in Illinois, Kansas, Oregon, Alaska, and Arizona.

Jim's interest in folklore began in 1974 when he was teaching at Emporia State University. His department head asked him to "represent the department" at a meeting of the Kansas Folklore Society in Lindsborg, KS. It turned out to be a life-changing experience. There he met Bill Koch and Sam Sackett (the "superheroes" of Kansas folklore), co-authors of the monumental book *Kansas Folklore* (1961). It was from Bill and Sam that Jim came to understand what an exciting and interesting field of study folklore is, as well as learning from them much of what he knows about how folklore is "done."

A couple of years later (in 1976 to be exact) Jim met Don Lance, an English professor at the University of Missouri in Columbia. Through Don, Jim met Dolf and Becky Schroeder, Ruth Barton, et al., and in 1977 joined them as a founding member of the reorganized Missouri Folklore Society. Jim has been deeply involved with Missouri folklore, in many capacities, ever since. It was after making these connections that he came to understand the value – besides entertainment – of the stories his great-grandmother had told his 10 year old self, and to understand that his personal family history pretty much mirrored the history of the westward movement in the U. S. – Jacob Van Der Grift, a magistrate in New Amsterdam, New Netherlands, in the 1670s; Mary Dodson Donoho, the first Anglo-American woman in Santa Fe, NM, in the 1830s; James M. Dodson, who settled in Missouri in 1832 on land that the Osage people considered theirs, but abandoned by moving west when the Europeans moved in; John Armstrong, Confederate soldier in Price's army and later newspaper publisher in the late 1800s, who fought in the Battle of Lone Jack and helped establish the Confederate Memorial is Higginsville, MO; and Harl Gibson, a deputy U.S. marshal in "The Nations" (as his Grandma Lizzie always called Oklahoma).

From his years with the Society and his association with it members, he has come to understand much about the "whys" of his own life-ways: Why the music? Why the food? Why the architectural forms? Why the toys and games? Why the accent and lexicon? Why the . . .? As Jim tells us, it has all been – and continues to be – great fun!

Though he never forgets his Missouri roots, Jim and his wife, fellow scholar and MFS member Donna Jurich, love living in Arizona, as well as spending time with Jim's daughter and her family since they moved to Tucson.

ABOUT THE EDITORS

Lyn Wolz

Lyn has called Kansas City home for nearly twenty years now, but she was born and raised in St. Louis by fourth-generation St. Louisans of German and Irish descent. Though a maternal great-grandfather played an ebony flute and her father played accordion as a child and bagpipes for an Army band (don't ask!), her main musical heritage consisted of singing camp songs as a Girl Scout and listening to groups like the Kingston Trio and Peter, Paul & Mary in the Sixties, before delving into true traditional music in college.

For most of the 1970s, Wolz lived in Columbia, Missouri, where she received her master's degree in library science from the University of Missouri and worked as a librarian at Columbia College, in addition to majoring in "hanging out and playing music" at the Chez Coffeehouse. In 1978, she moved to Chapel Hill to attend graduate school at the University of North Carolina, where she received her second master's degree in – what else? – folklore!

Before moving back to the Midwest to work at the University of Kansas in 1995, Lyn was a librarian at Ferrum College in the foothills of Virginia's Blue Ridge Mountains for sixteen years. She also served for many of those years as music director for the college's Jack Tale Players, a traveling music and theater company, and for the Blue Ridge Folklife Festival, still held on the campus on the fourth Saturday in October every year.

Lyn has been a member of the Missouri Folklore Society since its reactivation in 1977 and has served as board member, journal indexer, and all-around avid supporter for almost 40 years now. She was also president of the society in 2001 when she organized the annual MFS meeting in Independence.

One reflection of Lyn's interest in folk music and folk songs has been her work with archival folk song collections. Among the collections she has processed and indexed are the papers of three female folk song collectors—American Annabel Morris Buchanan and Englishwomen Anne Geddes Gilchrist and Janet Heatley Blunt. She has also established archival collections at State Historical Society of Missouri libraries—the Cross Currents/Foolkiller Collection, which includes the papers and memorabilia of a non-profit folk arts organization that has been active in Kansas City for more than forty years, and the Chez Coffeehouse Collection, which includes papers, recordings, and memorabilia from the non-profit coffeehouse that served as a home away from home for thousands of students in Columbia for more than forty years (ca. 1964-2004).

During her career in higher education, Lyn has produced nineteen articles and book chapters, almost all of them on folk music topics. Fifteen of these publications are now available online in the KU ScholarWorks repository (http://kuscholarworks.ku.edu; search "Author," then "Wolz"). Based on her career-long program of research into British and American folk music (with special focus on women who collected folk songs), Lyn was promoted by the faculty of the University of Kansas to the academic rank of full professor in 2012.

Now that her work on this issue of the journal is finished, Lyn plans to complete her index to the first thirty volumes of this journal before getting back to other pursuits, such as singing ballads and other folk songs while accompanying herself on guitar, dulcimer, or autoharp. After all, it was these pastimes that resulted in her nickname—"The Only Truck-Drivin,' Guitar-Pickin' Librarian in Town"! She is looking forward to retirement so that she can concentrate more of her time and energy on folk music and archive activities, while still making time for traveling with her partner Susan Bryson.

Elizabeth Freise
Elizabeth received her BA in Classics from Reed College in Portland, Oregon, and furthered her studies in Ancient Greek at Bryn Mawr College in Pennsylvania, where she received an MA. She also earned a master's degree in Library Science from the University of Alabama.

Before she started her academic career, Elizabeth worked in various industries, including a stint at famous independent book store Powell's in Oregon and a sojourn at American Century Investments in Kansas City. This variety of experiences gave her a unique set of qualifications that stood her in good stead during her nearly twenty-year career in academic libraries, 12 years of which were spent at the University of Kansas Regents Center Library in the suburbs of Kansas City. This phase of her life ended in 2014, when she left KU to pursue a career in freelance writing and editing.

Elizabeth, who resides in Overland Park, Kansas, is currently devoting herself to developing her new career while continuing to participate in long-time hobbies like gardening, dog training, knitting, sewing, and traveling.

Editor Lyn Wolz
(University of Kansas official photo, 2012)

Assistant Editor Elizabeth Freise
(Courtesy of Elizabeth Freise, 2013)

Publishing Statement

The *Missouri Folklore Society Journal* is published annually and distributed to approximately 300 members and institutional subscribers. No advertising is available in this publication.

The *Journal* publishes articles relating to any aspect of traditional folklife and cultural expression from all ethnic groups, geographic locations, and historical periods in the state of Missouri, or otherwise related to Missouri or Missourians.

Our aim is to present a mix of scholarly articles written in an accessible style and personal experience stories from tradition-bearers. In addition, we feature reviews of books, audio and video recordings, websites, exhibits, and other materials/events relating to folklore and culture in Missouri. Sometimes the *Journal* also includes obituaries of tradition bearers, academics, and others who have been important to the society or to the cultural history of the state of Missouri.

Authors are not required to be members of MFS. APA and MLA styles of documentation are acceptable. Authors must be able to document permission or public domain status for all images.

Please send manuscripts and editorial correspondence to the Editor at the society's post office box listed on the title page of this issue.

If you have suggestions for materials to be reviewed or if you have physical materials you would like someone to review, send them to the Review Editor in care of the Society's post office box listed on the title page of this issue.

www.ingramcontent.com/pod-product-compliance
Lightning Source LLC
Chambersburg PA
CBHW071605080526
44588CB00010B/1029